a guide to
The World Bank

a guide to
The World Bank

THE WORLD BANK
WASHINGTON, D.C.

Cover and interior design by Susan Brown Schmidler.

Photo credits

Cover photos (clockwise from top): World Bank; Yemen Social Fund; World Bank

Interior photos: p. 2, Yemen Social Fund; p. 6, World Bank; p. 10, World Bank; p. 32, World Bank; p. 68, World Bank; p. 109, World Bank

Soft cover: ISBN 0-8213-5344-6
Hard cover: ISBN 0-8213-5830-8

Library of Congress Cataloging-in-Publication Data

A guide to the World Bank Group.
    p. cm.
    Includes index.
    Soft cover: ISBN 0-8213-5344-6
    Hard cover: ISBN 0-8213-5830-8
      1. World Bank Group. 2. Developing countries—Economic conditions.
    I. World Bank.

HG3881.5.W57G853 2003
332.1'53—dc21

2003053457

Contents

CHAPTER 3

How the World Bank Group Operates   33

CHAPTER 4

World Bank Group Countries and Regions   69

Boxes

Figures

Tables

Foreword

The mission of the World Bank Group is to reduce poverty and encourage economic growth. The debate on globalization and the fight against terrorism have only served to increase awareness about how much is at stake in development. Our goals are ambitious: to improve the quality of life and extend economic benefits and empowerment broadly throughout societies. Now we are seeing a growing consensus: both a recognition by wealthier countries that they need to do more and a renewed commitment on the part of the international community to collaborate and harmonize the many efforts under way.

The different parts of the World Bank Group are involved in nearly every aspect of development, with activities ranging from economic research and analysis to financial and technical assistance for governments and private enterprises. We play an important supporting role as developing countries shape and implement their strategies to reduce poverty and stimulate growth. We also place a high priority on communicating knowledge about development, drawing on our own 60 years of experience and that of our 184 members, both developing and developed.

A Guide to the World Bank aims to make the World Bank more accessible, explaining how we are organized and what we do. It complements some well-established tools for learning about the Bank Group institutions: our annual reports, our Web sites, and our print publications that cover a wide range of topics. It explains how our institutions are organized, how we operate, and how we focus our efforts on world regions and major challenges in development. Throughout the text, we indicate where additional information may be found.

We hope this new publication will increase awareness and understanding of the World Bank Group's mission and activities among a wide range of audiences and stakeholders, and by doing so contribute to our collective fight against poverty.

Ian Goldin
Vice President, External Affairs
and United Nation Affairs

Acknowledgments

This book was conceived and edited by Paul McClure, adapting and expanding on numerous print publications and Internet resources of the World Bank Group. Additional research and writing were provided by Steven Kennedy, Afshin Molavi, and Stuart Tucker. Comments on development of the manuscript came principally from Dirk Koehler and from Guy Brussat, Nicole Frost, Angela Gentile, Gabriela Gold, Dana Lane, Jeffrey McCoy, Barbara Murek, and Santiago Pombo-Bejarano. The book benefited from the hard work and many ideas of staff in the World Bank Office of the Publisher.

Acronyms

ACS	Administrative and Client Support Network
AMSCO	African Management Services Company
APDF	Africa Project Development Facility
BP	Bank procedure
CAS	Country assistance strategy
CDF	Comprehensive Development Framework
CEB	U.N. System Chief Executives Board for Coordination
CGAP	Consultative Group to Assist the Poorest
CGIAR	Consultative Group on International Agricultural Research
CSR	Corporate social responsibility
CUP	Cooperative Underwriting Program
DACON	Data on Consultants
DEVCOMM	Development Communication Division
DGF	Development Grant Facility
EA	Environmental assessment
ECD	Early Child Development
ECOSOC	U.N. Economic and Social Council
ED	Executive director
EFA	Education for All
EKE	Education for the Knowledge Economy
ESSD	Environmentally and Socially Sustainable Development
FDI	Foreign direct investment
G-5, G-7, G-8	Group of Five, Group of Seven, Group of Eight
GDLN	Global Development Learning Network
GDP	Gross domestic product
GEF	Global Environment Facility
GICT	Global Information and Communication Technologies
GP	Good practice
HDN	Human Development Network
HIPC	Heavily Indebted Poor Countries
HNP	Health, nutrition, and population

IBRD	International Bank for Reconstruction and Development
ICSID	International Centre for Settlement of Investment Disputes
IDA	International Development Association
IFC	International Finance Corporation
IMF	International Monetary Fund
IMFC	International Monetary and Financial Committee
MAP	Multi-Country HIV/AIDS Program
MD	Managing director
MDB	Multilateral development bank
MDG	Millennium Development Goal
MIGA	Multilateral Investment Guarantee Agency
NEPAD	New Partnership for Africa's Development
NGO	Nongovernmental organization
OD	Operational directive
OECS	Organization for Eastern Caribbean States
OED	Operations Evaluation Department
OP	Operational policy
OPCS	Operations Policy and Country Services
PAD	Project Appraisal Document
PGD	Program Document
PIC	Public Information Center
PPIAF	Public-Private Infrastructure Advisory Facility
PREM	Poverty Reduction and Economic Management
PRSP	Poverty Reduction Strategy Paper
PSI	Private Sector Development and Infrastructure Network
QAG	Quality Assurance Group
REEF	Renewable Energy and Energy Efficiency Fund
SDP	Strategic Directions Paper
SFP	Strategic Framework Paper
SME	Small and medium enterprise
U.N.	United Nations
UNAIDS	Joint United Nations Programme on HIV/AIDS
UNCITRAL	U.N. Commission on International Trade Law
UNDG	U.N. Development Group
UNDP	United Nations Development Programme
VPU	Vice presidential unit
WBI	World Bank Institute
WorLD	World Links for Development
WTO	World Trade Organization

World Bank Group Mission Statement

Our dream is a world free of poverty

- To fight poverty with passion and professionalism for lasting results.
- To help people help themselves and their environment by providing resources, sharing knowledge, building capacity, and forging partnerships in the public and private sectors.
- To be an excellent institution able to attract, excite, and nurture diverse and committed staff with exceptional skills who know how to listen and learn.

Our principles

- Client centered, working in partnership, accountable for quality results, dedicated to financial integrity and cost-effectiveness, inspired and innovative.

Our values

- Personal honesty, integrity, commitment; working together in teams—with openness and trust; empowering others and respecting differences; encouraging risk-taking and responsibility; enjoying our work and our families.

A focus group meeting in a rural area in the Republic of Yemen

CHAPTER 1

Introduction

Conceived in 1944 to reconstruct war-torn Europe, the World Bank Group has evolved into one of the world's largest sources of development assistance, with a mission of fighting poverty with passion by helping people help themselves.

The Five World Bank Group Institutions

The World Bank Group is composed of five institutions:

- The *International Bank for Reconstruction and Development (IBRD)* lends to governments of middle-income and creditworthy low-income countries.

- The *International Development Association (IDA)* provides interest-free loans, called credits, to governments of the poorest countries.

- The *International Finance Corporation (IFC)* lends directly to the private sector in developing countries.

- The *Multilateral Investment Guarantee Agency (MIGA)* provides guarantees to investors in developing countries against losses caused by noncommercial risks.

- The *International Centre for Settlement of Investment Disputes (ICSID)* provides international facilities for conciliation and arbitration of investment disputes.

Although the World Bank Group consists of five institutions, only IBRD and IDA constitute the World Bank.

Through its five institutions (see box 1.1), the Bank Group works in more than 100 developing economies, bringing a mix of financing programs and ideas to improve living standards and eliminate the worst forms of poverty. This role has grown in relative importance in the world of international finance in recent years as private sector net financial flows to developing countries have declined (see figure 1.1).

The Bank Group is managed by its member countries (borrowers, lenders, and donors), whose representatives are resident at the Bank Group's headquarters in Washington, D.C., and at country offices around the world. Many developing countries use Bank Group assistance—ranging from loans and grants to technical assistance and policy advice. All Bank Group efforts are coordinated with a wide range of partners, including government agencies, nongovernmental organizations, other aid agencies, and the private sector. A rapidly increasing percentage of Bank Group staff members is based in the countries that receive assistance.

This book guides the reader into the conceptual work of the World Bank Group. Its goal is to serve as an introduction for the reader—a starting point for more in-depth inquiries into subjects of particular interest. It provides a glimpse of the wide array of activities conducted by the Bank Group institutions and directs the reader toward publication and Web site resources that have more detailed information.

The text is descriptive; it makes no attempt to justify the activities described (for that it refers you to institutional annual reports, presidential speeches, and many topical publications issued by the Bank Group). The length of specific descriptions does not convey any judgment about the relative importance of selected activities.

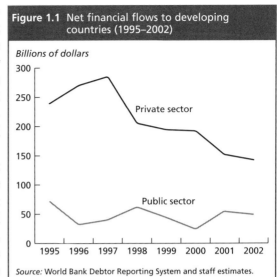

Figure 1.1 Net financial flows to developing countries (1995–2002)

Billions of dollars

Source: World Bank Debtor Reporting System and staff estimates.

This book is intended for the wide range of people around the world who need basic information about the work of the Bank Group. This audience includes people working in all aspects of development, students, members of the general public, and staff members of the Bank Group itself. Because this audience is so broad, the text emphasizes the organizational and conceptual divisions of the Bank Group's activities and guides readers to potential sources of more-detailed explanations of the development work in progress. The annual reports of the Bank Group institutions provide more details on the volume and types of development assistance. The annual *World Bank Group Directory* lists telephone contacts for individuals and departments.

The following chapters explain how the World Bank Group is organized; how it operates; and how its work focuses on countries, regions, and specific topics in development. Appendixes provide further information on Bank Group contacts, on the organization's history, on country membership and the voting shares in the institutions, on the sector and thematic categories for the Bank Group's activities, and on Bank Group resources in individual countries.

We welcome comments on this publication, as well as on the many projects and activities of the Bank Group institutions. To provide comments, visit <http://www.worldbank.org> and click on "Contact Us," or send an e-mail to <feedback@worldbank.org>.

The World Bank Group headquarters in Washington, D.C.

CHAPTER 2

How the World Bank Group Is Organized

This chapter explains how the World Bank Group is governed and how it is organized to do its work. It provides detailed information on the five World Bank Group institutions and other major organizational units. The final section explains the relationship of the World Bank Group to the International Monetary Fund and the United Nations.

Governance of the World Bank Group

Founding Documents

Each of the five institutions of the World Bank Group has its own articles of agreement or an equivalent founding document. These documents legally define the institution's purpose, organization, and operations, including the mechanisms by which it is owned and governed. By signing these documents and meeting the requirements set forth in them, a country can become a member of the Bank Group institutions.

Ownership by Member Countries

Each Bank Group institution is owned by its member countries (its shareholders). The number of member countries varies by institution, from 184 in the International Bank for Reconstruction and Development (IBRD) to 139 in the International Centre for the Settlement of Investment Disputes (ICSID), as of May 2003. The requirements for membership and the country classifications the Bank Group uses are explained in chapter 4 ("World Bank Group Countries and Regions").

In practice, member countries govern the Bank Group through the Board of Governors and the Board of Executive Directors. These bodies make all major policy decisions for the organization (see figure 2.1).

Figure 2.1 Relationship of member countries and the World Bank Group

Member countries
↓↓↓
Board of Governors
↓↓↓
Board of Executive Directors
↓↓↓
President
↓↓↓
Bank Group management and staff

Board of Governors

The World Bank Group operates under the authority of the Board of Governors. Each of the member countries of the Bank Group institutions is represented by one governor, who is usually a government official at the ministerial level. There is one Board of Governors serving IBRD, the International Finance Corporation (IFC), and the International Development Association (IDA), and a separate Board of Governors for the Multilateral Investment Guarantee Agency (MIGA). ICSID has an Administrative Council. Unless a government makes a contrary designation, its governor for the Bank sits ex officio on ICSID's Administrative Council.

Once a year the Boards of Governors of both the Bank Group and IMF meet in a joint session known as the Annual Meetings. More information on these meetings appears in the final section of this chapter. The views of member governments are represented throughout the year by the executive directors.

Executive Directors

General operation of the Bank Group is delegated to a smaller group of representatives, the Board of Executive Directors, with the president of the Bank Group serving as chairman of the board. The executive directors, sometimes referred to as EDs, are based at Bank Group headquarters in Washington, D.C. The Board of Executive Directors is responsible for policy decisions affecting the Bank Group's operation, and for approval of all loans. The executive directors normally meet twice a week to oversee the Bank Group's business. Each executive director also serves on one or more standing committees: Audit, Budget, Development Effectiveness, Personnel, and Executive Directors' Administrative Matters.

IBRD has 24 executive directors. The five largest shareholders—United States, Japan, Germany, France, and the United Kingdom—each appoints one executive director. The other countries are grouped into constituencies, each represented by an executive director who is elected by a country or group of countries. The members themselves decide how they will be grouped. Some countries—China, the Russian Federation, and Saudi Arabia—form single-country constituencies. The country groups more or less represent geographic regions with some political and cultural factors determining exactly how they are constituted.

Under the Articles of Agreement of IDA and IFC, the executive directors of IBRD serve ex officio as executive directors of IDA and as members of the Board of Directors of IFC. MIGA has its own Board of Directors, also consisting of 24 members. All members of the MIGA Board of Directors are elected.

The boards normally make decisions by consensus; however, the relative voting power of individual executive directors is based on the shares that are held by the countries they represent (see figure 2.2). For more on the constituencies, voting power, and elections of the executive directors, see appendixes D and E.

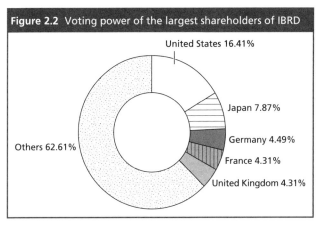

Figure 2.2 Voting power of the largest shareholders of IBRD

United States 16.41%

Japan 7.87%

Germany 4.49%

France 4.31%

United Kingdom 4.31%

Others 62.61%

World Bank Group President

The president is selected by the Board of Executive Directors and serves as president of each Bank Group institution. The Articles of Agreement do not

World Bank Group President James D. Wolfensohn

James D. Wolfensohn became president of the World Bank Group on June 1, 1995, and began a second five-year term in 2000. Born in Australia in December 1933, Mr. Wolfensohn is a naturalized U.S. citizen. He holds a B.A. and LL.B. from the University of Sydney and an M.B.A. from Harvard Business School.

Before joining the Bank Group, Mr. Wolfensohn was an international investment banker and founder of a firm advising major U.S. and international corporations. Previously, he held senior positions in finance firms, including Salomon Brothers in New York, Schroders Ltd. in London, J. Henry Schroders Banking Corp. in New York, and Darling & Co. in Australia. Earlier, in Australia, he worked as a lawyer, served in the air force, and competed on the Olympic fencing team.

Mr. Wolfensohn's cultural and volunteer work includes board membership for many foundations, business associations, and nonprofit groups. He has served as board chairman at Carnegie Hall in New York; at the Kennedy Center in Washington, D.C.; and at the Institute for Advanced Study at Princeton University.

specify the nationality of the president, but by custom the U.S. executive director makes a nomination. By a long-standing, informal agreement, the president of the Bank Group is a U.S. national, while the managing director of IMF is a European. The initial term for the president is five years; a second term could be five years or fewer. There is no mandatory retirement age.

Bank Group units report to the president, and through him to the executive directors—one exception being Operations Evaluation at the World Bank, which reports directly to the executive directors. The president delegates some of this oversight responsibility to the managing directors.

James D. Wolfensohn is president of the World Bank Group (see box 2.1). For information on previous presidents of the Bank Group, see appendix C.

Managing Directors

The five managing directors assist the president in broad oversight of the World Bank (IBRD and IDA). Each of the managing directors, or MDs, oversees several organizational units. One managing director also serves as executive vice president of IFC. A few senior officers of the World Bank report directly to the president rather than to a managing director; they include the Bank's general counsel and chief economist. The executive vice president of MIGA and the secretary-general of ICSID also report directly to the president.

The Five World Bank Group Institutions

The institutions that make up the World Bank Group specialize in different aspects of development, but they work collaboratively toward the overarching goal of poverty reduction. The terms "World Bank" and "the Bank" refer

Origin of the Term "World Bank"

The term "world bank" was first used in reference to the International Bank for Reconstruction and Development (IBRD) in an article in *The Economist* on July 22, 1944, in a report on the Bretton Woods Conference. The first meeting of the Boards of Governors of IBRD and the International Monetary Fund (IMF), which was held in Savannah, Georgia, in March 1946, was officially called the "World Fund and Bank Inaugural Meeting," and several news accounts of this conference, including one in the *Washington Post*, used the term "world bank." What began as a nickname became an official shorthand for IBRD and IDA in 1975.

only to IBRD and IDA, whereas the terms "World Bank Group" and "the Bank Group" include all five institutions (see box 2.2).

The World Bank: IBRD and IDA

Through its loans, policy advice, and technical assistance, the World Bank supports a broad range of programs aimed at reducing poverty and improving living standards in the developing world. It divides its work between IBRD, which assists middle-income and creditworthy poorer countries, and IDA, which focuses exclusively on the world's poorest countries. Working through both IBRD and IDA, the Bank uses its financial resources, a skilled staff, and an extensive knowledge base to help each developing country achieve stable, sustainable, and equitable growth.

IBRD and IDA are run on the same lines. They share the same staff and the same headquarters, report to the same senior management, and use the same standards when evaluating projects. Some countries borrow from both institutions. IDA merely takes its money out of a different "drawer." A country must be a member of IBRD before it can join IDA.

For all its clients, the Bank emphasizes the need for

- Investing in people, particularly through basic health and education
- Focusing on social development, inclusion, governance, and institution building as key elements of poverty reduction
- Strengthening the ability of the governments to deliver quality services efficiently and transparently
- Protecting the environment
- Supporting and encouraging private business development
- Promoting reforms to create a stable macroeconomic environment that is conducive to investment and long-term planning.

Effective poverty reduction strategies and poverty-focused lending are central to achieving the Bank's objectives. Bank programs give high priority to sustainable social and human development and to strengthened economic management, with a growing emphasis on inclusion, governance, and institution building. The Bank has helped build a consensus in the international community that developing countries must take the lead in creating their own strategies for poverty reduction. It also plays a key role in helping countries implement the Millennium Development Goals, which the United Nations and the broader international community seek to achieve by 2015.

In conjunction with IFC, the Bank is also helping countries strengthen and sustain the fundamental conditions they need to attract and retain private investment. With Bank Group support—both lending and advice—governments are reforming their overall economies and strengthening banking systems. Investments in human resources, infrastructure, and environmental protection help enhance the attractiveness and productivity of private investment.

IBRD: International Bank for Reconstruction and Development

IBRD, established in 1945, is the original institution of the World Bank Group and the source of the loans for which the Bank Group is best known. IBRD remains what many people mean when they refer to the World Bank. It has the largest country membership, the broadest mission, and the greatest number of staff in the Bank Group, both at headquarters and in the field (see box 2.3).

When IBRD was established, its first task was to help Europe recover from World War II. Today, IBRD plays an important role in poverty reduction, by providing the countries it now serves—middle-income and creditworthy poorer countries—with loans, guarantees, and analytical and advisory services. It provides these client countries with access to capital on favorable terms in larger volumes, with longer maturities, and in a more sustainable manner than the market provides. Specifically, IBRD

Box 2.3
Basic Facts: International Bank for Reconstruction and Development
Year established: 1945
Number of member countries: 184
Cumulative lending: US$371 billion
Fiscal 2002 lending: US$11.5 billion for 96 new operations in 40 countries
Web: http://www.worldbank.org/ibrd

- Supports long-term human and social development needs that private creditors do not finance
- Preserves borrowers' financial strength by providing support in crisis periods, when poor people are most adversely affected
- Uses the leverage of financing to promote key policy and institutional reforms (such as safety-net or anticorruption reforms)
- Creates a favorable investment climate in order to catalyze private capital

- Provides financial support (in the form of grants made available from IBRD net income) in areas that are critical to the well-being of poor people in all countries.

IBRD raises most of its funds on the world's financial markets. It is a AAA-rated financial institution, but one with some unusual characteristics. Its shareholders are sovereign governments. Its member borrowers have a voice in setting its policies. IBRD loans (and IDA credits) are typically accompanied by nonlending services to ensure more-effective use of funds. Also, unlike commercial banks, IBRD is driven by development impact rather than by profit maximization.

IBRD borrowers are typically middle-income countries that have some access to private capital markets. Some countries are eligible for IDA lending because of low per capita incomes but also are eligible for some IBRD borrowing because of their creditworthiness. These countries are known as "blend" borrowers (see table 2.1). Countries that receive IBRD lending contain 75 percent of the world's people who live on less than US$1 per day; even excluding IBRD loans to the "blend" countries, the remaining IBRD borrowers contain 25 percent of those who live on less than US$1 a day. (For more on country classifications, see *World Development Indicators* or the *World Bank Annual Report*.)

Countries are considered to have graduated from IBRD borrowing when they cease to borrow because their per capita income exceeds the level that the Bank classifies as middle income. For more information, including a list of IBRD graduates, see chapter 4 ("World Bank Group Countries and Regions") and box 4.2.

Although IBRD does not maximize profit, it has earned a positive net income each year since 1948. This income funds developmental activities and ensures financial strength, enabling low-cost borrowings in capital markets and good terms for borrowing clients. IBRD links member countries' voting power to their capital subscriptions, which in turn are based on their relative economic strength. Additional information on IBRD loans appears in the next chapter. For more on capital subscriptions, see chapter 4 ("World Bank Group Countries and Regions") and the list of member countries in appendix E.

IDA: International Development Association

After the rebuilding of Europe following World War II, the Bank turned its attention to the developing countries. It became clear that the poorest developing countries could not afford to borrow capital for development on the terms offered by the Bank; hence, a group of Bank member countries decided to found IDA as an institution that could lend to very poor developing nations on easier terms. To imbue

Table 2.1 Country Eligibility for Borrowing from the World Bank (as of July 1, 2002)

Income group and country	2001 GNI per capita[a]	Income group and country	2001 GNI per capita[a]
Countries eligible for IBRD funds only			
Per capita income over $5,185		Dominican Republic	2,230
Slovenia	9,780	Marshall Islands	2,190
Korea, Republic of	9,400	Micronesia, Federated States of	2,150
Antigua and Barbuda	9,070	Fiji	2,130
Argentina	6,960	Tunisia	2,070
St. Kitts and Nevis	6,880	El Salvador	2,050
Palau	6,730	Peru	2,000
Uruguay	5,670	Thailand	1,970
Mexico	5,540	Namibia	1,960
Trinidad and Tobago	5,540	Colombia	1,910
Czech Republic	5,270	Iran, Islamic Republic of	1,750
Seychelles	—	Jordan	1,750
		Russian Federation	1,750
Per capita income $2,976–$5,185		Romania	1,710
Hungary	4,800	Macedonia, former Yugoslav Republic of	1,690
Venezuela, República Bolivariana de	4,760	Suriname	1,690
Croatia	4,550	Guatemala	1,670
Chile	4,350	Algeria	1,630
Poland	4,240	Bulgaria	1,560
Lebanon	4,010	Egypt, Arab Republic of	1,530
Costa Rica	3,930		
Mauritius	3,830	**Per capita income $746–$1,435**	
Estonia	3,810	Kazakhstan	1,360
Slovak Republic	3,720	Paraguay	1,300
Malaysia	3,640	Swaziland	1,300
Botswana	3,630	Ecuador	1,240
Panama	3,290	Belarus	1,200
Latvia	3,260	Morocco	1,180
Gabon	3,160	Philippines	1,050
Lithuania	3,080	Syrian Arab Republic[b]	1,000
Brazil	3,070	Turkmenistan	950
		China	890
Per capita income $1,436–$2,975		Iraq[c]	—
Belize	2,910		
South Africa	2,900	**Per capita income less than $746**	
Jamaica	2,700	Ukraine	710
Turkey	2,530	Equatorial Guinea	700
Countries eligible for a blend of IBRD and IDA funds[d]			
Per capita income $2,976–$5,185		**Per capita income less than $746**	
St. Lucia[e]	3,970	Indonesia	680
Grenada[e]	3,720	Azerbaijan	650
Dominica[e]	3,060	Papua New Guinea	580
		Uzbekistan	560
Per capita income $1,436–$2,975		Zimbabwe[c]	480
St. Vincent and the Grenadines[e]	2,690	India	460
		Pakistan	420
Per capita income $746–$1,435		Nigeria	290
Bosnia and Herzegovina	1,270		
Bolivia	940		
Yugoslavia, Fed. Rep. (Serbia and Montenegro)[c]	—		
Countries eligible for IDA funds only[d]			
Per capita income $1,436–$2,975		Vanuatu[e]	1,050
Maldives[e]	2,040	Djibouti	890
Tonga[e]	1,530	Honduras	890
Samoa[e]	1,520	Guyana	840
		Kiribati	830
Per capita income $746–$1,435		Sri Lanka	830
Cape Verde[e]	1,310		
Albania	1,230		

Table 2.1 Country Eligibility for Borrowing from the World Bank (continued)

Income group and country	2001 GNI per capita[a]	Income group and country	2001 GNI per capita[a]
Per capita income less than $746		São Tomé and Principe	280
Congo, Republic of	700	Tanzania	280
Bhutan	640	Uganda	280
Côte d'Ivoire	630	Central African Republic[c]	270
Solomon Islands[c]	580	Cambodia	270
Cameroon	570	Togo[c]	270
Georgia	570	Madagascar	260
Armenia	560	Nepal	240
Lesotho	550	Rwanda	220
Angola	500	Burkina Faso	210
Haiti[c]	480	Mali	210
Senegal	480	Mozambique	210
Yemen, Republic of	460	Chad	200
Vietnam	410	Eritrea	190
Guinea	400	Malawi	170
Mongolia	400	Niger	170
Moldova	390	Guinea-Bissau	160
Comoros	380	Tajikistan	160
Bangladesh	370	Sierra Leone	140
Benin	360	Burundi	100
Mauritania	350	Ethiopia	100
Kenya	340	Afghanistan[c]	—
Gambia, The	330	Congo, Democratic Republic of[c]	—
Sudan[c]	330	Liberia[c]	—
Zambia	320	Myanmar[c]	—
Lao People's Democratic Republic	310	Nicaragua	—
Ghana	290	Somalia[c]	—
Kyrgyz Republic	280		

— Precise figures are not available.
[a]World Bank Atlas methodology; per capita GNI (gross national income, formerly GNP) figures are in 2001 U.S. dollars.
[b]Loans/credits in nonaccrual status as of June 30, 2002.
[c]Loans/credits in nonaccrual status as of July 1, 2002.
[d]Countries are eligible for IDA on the basis of (a) relative poverty and (b) lack of creditworthiness. The operational cutoff for IDA eligibility for fiscal 2003 is a 2001 GNI per capita of $875, using Atlas methodology. To receive IDA resources, countries also meet tests of performance. In exceptional circumstances, IDA extends eligibility temporarily to countries that are above the operational cutoff and are undertaking major adjustment efforts but are not creditworthy for IBRD lending. An exception has been made for small island economies (see footnote e).
[e]An exception to the GNI per capita operational cutoff for IDA eligibility ($875 for fiscal 2003) has been made for some small island economies, which otherwise would have little or no access to Bank Group assistance because they lack creditworthiness. For such countries, IDA funding is considered case by case for the financing of projects and adjustment programs designed to strengthen creditworthiness.

IDA with the discipline of a bank, these countries agreed that IDA should be part of the World Bank. IDA began operating in 1960 (see box 2.4).

IDA helps the world's poorest countries reduce poverty by providing credits, which are loans at zero interest with a 10-year grace period and maturities of 35 to 40 years. These credits are often referred to as concessional lending. IDA credits help build the human capital, policies, institutions, and physical infrastructure that these countries urgently need to achieve faster, environmentally sustainable growth. IDA's goal is to reduce disparities across and within countries—especially in terms of access to primary education, basic health, and water supply and sanitation—and to bring more people into the economic mainstream by raising their productivity.

IDA is funded largely by contributions from the governments of the industrial member countries (see table 2.2). Representatives of donor countries meet every three years to replenish IDA funds. Their cumulative contributions since IDA's beginning total some US$109 billion. Additional funds come from repayments of earlier IDA credits and from IBRD's net income. Donors also use the replenishment meeting as an opportunity to discuss IDA's future direction; in 2001, for the first time, representatives of borrowing countries joined donors in these discussions. The three-year cycles of IDA funding are commonly referred to by number. For example, the cycle that covers lending during fiscal 2003 to 2005 is the 13th Replenishment of IDA, or IDA-13.

IDA lends to countries that have very low per capita income—less than US$875 in 2002—and that lack the financial ability to borrow from IBRD. At present, the countries that are eligible to borrow from IDA are home to 2.5 billion people, constituting half of the total population of the developing countries. In most of these countries, the vast majority of people live on less than US$2 a day, whereas 4 out of 10 people—an estimated 1.1 billion people—survive on less than US$1 a day. As noted in the section on IBRD, some countries are eligible for IDA borrowing because of their low per capita incomes but are also eligible for some IBRD borrowing because of their creditworthiness. Examples of such "blend" borrowers are India and Indonesia.

IDA eligibility is a transitional arrangement, allowing the poorest countries access to substantial resources before they can obtain from the markets the financing they need in order to invest. As their economies grow, countries graduate from IDA eligibility. The repayments, or "reflows," that they make on IDA loans then help finance new IDA loans to the remaining poor countries. Over the years, more than 20 countries have seen their economies develop and grow beyond the IDA-eligibility threshold. Examples include Costa Rica, Chile, the Arab Republic of Egypt, Morocco, Thailand, and Turkey. Some countries donate to IDA while continuing to borrow from IBRD.

The International Finance Corporation

 IFC promotes economic development through the private sector (see box 2.5). Working with business partners, IFC invests in sustainable private enterprises in developing countries

Table 2.2 Cumulative IDA Subscriptions and Contributions

Member	Cumulative IDA subscriptions and contributions (millions of U.S. dollars)	Cumulative IDA subscriptions and contributions (percent of total)
United States	25,841.78	23.62
Japan	24,137.67	22.07
Germany	12,467.53	11.40
United Kingdom	8,068.19	7.38
France	7,562.38	6.91
Canada	4,763.45	4.35
Italy	4,462.91	4.08
Netherlands	4,054.32	3.71
Sweden	2,802.32	2.56
Saudi Arabia	2,158.21	1.97
Australia	1,824.58	1.67
Belgium	1,778.30	1.63
Denmark	1,475.61	1.35
Switzerland	1,449.61	1.33
Norway	1,398.50	1.28
Austria	905.86	0.83
Kuwait	707.35	0.65
Finland	698.02	0.64
Spain	667.87	0.61
Korea, Republic of	309.80	0.28
Brazil	305.33	0.28
Russian Federation	174.00	0.16
Ireland	142.74	0.13
Mexico	137.83	0.13
New Zealand	131.49	0.12
Turkey	113.79	0.10
South Africa	91.70	0.08
Argentina	69.80	0.06
Luxembourg	66.62	0.06
Poland	59.09	0.05
Portugal	58.38	0.05
Hungary	45.63	0.04
Greece	41.24	0.04
Czech Republic	35.34	0.03
Colombia	24.43	0.02
Iceland	23.22	0.02
Israel	13.19	0.01
Slovak Republic	12.57	0.01
Yugoslavia, Fed. Rep. (Serbia and Montenegro)	6.80	0.01
United Arab Emirates	5.58	0.01
Croatia	5.54	0.01
Slovenia	3.00	0.00
Bosnia and Herzegovina	2.34	0.00
Botswana	1.61	0.00
Oman	1.33	0.00
Macedonia, former Yugoslav Republic of	1.03	0.00
Barbados	0.63	0.00
Total donors	109,108.51	99.74
Total nondonors	279.20	0.26
Grand total	109,387.71	100.00

Note: Amounts may not add to totals because of rounding.

without accepting government guarantees. This direct lending to businesses is the fundamental contrast between IFC and the World Bank: under their Articles of Agreement, IBRD and IDA can lend only to the governments of member countries. IFC was founded specifically to address this limitation in World Bank lending.

IFC provides equity, long-term loans, loan guarantees, risk management products, and advisory services to its clients. It is the largest multilateral source of loan and equity financing for private sector projects in developing countries. It seeks to reach businesses in regions and countries that otherwise would have limited access to capital. It provides financing programs in markets that would be deemed too risky by commercial investors in the absence of IFC participation. IFC further supports the projects it finances by providing corporate governance, environmental and social expertise, and advice and technical assistance to businesses and governments.

Project financing

IFC offers an array of financial products and services to companies in its developing member countries, including

- Long-term loans in major and local currencies, at fixed or variable rates
- Equity investments
- Quasi-equity instruments (such as subordinated loans, preferred stock, income notes, and convertible debt)
- Syndicated loans
- Risk management (such as intermediation of currency and interest rate swaps, and provision of hedging facilities)
- Intermediary financing

IFC can provide financial instruments singly or in whatever combination is necessary to ensure that projects are adequately funded from the outset. It can also help structure financial packages by coordinating financing from foreign and local banks and companies and from export credit agencies.

IFC charges market rates for its products and does not accept government guarantees; therefore, it carefully reviews the likelihood of success for each enterprise. To be eligible for IFC financing, projects must be profitable for investors, benefit the economy of the host country, and comply with stringent environmental and social guidelines. IFC finances projects in all types of industries and sectors; examples include manufacturing, infrastructure, tourism, health and education, and financial services. Financial service projects represent a significant share of new approvals; they range from investments in nascent leasing, insurance, and mortgage markets to student loans and credit lines, to local banks, which in turn provide microfinancing or business loans to small and medium enterprises. Although IFC is primarily a financier of private sector projects, it may provide financing for a company with some government ownership, provided there is private sector participation and the venture is run on a commercial basis. It can finance companies that are wholly locally owned as well as joint ventures between foreign and local shareholders.

To ensure the participation of investors and lenders from the private sector, IFC limits the total amount of own-account debt and equity financing it will provide for any single project. For new projects, the maximum is 25 percent of the total estimated project costs or, on an exceptional basis, up to 35 percent for small projects. For expansion projects, IFC may provide up to 50 percent of the project cost, provided its investments do not exceed 25 percent of the total capitalization of the project company. On average, for every US$1 of IFC financing, other investors and lenders provide more than US$5.

IFC investments typically range from US$1 million to US$100 million. IFC funds may be used for permanent working capital or for foreign or local expenditures in any IBRD member country to acquire fixed assets. Because IFC operates on commercial terms that target profitability, it has made a profit every year since its inception.

Resource mobilization

IFC participates in an investment only when it can make a special contribution that complements the role of market operators. Owing to its success record and its special standing as a multilateral institution, it is able to act as a catalyst for private investment. Its participation in a project enhances investor confidence and attracts other lenders and shareholders. IFC mobilizes financing directly for sound companies in developing countries by syndicating loans with international commercial banks and by underwriting investment funds and corporate securities issues. It also handles private placements of securities.

Advisory services

IFC's particular focus is to promote economic development by encouraging the growth of private enterprises and efficient capital markets in its member countries. In this context, IFC advises business in developing countries on a wide variety of matters, including physical and financial restructuring; formulating business plans; identifying markets, products, technologies, and financial and technical partners; and mobilizing project financing. IFC can provide advisory services in the context of an investment or can provide them independently for a fee, in line with market practice.

IFC also advises governments in developing countries on how to create an enabling business environment, and it provides guidance on attracting foreign direct investment (FDI). For example, it helps develop domestic capital markets. It also provides assistance in areas such as restructuring and privatizing state-owned enterprises.

The Multilateral Investment Guarantee Agency

MIGA encourages foreign investment in developing countries by providing guarantees to foreign investors against losses caused by noncommercial risks, such as expropriation, currency inconvertibility and transfer restrictions, war and civil disturbance, or breach of contract (see box 2.6). In addition, MIGA provides technical assistance to help countries disseminate information on investment opportunities. The agency also provides investment dispute mediation services upon request.

MIGA has four guiding principles:

- *Focus on clients:* serve investors, lenders, and host-country governments by supporting private enterprise and promoting foreign investment.
- *Engage in partnerships:* work with other insurers, government agencies, and international organizations to ensure complementarity of services and approach.
- *Promote developmental impact:* strive to improve the lives of people in emerging economies, consistent with the goals of host countries and with sound business, environmental, and social principles.
- *Ensure financial soundness:* balance developmental goals and financial objectives through prudent underwriting and sound risk management.

MIGA membership is open to all World Bank members. The agency has a capital stock of US$1 billion. In March 1999, MIGA's Council of Governors adopted a resolution for a capital increase of approximately US$850 million. The agency received another US$150 million in operating capital from the World Bank.

Development impact

Projects supported by MIGA have widespread benefits. They create local jobs, generate tax revenue, and transfer skills and technological know-how. Local communities often receive significant secondary benefits through improved infrastructure, including roads, electricity, hospitals, schools, and clean water. FDI supported by MIGA also encourages similar local investments and spurs the growth of local businesses that supply related goods and services. As a result, developing countries have a greater chance to break the cycle of poverty.

MIGA's guarantee coverage requires investors to adhere to social and environmental standards that are considered to be the world's best. MIGA both supports and draws on the extensive resources of the World Bank Group, applying unparalleled knowledge of emerging economies to the projects it guarantees.

An umbrella of deterrence

MIGA acts as an umbrella of deterrence against government actions that could disrupt investments, and this role allows it to influence the resolution of potential disputes. MIGA's capacity to serve as an objective intermediary enhances investor confidence that an investment in an emerging economy will be protected against noncommercial risks.

Concerns about uncertain political environments and perceptions of political risk often inhibit investment, with FDI often going to a handful of countries, leaving the world's poorest economies largely ignored. MIGA is an important catalyst, increasingly promoting FDI—a key driver of growth—in developing countries through its guarantees, technical assistance, and legal services.

Since its inception, MIGA has issued more than 500 guarantees for projects in 78 developing countries. As of June 2001, total coverage issued exceeded US$9 billion, bringing the estimated amount of FDI facilitated since inception to more than US$41 billion. The agency mobilized an additional US$153 million in investment coverage in fiscal 2001 through its Cooperative Underwriting Program (CUP), which encourages private sector insurers to insure transactions they would not otherwise undertake and helps the agency serve more clients.

MIGA's technical assistance services also play an integral role in catalyzing FDI, by helping developing countries around the world define and implement strategies to promote investment. MIGA develops and deploys tools and technologies to support the spread of information on investment opportunities. Thousands of users take advantage of MIGA's suite of online investment information services, which complement country-based capacity building work.

The agency also uses its legal services to smooth possible impediments to investment. Through its dispute mediation program, MIGA helps governments and investors resolve their differences and ultimately improve the country's investment climate.

MIGA's activities complement the activities of other investment insurers. It works with partners through its coinsurance and reinsurance programs to expand the income capacity of the political risk insurance industry. To date, MIGA has officially established 18 such partnerships.

The International Centre for Settlement of Investment Disputes

ICSID helps encourage foreign investment by providing international facilities for conciliation and arbitration of investment disputes, thus helping foster an atmosphere of mutual confidence between states and foreign investors (see box 2.7). Many

Box 2.7

Basic Facts: International Centre for Settlement of Investment Disputes

Year established: 1966

Number of member countries: 139

Total cases registered: 103

Fiscal 2002 cases registered: 16

Web: http://www.worldbank.org/icsid

international agreements concerning investment refer to ICSID's arbitration facilities. ICSID also carries out research and publishing in the areas of arbitration law and foreign investment law.

ICSID was established under the Convention on the Settlement of Investment Disputes between States and Nationals of Other States. The ICSID Convention came into force in 1966. ICSID has an Administrative Council and a Secretariat. The Administrative Council is chaired by the World Bank's president; it consists of one representative of each state that has ratified the ICSID Convention. Annual meetings of the Administrative Council are held in conjunction with the joint annual meetings of the Bank Group and IMF.

ICSID is an autonomous international organization, but it has close links with the World Bank. All of ICSID's members are also members of the Bank. Unless a government makes a contrary designation, its governor for the Bank sits ex officio on ICSID's Administrative Council. The expenses of the ICSID Secretariat are financed through the Bank's budget, although the costs of individual proceedings are borne by the parties involved.

ICSID provides three types of services:

- *Facilities for the conciliation and arbitration of disputes between member countries and investors who qualify as nationals of other member countries.* Recourse to ICSID conciliation and arbitration is entirely voluntary; however, after the parties have consented to arbitration under the ICSID Convention, neither can unilaterally withdraw its consent. Moreover, all ICSID contracting states, whether they are parties to the dispute or not, are required by the ICSID Convention to recognize and enforce ICSID arbitral awards.

- *Certain types of proceedings between states and foreign nationals that fall outside the scope of the ICSID Convention.* These proceedings include conciliation and arbitration proceedings when either the state party or the home state of the foreign national is not a member of ICSID. "Additional Facility" conciliation and arbitration are also available for cases in which the dispute is not an investment dispute, provided it relates to a transaction that has features that distinguish it from an ordinary commercial transaction. The Additional Facility Rules further allow ICSID to administer a type of proceedings not provided for in the ICSID Convention—namely, fact-finding proceedings to which any state or foreign national may have recourse if he or she wishes to institute an inquiry to examine and report on facts.

- *Appointment of arbitrators for ad hoc (that is, noninstitutional) arbitration proceedings.* These appointments are most commonly made in the context of arrangements for arbitration under the Arbitration Rules of the United Nations Commission on International Trade Law (UNCITRAL), which are specially designed for ad hoc proceedings.

Organizing Principles

This section explains the basic principles upon which the World Bank Group organizes its work. It also lists the major organizational units. Later chapters focus on the substance of what the Bank Group is doing.

The Matrix: Networks and Regions
As part of an institutional renewal effort that began in the mid-1990s, the World Bank Group organizes most of its development work along two dimensions—in addition to the long-established units that focus on world regions, the Bank Group now also has thematic networks of expertise in specific aspects of development cutting across the various regions. As a result of this matrix arrangement, a Bank Group staff member may work for a thematic network but be deployed to work in operations in a specific region or country.

Vice Presidential Units
The vice presidential unit is the main organizational unit of the World Bank Group. Such units are commonly referred to as vice presidencies, or VPUs. With a few exceptions that report directly to the president, each of these units reports to a managing director. In general, each vice presidency corresponds to a world region, a thematic network, or a central function.

Following is information on VPUs and other major Bank units. For additional information see <http://www.worldbank.org/vpu>.

Network vice presidencies and sectors
The Bank Group has created networks to link communities of staff members who work in the same fields of development and to link these staff members more effectively with partners outside the Bank Group. The networks help draw out lessons learned across countries and regions and help bring global best practices to bear in meeting country-specific needs. In practice, many staff members in the networks sell their time to the regional departments.

Each of the thematic networks covers several related sectors of development; in organizational terms, there is generally a subunit dedicated to each sector. Each sector has its own board, with representatives drawn from the regions as well as from the network itself. The sector boards are accountable to a network council. Sector boards also identify "themes"—topics in development that are narrower than the work of the sector itself—on which a small number of staff members will focus, often in partnership with other organizations.

A central function of the sectors—and by extension of the networks themselves—is to create coherent sector strategies for all the Bank Group's work in a given aspect of development. Networks and sectors have also created advisory services or help desks to field queries from Bank Group staff members—and, in most cases, from members of the general public—in the areas of their expertise.

The thematic networks and the sectors they cover are as follows. The sectoral programs correspond broadly to the sections in chapter 5 ("Topics in Development"), which provides information on dozens of sectoral programs within the World Bank and IFC. It is important to note that the term "sector" is not used consistently in the names of the networks and their subunits. For a full list of World Bank sectors, see appendix F.

- *Environmentally and Socially Sustainable Development (ESSD) Network*. The sectors—also referred to as "families of practice"—are environment, rural development, and social development.
- *Financial Sector Network*. The specialist financial units are financial sector operations and policy; global operations; and financial market integrity. There is a single sector board for this network.
- *Human Development Network (HDN)*. The sectors are education; health, nutrition, and population; and social protection.
- *Poverty Reduction and Economic Management (PREM) Network*. The sectors are economic policy; gender; governance and public sector reform; and poverty.
- *Private Sector Development and Infrastructure (PSI) Network*. The sectors are energy; information and communication technologies; mining; oil, gas, and petrochemicals; private sector; transport; urban development; and water supply and sanitation. Some of these sectors are handled by joint World Bank–IFC units.

A few parts of the Bank Group that have a more-administrative mission have adopted certain features of a network organization. They include Operations Policy and Country Services (OPCS), described under "Other Major World Bank Group Units," below; the Information Solutions Network, comprising all staff members working in information technology; CommNet, an association of communications professionals across Bank Group headquarters and country offices; and the Administrative and Client Support (ACS) Network, comprising all staff members in office support positions.

Regional vice presidencies and country offices

Bank Group institutions have long organized much of their work around major world regions and have carried it out through offices in member countries. In recent years, the same institutional renewal effort that created the thematic networks has made decentralization a top priority. The goal is to bring a higher proportion of Bank Group staff members into closer proximity to their clients in member countries. The World Bank, for example, has relocated two-thirds of its country directors from its headquarters in Washington, D.C., to the field since the mid-1990s. The percentage of staff members assigned to the regions who work in the field has also increased significantly.

All Bank Group institutions share this increased emphasis on countries and regions, but the World Bank and IFC vary somewhat in how they organize their regional and country efforts. The following paragraphs give a brief overview of these organizational units. The substance of Bank Group work in the regions, with the countries covered, is summarized in chapter 4 ("World Bank Group Countries and Regions"). The full list of addresses of Bank Group offices outside Washington, D.C., appears in appendix G.

The World Bank has six regional vice presidencies: Africa (Sub-Saharan), East Asia and the Pacific, Europe and Central Asia, Latin America and the Caribbean, Middle East and North Africa, and South Asia. The Bank operates offices in more than 100 member countries, as well as at the United Nations (New York) and at its VPUs in Europe (Paris) and Japan (Tokyo). The Paris and Tokyo offices and many offices in developing countries also serve as Public Information Centers (PICs) for the World Bank Group. Country offices coordinate their activities with member governments, representatives of civil society, and other international donor agencies operating in the country, and with the country team at headquarters.

IFC defines its regions somewhat differently from the Bank. It assigns directors to the following regions: Central and Eastern Europe, East Asia and the Pacific, Latin America and the Caribbean, Middle East and North Africa, South Asia, Southern Europe and Central Asia, and Sub-Saharan Africa. A few countries are assigned to regions different from the Bank's regions. The regional directors all report to the IFC vice president for operations. IFC maintains its own network of more than 60 offices in member countries; in some cases, these offices share quarters with a World Bank office.

MIGA has representatives resident in Europe, Africa, and Asia.

Other major World Bank Group units or activities

The following paragraphs describe other major units of the World Bank Group—VPUs or the equivalent. Note that some functions are handled by a single unit for all Bank Group organizations; in other cases there are separate units for each organization. Note also that this list is not intended to be comprehensive.

Corporate Secretariat

This unit supports the day-to-day operation of the Board of Executive Directors of the World Bank Group. It is responsible for administration of matters connected with membership, including Annual Meetings of the Board of Governors and capital subscriptions. It also provides support to the independent Inspection Panel (see below under "Operations Evaluation").

Development Economics

This main research unit of the World Bank is headed by the chief economist. The unit provides data, development prospects analysis, research findings, analytical tools, and policy advice in support of Bank operations as well as advice to clients. More information on Bank Group research and data appears in chapter 3 ("How the World Bank Group Operates").

IFC has its own economics department, which is headed by the IFC chief economist.

External Affairs

External Affairs and U.N. Affairs at the World Bank manages communications on major Bank-related issues; handles relations with the public, the media, other organizations, governments of donor countries, and the local community; arranges speaking engagements for Bank representatives; produces and disseminates publications; coordinates the Bank's PICs worldwide; and maintains the Bank's external Web site. Programs include Development Communications, CommNet, and the Development Dialogue on Values and Ethics. The Bank's offices in New York, Western Europe, and Japan are part of External Affairs.

IFC and MIGA each maintains a corporate relations unit.

Financial Management

For such staff positions and departments as chief financial officer, controller, treasury, loans and portfolio management, and guarantees, there are substantial differences in how the World Bank, IFC, and MIGA are organized.

The World Bank has vice presidencies for

- Chief financial officer
- Controller (oversees the accounting and loan departments)
- Resource mobilization and cofinancing (oversees mobilization of funds for IDA and key environmental and debt relief initiatives; manages trust funds and development grants; and is responsible for interaction with bilateral partners, multilateral development banks, and foundations)
- Strategy and resource management (oversees reforms of the Bank budget and improvement of analytic capacity in resource management)

- Treasury (oversees activities in asset and liability management, including technical assistance to borrowing countries; capital markets and financial engineering; financial products and services; and investment management).

IFC groups the following units under its vice president for portfolio and risk management: controller and budgeting, chief information officer, corporate portfolio management, credit review, financial operations, risk management and financial policy, special operations, and trust funds.

At MIGA, the following units report directly to the executive vice president: guarantees and underwriting, chief financial officer and finance and risk management, and investment marketing services.

General Services

This unit is responsible for design and maintenance of office space at Bank Group headquarters and overseas; procurement of goods and services; translation and interpretation; security; travel and shipping support; printing and graphic design; and mail, messenger, and food services. IFC and MIGA handle some of these responsibilities through their own offices for facilities management and administration.

Human Resources

This unit manages all personnel issues. It provides information on job opportunities and internships. There are separate human resources VPUs at the World Bank and IFC; at MIGA, human resources are handled by the Office of Central Administration. The World Bank human resources VPU conducts an orientation of all new staff members at the Bank Group and a staff exchange program with other organizations and companies.

Separate from these human resources units is the Bank Group's Conflict Resolution System, a group of independent offices that address problems in the workplace, such as ethical issues and disputes regarding staff rules, pay, career advancement, and benefits. In addition to these units the World Bank Group Staff Association, an independent, voluntary organization, advocates for the rights and welfare of staff members.

Information Solutions Group

This unit builds and operates the Bank Group's infrastructure for information and communications technologies. It falls under the direction of the chief information officer, who also is responsible for library oversight. IFC has a separate unit to provide support in this area.

Legal

There are separate legal VPUs at the World Bank, IFC, and MIGA, each of which is headed by its own general counsel. Each of these units provides legal services for its respective institution and helps ensure that all activities comport with the institution's charter, policies, and rules. The focus includes legal and judicial reform in developing countries.

Office of the President

This office provides support to the World Bank Group president and maintains information on the president's speeches, interviews, and travels.

Operations Evaluation

At the World Bank, the Operations Evaluation Department (OED) is an independent unit that reports directly to the Board of Executive Directors. The separate operations evaluation units at IFC and MIGA each report to the executive vice president of their institution. All of these units are tasked with assessing the results of the Bank Group's work and offering relevant recommendations. The work of OED occurs in the evaluation phase of all World Bank projects, as outlined in chapter 3 ("How the World Bank Operates"). The unit also supports development of evaluation capacity in recipient countries.

Other units with related missions include the Compliance Advisor/ Ombudsman for IFC and MIGA; the Conflicts of Interest Office, which deals with joint Bank–IFC units; and the Quality Assurance Group at the World Bank.

In addition, the World Bank has set up an independent Inspection Panel, a three-member body to whom citizens of developing countries can bring their concerns if they believe that they or their interests have been or could be directly harmed by a project financed by the World Bank.

Operations Policy and Country Services

Organized much like the thematic networks, this unit provides leadership and coordination on all policy-related operational matters. It monitors compliance with Bank policies and works to ensure that operational teams can count on strong support from staff members and units that provide essential core services. See chapter 3 ("How the World Bank Operates") for detailed information on Bank Group policies and procedures.

World Bank Institute

Often abbreviated WBI, this unit is the main training and educational unit of the Bank Group. WBI conducts training, consults on policy, and creates and supports knowledge networks related to international economic and social development. Its focus includes distance learning and other emerging technologies for education and training. WBI serves member countries, Bank Group staff members and clients, and other people working on poverty reduction and sustainable development.

For more information about World Bank Group organizational units, see <http://web.worldbank.org/WBSITE/EXTERNAL/EXTABOUTUS/0,,content MDK:20040598~menuPK:34619~pagePK:34542~piPK:36600~theSitePK: 29708,00.html>.

Relationship to the IMF and the United Nations

The World Bank Group is an independent specialized agency of the United Nations, and it works in particularly close cooperation with another independent specialized U.N. agency, the IMF. These relationships are explained below (see also the history timeline in appendix B).

The Bretton Woods Institutions

The World Bank and the IMF were both established in 1944 at a conference of world leaders in Bretton Woods, New Hampshire, with the aim of placing the international economy on a sound footing after World War II. As a result of their shared origin, the two entities—the IMF and the expanded World Bank Group—are sometimes referred to collectively as the Bretton Woods institutions. The Bank Group and the IMF work closely together, have similar governance structures, have a similar relationship with the U.N., and are headquartered in close proximity in Washington, D.C. Membership in the Bank Group organizations is in fact open only to countries that are already members of the IMF. However, the Bank Group and the IMF remain separate institutions. Their work is complementary, but their individual roles are quite different.

Key differences between the work of the World Bank Group and that of the IMF include the following:

- The Bank Group lends only to developing or transition economies, whereas all member countries, rich or poor, can draw on the IMF's services and resources.
- The IMF's loans address short-term economic problems; they provide general support of a country's balance of payments and international reserves while the country takes policy action to address its difficulties. The Bank Group is concerned mainly with longer-term issues; it seeks to integrate countries into the wider world economy and to promote economic growth that reduces poverty.
- The IMF focuses on the macroeconomic performance of world economies, as well as on macroeconomic and financial sector policy. The Bank Group's focus extends further into the particular sectors of a country's economy and includes specific development projects as well as broader policy issues.

There are a few joint Bank Group–IMF units, including the Library Network, Health Services, and the Bank/Fund Conferences Office, which plans and coordinates the Annual and Spring Meetings. The staff members of the two institutions have formed the joint Bank–Fund Staff Federal Credit Union, but this entity is independent of the institutions themselves.

Development Committee and International Monetary and Financial Committee

The Development Committee is a forum of the Bank Group and the IMF that facilitates intergovernmental consensus building on development issues. Known formally as the Joint Ministerial Committee of the Boards of the Bank and Fund on the Transfer of Real Resources to Developing Countries, the committee was established in 1974.

The committee's mandate is to advise the Boards of Governors of the two institutions on critical development issues and on the financial resources required to promote economic development in developing countries. Over time, the committee has interpreted this mandate to include trade and global environmental issues in addition to traditional development matters.

The committee has 24 members, usually ministers of finance and development, who represent the full membership of the Bank Group and the IMF. They are appointed by each of the countries—or groups of countries—represented on the Boards of Executive Directors of the two institutions. The chair is selected from among the committee's members and is assisted by an executive secretary elected by the committee. The Development Committee meets twice a year.

The International Monetary and Financial Committee, or IMFC, has a similar structure, selection process for members, and schedule for meetings. It serves in an advisory role to the IMF Board of Governors; however, unlike the Development Committee, the IMFC is solely an IMF entity.

Annual and spring meetings

Each September or October, the Boards of Governors of the World Bank Group and IMF hold joint Annual Meetings to discuss a range of issues related to poverty reduction, international economic development, and finance. These meetings provide a forum for international cooperation and enable the two institutions to serve their member countries more effectively. In addition, the Development Committee and the IMFC are officially convened.

These meetings traditionally have been held in Washington, D.C., two years out of three, and in a different member country every third year. Recent meetings outside Washington, D.C., have been held in Hong Kong, China (1997), and Prague, Czech Republic (2000). The 2003 meetings are scheduled to be held in Dubai, United Arab Emirates. Around these meetings, the

Bank Group and the IMF organize a number of forums to facilitate the interaction of governments and Bank Group–IMF staff members with non-governmental organizations (NGOs), journalists, and the private sector.

The Development Committee and the IMFC also meet in March or April of each year to discuss progress on the work of the Bank Group and the IMF. As with the Annual Meetings, a number of activities are organized at these spring meetings to involve the press, the NGOs, and the private sector. However, plenary sessions of the two institutions' Boards of Governors are scheduled only during the Annual Meetings in September or October.

Specialized Agency of the United Nations

Cooperation between the Bank Group and the U.N. has been in place since the founding of the two organizations (in 1944 and 1945, respectively) and focuses on economic and social areas of mutual concern such as reducing poverty, promoting sustainable development, and investing in people. In addition to a shared agenda, the Bank Group and the U.N. have almost the same membership: only a handful of U.N. member countries are not members of IBRD.

The World Bank's formal relationship with the U.N. is defined by a 1947 agreement that recognizes the Bank (now the Bank Group) as an independent specialized agency of the U.N.—as well as an observer in many U.N. bodies, including the General Assembly. As an independent specialized agency, the Bank Group officially falls under the purview of the Economic and Social Council (ECOSOC). In recent years ECOSOC has conducted a special high-level meeting with the Bretton Woods institutions immediately after the spring meeting of the Bank Group and the IMF. The Bank Group president is also a member of the U.N. System Chief Executives Board for Coordination (CEB), which meets twice annually. The Bank also plays a key role in supporting U.N.-led processes, such as the International Conference on Financing for Development and the World Summit on Sustainable Development. The Bank provides knowledge about country-level challenges and helps formulate international policy recommendations.

In terms of operations, the Bank Group works with other U.N. funds and programs to coordinate policies, aid, and implementation of projects. The Bank Group also helps prepare for and participates in most of the U.N. global conferences, and plays an important role in follow-up, especially in the implementation of goals at the country level.

Further information on the Bank Group's collaboration with U.N. agencies can be found under "Partnerships" in chapter 3 ("How the World Bank Group Operates").

The World Bank Treasury trading room

How the World Bank Group Operates

This chapter covers the basics of Bank Group operations. Many aspects of these operations are interconnected, but the chapter is organized into sections as follows:

- *Strategies.* This section explains the Bank Group's overall framework for its fight against poverty, as well as strategies that are specific to individual countries and to various sectors of development.
- *Policies and Procedures.* This section gives an overview of the policies and guidelines that the Bank Group has established for its operations, to help ensure quality and fairness in its projects.
- *The Bank Group's Finances.* This section offers a quick primer on how the Bank Group institutions are funded and what they do with their money.
- *Products and Services.* The Bank Group offers a wide range of services to support development and poverty reduction activities in member countries. Subsections here provide details on the World Bank, the International Finance Corporation (IFC), the Multilateral Investment Guarantee Agency (MIGA), and the International Centre for Settlement of Investment Disputes (ICSID).
- *World Bank Projects.* This section covers the typical phases of a World Bank project, the documentation that each phase creates, and the resources for locating detailed information about Bank projects.
- *IFC Projects.* This section covers the typical phases of an IFC project.
- *Partnerships.* This section provides an overview of the types of partners the Bank Group works with, including the affiliates whose secretariats are located at Bank Group headquarters.
- *Staff, Consultants, and Vendors.* Here are details about the Bank Group's staff and related opportunities: job openings, internships, and scholarships. The section also provides links to basic information on doing business with the Bank Group.

Strategies

This section covers the main strategies guiding the work of the Bank Group. More information on strategies can be found online at <http://www.developmentgoals.org>.

Millennium Development Goals

The Millennium Development Goals identify—and quantify—specific gains that can be made to improve the lives of the world's poor people. The aim is to reduce poverty while improving health, education, and the environment. These goals were endorsed by 189 countries at the September 2000 U.N. Millennium General Assembly in New York. They provide a focus for the efforts of the World Bank Group, other multilateral organizations, governments, and other partners in the development community—a focus on significant, measurable improvements.

Sometimes abbreviated as MDGs, the Millennium Development Goals grew out of the agreements and resolutions of world conferences organized by the U.N. in the past decade. Each goal is to be achieved by 2015, with progress to be measured by comparison with 1990 levels.

For a list of the goals, see box 3.1. Although the goals are sometimes numbered, the numbers are not intended to indicate any differences of priority or urgency.

The goals establish yardsticks for measuring results, not just for developing countries but also for the rich countries that help fund development programs and for the multilateral institutions that help countries implement them. The first seven goals are mutually reinforcing and are directed at reducing poverty in all its forms. The last goal—global partnership for development—is directed at the means to achieve the first seven. Many of the poorest countries will need additional assistance and must look to the rich countries to provide it. Countries that are poor and heavily indebted will need further help in reducing their debt burdens. All countries will benefit if trade barriers are lowered, allowing a freer exchange of goods and services.

Because achieving the goals is an enormous challenge, partnerships between the Bank Group, the U.N. Development Group (UNDG), and other organizations is the only way to ensure coordinated and complementary efforts. The UNDG is made up of the many U.N. programs, funds, and agencies engaged in development assistance and related activities. The Bank Group participates in the UNDG and supports its framework for greater coherence and cooperation in U.N. development operations.

For the Bank Group, as for other agencies, the challenge of implementing the Millennium Development Goals now provides a starting point for all operations. The Web site of the Millennium Development Goals is at <http://www.developmentgoals.org>.

Millennium Development Goals for 2015

Eradicate extreme poverty and hunger
- Halve the proportion of people living on less than one dollar a day.
- Halve the proportion of people who suffer from hunger.

Achieve universal primary education
- Ensure that boys and girls alike complete primary schooling.

Promote gender equality and empower women
- Eliminate gender disparity at all levels of education.

Reduce child mortality
- Reduce by two-thirds the under-five mortality rate.

Improve maternal health
- Reduce by three-quarters the maternal mortality rate.

Combat HIV/AIDS, malaria, and other diseases
- Reverse the spread of HIV/AIDS.
- Reverse the incidence of malaria and other major diseases.

Ensure environmental sustainability
- Integrate sustainable development into country policies and reverse loss of environmental resources.
- Halve the proportion of people without access to potable water.
- Significantly improve the lives of at least 100 million slum dwellers.

Develop a global partnership for development
- Raise official development assistance.
- Expand market access.
- Encourage debt sustainability.

Strategic Framework and Directions

In 2001, two papers outlined the strategy for the World Bank Group's work for the following five years. The Strategic Framework Paper (SFP) aligns the Bank Group's efforts with the international development goals confirmed in the Millennium Declaration and indicates how these goals will be supported while pointing to the challenges ahead. The Strategic Directions Paper (SDP) sets out the plan for fiscal 2002 to 2004 for implementing major elements of the strategy outlined in the SFP.

Thematic and Sector Strategies

Thematic and sector strategies address cross-cutting facets of poverty reduction, such as HIV/AIDS, the environment, and participation and decentralization in government. In addition to assessing the appropriateness and impact of related Bank Group policies, these strategies provide a vision to guide future work in a given sector. The strategies are revised on a

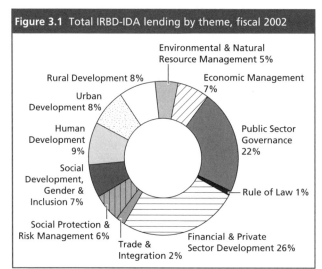

Figure 3.1 Total IRBD-IDA lending by theme, fiscal 2002

Environmental & Natural Resource Management 5%

Rural Development 8%

Economic Management 7%

Urban Development 8%

Human Development 9%

Public Sector Governance 22%

Social Development, Gender & Inclusion 7%

Rule of Law 1%

Social Protection & Risk Management 6%

Trade & Integration 2%

Financial & Private Sector Development 26%

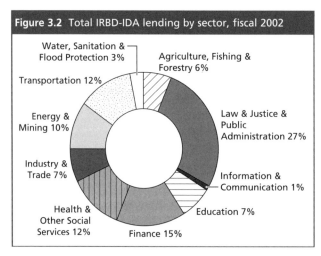

Figure 3.2 Total IRBD-IDA lending by sector, fiscal 2002

Water, Sanitation & Flood Protection 3%

Agriculture, Fishing & Forestry 6%

Transportation 12%

Energy & Mining 10%

Law & Justice & Public Administration 27%

Industry & Trade 7%

Information & Communication 1%

Health & Other Social Services 12%

Education 7%

Finance 15%

rolling basis every three years, through extensive consultation with a wide variety of stakeholders. The process helps build consensus within the Bank Group and strengthen relationships with external partners. See figures 3.1 and 3.2 regarding the current overall shares of lending by theme and sector.

Many sector strategies are posted on the World Bank's Web sites; some are available for purchase from World Bank Publications. See appendix G for a list of sectors and themes and their codes.

Comprehensive Development Framework

The Comprehensive Development Framework, or CDF, is an approach to development whereby countries become the leaders and owners of their own development and poverty reduction policies. The CDF emphasizes the interdependence of all aspects of development: social, structural, human, governance-related, environmental, economic, and financial. It aims to correct historical shortcomings of many aid programs, which often were implemented with a limited focus and little support in the affected country.

Specifically, the CDF advocates

- A holistic long-term strategy with the country in the lead, both owning and directing the development agenda, while the Bank Group and other partners each define their support in their respective business plans

- Stronger partnerships between governments, donors, civil society, the private sector, and other development stakeholders in implementing the country strategy
- A transparent focus on development results to ensure better practical success in reducing poverty.

The CDF is not a blueprint to be applied to all countries in a uniform manner, but a new way of doing business to make development efforts more effective in a world challenged by poverty and distress. The related Web site is <http://www.worldbank.org/cdf>.

Poverty Reduction Strategies

Poverty reduction strategies represent the tangible outcome of the new approach defined by the CDF. In contrast to the model plans, which were once applied to countries by the donor organizations, poor countries now write their own strategies for reducing poverty (see box 3.2). The resulting

---

Box 3.2

Poverty Reduction Strategies: Key Steps

There is no blueprint for building a country's poverty reduction strategy. Rather, the process reflects a country's individual circumstances and characteristics. Recommended features of the Poverty Reduction Strategies Paper (PRSP) include the following:

- *A description of the participatory process used in preparing the strategy.* A PRSP needs to describe the format, frequency, and location of consultations; summarize the main issues raised and the views of participants; give an account of the impact of the consultations on the design of the strategy; and discuss the role of civil society in future monitoring and implementation.

- *Comprehensive poverty diagnostics.* A PRSP needs to describe who the poor are and where they live, using existing data. Building on this description, the PRSP can analyze the macroeconomic, social, structural, and institutional constraints on faster growth and poverty reduction.

- *Clear priorities and cost assessments for macroeconomic, structural, and social policies.* In light of a deeper understanding of poverty and its causes, the PRSP needs to set out the macroeconomic, structural, and social policies comprised in a comprehensive strategy for achieving poverty reduction. It is important that policies be prioritized as much as possible, with cost assessments, so that they are not reduced to a wish list.

- *Appropriate targets, indicators, and systems for monitoring and evaluating progress.* A PRSP needs to define medium- and long-term goals for poverty reduction outcomes (monetary and nonmonetary), establish indicators of progress, and set annual and medium-term targets. The indicators and targets should be appropriate given the assessment of poverty and the institutional capacity to monitor progress; the indicators and targets should also be consistent with the policy choices in the strategy. Finally, a PRSP needs to include an assessment of the country's monitoring and evaluation systems and identify participatory mechanisms for this assessment wherever possible.

Poverty Reduction Strategies Papers, or PRSPs, then become the basis for International Development Association (IDA) lending from the World Bank, for comparable lending from the Poverty Reduction Growth Facility of the International Monetary Fund (IMF), and for debt relief under the Heavily Indebted Poor Countries initiative.

A PRSP is an annually updated document that a country prepares in collaboration with the Bank and IMF. The PRSP is expected to be comprehensive in scope and partnership-oriented, with participation from civil society and the private sector in its preparation. The PRSP describes the country's plans to foster growth and reduce poverty through three-year economic adjustment programs that include macroeconomic, structural, and social policies. In addition, it describes associated external financing needs and major sources of financing. The World Bank has produced the *Poverty Reduction Strategy Sourcebook,* with chapters addressing the various sectors of development, as a resource to help countries in producing their PRSPs. While this is an evolving Web document, a CD version is available. The Web site for PRSPs, with links to the documents themselves, is at <http://www.worldbank.org/prsp>.

While preparing a PRSP, a country can submit an interim PRSP in order to avoid delays in receiving assistance. The interim document must take stock of a country's current poverty reduction strategy and lay out a road map of how the country is going to develop its complete PRSP. On receiving the interim or final document, the World Bank and IMF conduct a joint staff assessment; this assessment helps the boards of the institutions judge whether the document provides a sound basis on which to proceed with assistance and debt relief.

Country Assistance Strategies

The Bank Group develops a Country Assistance Strategy (CAS) for each of its client countries. The CAS is the central vehicle used by the Board of Executive Directors to review the Bank Group's assistance strategy for borrowers from IDA and the International Bank for Reconstruction and Development (IBRD). On the basis of an assessment of the country's priorities, past portfolio performance, and creditworthiness, the CAS sets the level and composition of financial and technical assistance that the Bank seeks to provide to the country.

The country's government participates in preparing the CAS. The key elements of the CAS are discussed with the government and often with representatives of civil society before the board considers the CAS. However, it is not a negotiated document. Any differences between the country's own agenda and the strategy advocated by the Bank Group are highlighted in the CAS. Although the country owns its development strategy as outlined in the PRSP, the Bank Group uses the CAS specifically to account to its shareholders for its diagnosis and the programs it supports.

The CAS normally provides a three-year focus for Bank Group activities. CASs for larger countries are revised more frequently, some annually. The Bank's Board reviews all CASs; the Bank then issues a CAS Public Information Notice and the chair's summary of the Board discussion. At government request, the full text of the CAS may also be disclosed.

More information on the purpose, process, and content of CASs—as well as a CAS calendar—can be found at <http://www.worldbank.org/cas>.

Policies and Procedures

The World Bank Group has established policies and procedures that help ensure its operations are economically, financially, socially, and environmentally sound, thereby improving the impact of its operations on poor people. Each operation must follow these policies and procedures to ensure quality, integrity, and adherence to the Group's mission, corporate priorities, and strategic goals. These policies and procedures—including rigorous safeguard policies on projects affecting women, the environment, indigenous peoples, and other sensitive issues—are codified in the Operational Manual. They are subject to extensive review while being formulated and to compliance monitoring after being approved.

The Operations Policy and Country Services (OPCS) vice presidency provides leadership and coordination on all operations policy-related matters. The thematic network vice presidencies are responsible for formulating and reviewing policies and for monitoring compliance. The regional vice presidencies are fully accountable for compliance with all operational policies and procedures.

Operational Manual
The World Bank Group's Operational Manual is available online. Volume I deals with the Bank's core development objectives and goals, as well as the instruments for pursuing them. Volume II covers the requirements applicable to Bank-financed lending operations. The manual covers several different kinds of operational statements: operational policies, bank procedures, good practices, and operational directives. It is available at <http://www.worldbank.org/opmanual>.

Policy definitions and documentation
Operational policies (OPs) are short, focused statements that follow from the Bank's Articles of Agreement, the general conditions and policies approved by the Board of Executive Directors. They establish the parameters for conducting operations, describe the circumstances in which exceptions to policy are admissible, and spell out who authorizes exceptions. Bank procedures (BPs) explain how Bank staff members carry out the OPs, by

describing the procedures and documentation required to ensure Bank-wide consistency and quality. Good practices (GPs) contain advice and guidance on policy implementation such as the history of the issue, the sectoral context, the analytical framework, and examples of good practice. Operational directives (ODs) contain a mixture of policies, procedures, and guidance; they are gradually being replaced by OPs, BPs, and GPs.

OPs and BPs are detailed in the Operations Manual. ODs that are still in effect can also be found in the manual. GPs are maintained and made available by the various Bank units responsible for specific policies.

Safeguard policies

Safeguard policies help ensure that Bank operations assist people and the environment rather than harm them. There are 10 safeguard policies, consisting of the Bank's policy on environmental assessment (EA) and those policies that fall within the scope of EA: cultural property, disputed areas, forestry, indigenous peoples, international waterways, involuntary resettlement, natural habitats, pest management, and safety of dams.

The Bank conducts environmental screening of each proposed project to determine the appropriate extent and type of EA to be undertaken and to ascertain whether the project may trigger other safeguard policies. The Bank classifies the proposed project into one of four categories (A, B, C, and FI) depending on the type, location, sensitivity, and scale of the project and the nature and magnitude of its potential environmental impacts.

Category A requires the project to undergo the most comprehensive environmental assessment, Category B requires a narrower assessment, and Category C requires no environmental assessment. A project could be classified as A, B, or C and trigger other safeguard policies. In that case, additional assessments specifically related to those policies are required. Category FI identifies subprojects that are funded by the Bank through financial intermediaries and that may affect the environment adversely. Assessments provide mechanisms for public review and scrutiny.

The borrower is responsible for any assessment required by the safeguard policies, with general assistance provided by Bank staff members. The Bank's legal vice presidency monitors compliance with the policies addressing international waterways and disputed areas. The Environmentally and Socially Sustainable Development (ESSD) network monitors all other safeguard policies.

Policy formulation and review

The Bank's OPCS vice presidency guides policy formulation and review, a process that is managed by the appropriate network vice presidency. Formulation or review of a policy entails bringing together experienced regional and network staff members, legal experts, and policy writers. If the policy is complex, the task may take several years and may entail an iterative process of drafting and revising. An initial draft is prepared, often based on sector or thematic strategy work relevant to the policy. The draft statement is then circulated for comments to internal experts, clients, external experts and partners such as nongovernmental organizations, and the public. Finally, the policy is submitted for comments and approval to responsible units, the Bank's managing directors, and the Board of Executive Directors.

Policies on adjustment lending, extractive industries, forests, involuntary resettlement, and the IMF–World Bank Poverty Reduction Strategy Program are among those recently reviewed or still under review.

Compliance monitoring

The Bank's credibility rests on effective implementation of its policies. Monitoring compliance with policies is the responsibility of OPCS. OPCS works to strengthen systems for monitoring compliance. It works in collaboration with the Bank's other vice presidencies and with other World Bank Group organizations.

The Bank has also set up the Inspection Panel, an independent forum for private citizens who believe that their rights or interests have been or could be directly harmed by a Bank-financed project. If people living in a project area believe that harm has resulted or will result from the failure of the Bank to follow its policies and procedures, they or a representative may request a review of the project by the Inspection Panel. The Panel's Web site is at <http://www.worldbank.org/inspectionpanel>.

Disclosure of information

The Bank has established its disclosure policy to support important goals: to be open about its activities, to explain its work to the widest possible audience, and to promote overall accountability and transparency in the development process. The Bank seeks to provide balanced information, reporting, and learning from the failures or disappointments in its operations as well as from the successes.

Recent extensions of the disclosure policy include the release of a greater number of project-related documents, disclosure of the chair's summaries of discussions on CASs and Sector Strategy Papers by the Board of Executive Directors, and a more systematic approach to accessing Bank archives. The Bank continues to review the provisions and implementation of its disclosure policy on a regular basis. More about disclosure is available at <http://www1.worldbank.org/operations/disclosure>.

Fiduciary policies

The Bank's fiduciary policies, set forth in volume II of the Operational Manual, govern the use and flow of Bank funds, including procurement.

OPCS provides guidelines for the procurement of goods and services in Bank projects. The guidelines help ensure that funds are used for their intended purposes and with economy, efficiency, and transparency. They also ensure competitive bidding and help protect Bank-funded projects from fraud and corruption (see box 3.3). The procurement policy Web site is at <http://www.worldbank.org/procure>.

Bank projects are audited periodically by independent firms to make sure that the procurement rules are being followed. Any allegations of fraud or corruption that surface are referred to the Oversight Committee for follow-up, including investigations where appropriate. If the allegations prove true, the Bank may terminate the employment of a staff member, debar the firms implicated, and cancel the funds allocated to the contract in question.

Box 3.3

Reporting Fraud or Corruption

Since 1998, the World Bank has operated a telephone hotline to facilitate the reporting of allegations of fraud and corruption within the World Bank Group or in connection with Bank Group–financed projects. Both Bank staff members and members of the general public may use the hotline, which is operated 24 hours a day, seven days a week by an outside firm staffed by trained specialists. Interpreters are available upon request. The toll-free number is (1-800) 831-0463.

This number is accessible from most countries by contacting an international operator and asking to be connected to the World Bank's hotline number. A list of direct access numbers for AT&T operators throughout the world is available on AT&T's Web site at <http://www.consumer.att.com/global/english>.

Callers may remain anonymous. Calls are not recorded, and no attempt is made to determine the source number. The Bank does not reveal any information that might disclose a caller's identity to anyone outside the investigative team unless the Bank determines that a caller has committed a crime.

Because the hotline number is not accessible from all countries of the world, two additional mechanisms have been established to allow both Bank Group staff members and members of the public to contact the Bank to report fraudulent and corrupt practices:

- *Collect call hotline number.* Individuals may use a collect call number to contact the World Bank hotline from anywhere in the world at no expense to the caller. The call will be answered with the greeting "International Line." The collect call hotline number is (1-704) 556-7046.
- *Hotline post office box.* Individuals who do not have access to a telephone or do not wish to communicate by telephone may now contact the World Bank hotline through a post office box at the following address:

PMB 137
4736 Sharon Road, Suite W
Charlotte, NC 28210, USA

Policies at IFC, MIGA, and ICSID

The policies and procedures of the World Bank Group apply also to IFC and to MIGA, with some specific variations in guidelines as appropriate to their clients:

- For a list of IFC policies, see "IFC Projects & Policies" at <http://www.ifc.org/policies>.
- For a list of MIGA policies, see "Environment and Disclosure Policies" at <http://www.miga.org/screens/policies/policies.htm>.
- ICSID policies are set forth in its basic documents, additional facility documents, and other documents available at its Web site at <http://www.worldbank.org/icsid>.

The Bank Group's Finances

This section provides an overview of how the Bank Group institutions are financed, how they provide assistance in developing countries, and how they report on their finances. More details about Bank Group loans and other assistance follow in the next section, "Products and Services."

IBRD and IDA Funding and Lending

The World Bank raises money for its development programs by tapping the world's capital markets and, in the case of the IDA, by raising contributions from wealthier member governments.

IBRD, which facilitates more than half of the Bank's annual lending, raises almost all its money in financial markets. IBRD sells AAA-rated bonds and other debt securities to pension funds, insurance companies, corporations, other banks, and individuals around the globe. IBRD charges interest to its borrowers at rates that reflect its cost of borrowing. Loans must be repaid in 15 to 20 years; there is a 3- to 5-year grace period before repayment of principal begins.

Less than 5 percent of IBRD's funds are paid in by countries when they join the Bank. Member governments purchase shares, the number of which is based on their relative economic strength, but pay in only a small portion of the value of those shares. The unpaid balance is "on call" in case the Bank should suffer losses so grave that it could no longer pay its creditors—something that has never happened. This guaranteed capital can be used only to pay bondholders, not to cover administrative costs or to make loans. IBRD's rules require that loans outstanding and disbursed may not exceed the combined total of capital and reserves.

IDA provides assistance to countries that are too poor to borrow at commercial rates, using interest-free loans known as IDA credits. These credits account for more than one-fourth of all Bank lending. Borrowers pay a fee of less than 1 percent of the loan to cover administrative costs. Repayment is required in 35 or 40 years, with a 10-year grace period.

Nearly 40 countries contribute to IDA's funding, which is replenished every three years. Donor nations include not only industrial member countries such as France, Germany, Japan, the United Kingdom, and the United States but also developing countries such as Botswana, Brazil, Hungary, the Republic of Korea, the Russian Federation, and Turkey, some of which were once IDA borrowers. IDA's funding is managed in the same way as IBRD's. As with IBRD, there has never been a default on an IDA credit.

Cumulative lending by IBRD and IDA as of June 30, 2002, amounted to more than US$506 billion (see table 3.1). More information on IBRD and IDA product lines and lending instruments follows in the next section, "Products and Services." Grants and loans obtained from cofinanciers and partnerships often complement government funds and World Bank lending to make up the total package of assistance to a country.

Funding of IFC, MIGA, and ICSID

IFC and MIGA each have share capital, which is paid in by member countries, which vote in proportion to the number of shares they hold.

IFC makes loans and equity investments. The corporation's equity and quasi-equity investments are funded out of paid-in capital and retained earnings from these investments. Strong shareholder support, AAA ratings, and the substantial paid-in capital base have allowed IFC to raise funds for its lending activities on favorable terms in the international capital markets.

In addition to its share capital, MIGA receives funding for some of its operating expenses from the World Bank. MIGA also charges fees for the services it provides.

The operating expenses of the ICSID Secretariat are funded through the World Bank's budget, although the costs of individual proceedings are borne by the parties involved.

Trust Funds

Trust funds are financial arrangements between a Bank Group institution and a donor under which the donor entrusts the Bank Group with funds for a specific development-related activity.

At the World Bank, the number and dollar amount of total trust funds have grown rapidly over the past few years, so that there are now more than 850 active trust funds with an annual level of disbursements of more than US$1 billion. The Resource Mobilization and Cofinancing unit is responsible for overall oversight of trust fund management, as well as the mobilization of trust fund resources. It also administers several of the Bank's most important trust fund programs, including the Policy and Human Resources Development Fund, Japan Social Development Fund, Asia–Europe

Country	Total Number	Total Amount	Country	Total Number	Total Amount
Afghanistan	24	330.1	Georgia	28	649.8
Africa	13	310.3	Ghana	110	4,223.4
Albania	47	656.9	Greece	17	490.8
Algeria	70	5,728.4	Grenada	4	26.5
Angola	11	310.8	Guatemala	38	1,325.3
Argentina	114	18,947.4	Guinea	59	1,368.4
Armenia	28	695.9	Guinea-Bissau	23	285.9
Australia	7	417.7	Guyana	29	387.6
Austria	9	106.4	Haiti	37	629.1
Azerbaijan	18	531.1	Honduras	63	1,975.8
Bahamas, The	5	42.8	Hungary	40	4,333.6
Bangladesh	174	9,959.8	Iceland	10	47.1
Barbados	12	118.4	India	434	58,535.0
Belarus	4	192.8	Indonesia	297	29,040.4
Belgium	4	76.0	Iran, Islamic Republic of	41	2,290.1
Belize	9	86.2	Iraq	6	156.2
Benin	53	784.5	Ireland	8	152.5
Bhutan	9	64.3	Israel	11	284.5
Bolivia	79	2,051.5	Italy	8	399.6
Bosnia and Herzegovina	39	811.5	Jamaica	66	1,531.0
Botswana	25	296.5	Japan	31	862.9
Brazil	277	31,945.6	Jordan	68	2,127.0
Bulgaria	26	1,533.1	Kazakhstan	22	1,883.6
Burkina Faso	56	1,187.4	Kenya	125	4,438.2
Burundi	52	829.3	Korea, Republic of	120	15,757.8
Cambodia	19	478.3	Kyrgyz Republic	25	621.4
Cameroon	72	2,473.8	Lao People's		
Cape Verde	17	178.4	Democratic Republic	32	662.6
Caribbean	6	126.0	Latvia	18	395.8
Central African Republic	27	448.5	Lebanon	20	1,048.6
Chad	42	876.0	Lesotho	31	486.8
Chile	63	3,703.9	Liberia	33	270.5
China	239	36,075.9	Lithuania	17	490.9
Colombia	165	10,518.6	Luxembourg	1	12.0
Comoros	18	119.1	Macedonia, former		
Congo, Democratic			Yugoslav Republic of	26	654.7
Republic of	68	1,981.5	Madagascar	86	2,197.4
Congo, Republic of	24	490.0	Malawi	79	2,080.7
Costa Rica	40	944.0	Malaysia	88	4,150.6
Côte d'Ivoire	87	4,930.4	Maldives	7	64.9
Croatia	18	983.6	Mali	65	1,567.2
Cyprus	30	418.8	Malta	1	7.5
Czech Republic	3	776.0	Mauritania	52	882.7
Denmark	3	85.0	Mauritius	37	479.9
Djibouti	15	125.6	Mexico	182	33,821.1
Dominica	5	20.3	Moldova	18	504.3
Dominican Republic	34	918.7	Mongolia	17	300.4
East Africa	1	45.0	Morocco	131	8,596.2
Ecuador	77	2,760.1	Mozambique	42	2,262.1
Egypt, Arab Republic of	105	6,531.5	Myanmar	33	837.4
El Salvador	35	988.8	Nepal	72	1,634.5
Equatorial Guinea	9	45.0	Netherlands	8	244.0
Eritrea	11	385.4	New Zealand	6	126.8
Estonia	8	150.7	Nicaragua	58	1,323.8
Ethiopia	82	3,888.1	Niger	50	1,030.9
Fiji	12	152.9	Nigeria	107	7,832.5
Finland	18	316.8	Norway	6	145.0
France	1	250.0	OECS countries	3	37.1
Gabon	14	227.0	Oman	11	157.1
Gambia, The	28	259.2	Pakistan	196	13,256.7

(continued)

Country	Total Number	Total Amount	Country	Total Number	Total Amount
Panama	45	1,273.2	Swaziland	14	112.6
Papua New Guinea	44	899.8	Syrian Arab Republic	20	660.5
Paraguay	43	862.4	Taiwan, China	18	344.7
Peru	87	5,298.2	Tajikistan	17	302.1
Philippines	162	11,432.9	Tanzania	120	4,229.5
Poland	37	5,384.8	Thailand	124	8,104.2
Portugal	32	1,338.8	Togo	42	753.5
Romania	66	5,498.4	Tonga	3	10.9
Russian Federation	51	12,560.0	Trinidad and Tobago	21	313.6
Rwanda	54	1,073.0	Tunisia	120	5,028.7
Samoa	10	66.0	Turkey	145	20,296.4
São Tomé and Principe	10	68.9	Turkmenistan	3	89.5
Senegal	100	2,327.8	Uganda	83	3,410.5
Seychelles	2	10.7	Ukraine	22	3,222.8
Sierra Leone	30	555.9	Uruguay	49	1,815.1
Singapore	14	181.3	Uzbekistan	12	539.1
Slovak Republic	4	335.8	Vanuatu	5	18.9
Slovenia	5	177.7	Venezuela, República Bolivariana de	40	3,328.4
Solomon Islands	8	49.9	Vietnam	36	3,862.5
Somalia	39	492.1	West Africa	5	68.0
South Africa	12	287.8	Yemen, Republic of	125	1,995.9
Spain	12	478.7	Yugoslavia, Fed. Rep. (Serbia and Montenegro)	4	171.8
Sri Lanka	89	2,639.4	Yugoslavia, former	89	6,090.7
St. Kitts and Nevis	3	12.4	Zambia	78	3,171.4
St. Lucia	7	43.6	Zimbabwe	36	1,645.2
St. Vincent and the Grenadines	4	16.9			
Sudan	55	1,518.9	Total	8,070	506,545.3

Meeting Trust Fund, Bank–Netherlands Partnership Program, and the Consultant Trust Fund Program. The main Web page for Bank trust funds is at <http://www.worldbank.org/rmc/tf>.

IFC uses donor-supported trust funds to help with the technical assistance of various projects. IFC initiated the Technical Assistance Trust Funds Program in 1988 in an effort to identify and support viable business projects in developing countries at an early stage. Among other forms of technical assistance, the program provides technical assistance to entrepreneurs preparing projects and designing proposals that meet the criteria of prospective investors, including IFC. Since its inception, the program has supported approximately 1,000 technical assistance projects in a broad range of sectors. It also supports some of IFC's privatization advisory services and capital markets activities aimed at strengthening private sector institutions. IFC issues an annual report on trust funds, which is available at <http://www.ifc.org/tatf/ar2002>.

Financial Reporting: Bank Group Annual Reports

Each of the Bank Group institutions provides detailed financial statements through its annual report. The fiscal year for these institutions runs from July 1 of a given year to June 30 of the following calendar year. The reports catalog financial performance and new activities; they include comparative information on the world regions and development sectors in which the institutions have provided assistance. These reports are available for free to the public, both in print and on the Internet. The reports are published in multiple languages, and the Web sites include past editions. For Web links to the Bank Group's annual reports, see "Contacting the World Bank Group" in appendix A.

Products and Services

This section explains specific products and services that the World Bank Group provides (see box 3.4 for Web links). Though known best for its financial services, the Bank Group also provides analytic and advisory services and is involved in learning and capacity building in developing countries worldwide.

World Bank Products and Services

Lending instruments

The World Bank offers two basic types of lending instruments to its client governments: investment loans and adjustment loans. Depending on its eligibility, a member country will draw on loans from either IBRD or IDA to support a lending project. Whether the money is lent through IBRD or IDA determines the terms of the loan (see box 3.5 regarding key terms and rates).

Box 3.4

Web Links for Products and Services

World Bank
What we do: http://www.worldbank.org

What IDA is: http://www.worldbank.org/ida

Lending instruments: http://www.worldbank.org/projects

Loans and credits: http://www.worldbank.org/loansandcredits

IFC
What we do: http://www.ifc.org/about/what/what.html

Products and services: http://www.ifc.org/proserv

MIGA
Products and services: http://www.miga.org/screens/services/services.htm

ICSID
Cases: http://www.worldbank.org/icsid/cases/cases.htm

Financial Terms for New World Bank Loans

IBRD

Front-end fee: 1.0 percent of the loan amount, payable on loan effectiveness

Lending rate: Product specific; for some products, also currency specific

Commitment fee: varies by product but 0.75 percent on undisbursed balance for most loans; partial waiver may apply

Maturity: 15 to 20 years, with a 3- to 5-year grace period

IDA

Service charge: 0.75 percent

Commitment fee: 0.0 to 0.5 percent on undisbursed balance (set annually, but has been 0.0 percent since 1989)

Maturity: 40 years (35 years for IBRD–IDA blend countries), with a 10-year grace period

Contact information
Financial Products and Services Group

The World Bank
1818 H Street, NW
MS MC7-708
Washington, DC 20433, USA
Tel: (1-202) 458-1122
Fax: (1-202) 522-2102
E-mail: fps@worldbank.org

Loans are made as part of the comprehensive lending program set out in the CAS, which tailors Bank assistance (both lending and services) to each borrower's development needs. For more about the CAS, see above under "Country Assistance Strategies." Lending operations are developed in several phases, as outlined in the section on "World Bank Projects" later in this chapter.

Full descriptions of the Bank's various lending instruments are included in its "Lending Instruments Brochure," which is available online at <http://www.worldbank.org/projects>. Additional information is available from the Financial Products and Services Group (see above).

The Bank has a searchable online database of all projects: click "Projects" on the home page of the Bank's Web site. In addition, it posts information on the loans and credits most recently approved by its Board of Executive Directors: this listing appears under "News" on the Bank's Web site. For more information, see "Project Information" below under "World Bank Projects" and box 3.7.

Investment lending

Investment loans provide long-term financing for a range of activities aimed at creating the physical and social infrastructure necessary for poverty alleviation and sustainable development. Over the past two decades, investment lending has, on average, accounted for 75 to 80 percent of all Bank lending.

The nature of investment lending has evolved over time. Originally focused on hardware, engineering services, and bricks and mortar, investment lending has come to focus more on institution building, social development, and the public policy infrastructure needed to facilitate private sector activity. Examples of areas in which recent projects have been funded include

- Urban poverty reduction (involving private contractors in new housing construction)
- Rural development (formalizing land tenure to increase the security of small farmers)
- Water and sanitation (improving the efficiency of water utilities)
- Natural resource management (providing training in sustainable forestry and farming)
- Postconflict reconstruction (reintegrating soldiers into communities)
- Education (promoting the education of girls)
- Health (establishing rural clinics and training health care workers).

Adjustment lending

Adjustment loans provide quick-disbursing assistance to support structural reforms in a sector or the economy as a whole. They support the policy and institutional changes needed to create an environment conducive to sustained and equitable growth. Over the past two decades, adjustment lending has accounted, on average, for 20 to 25 percent of total Bank lending.

Adjustment loans were designed to provide support for macroeconomic policy reforms, including reforms in trade policy and agriculture. Over time, they have evolved to focus more on structural, financial sector, and social policy reform and on improving public sector resource management. Objectives of such loans now include the following:

- Promoting competitive market structures (legal and regulatory reform)
- Correcting distortions in incentive regimes (taxation and trade reform)
- Establishing appropriate monitoring and safeguards (financial sector reform)
- Creating an environment conducive to private sector investment (judicial reform and adoption of a modern investment code)

- Encouraging private sector activity (privatization and public–private partnerships)
- Promoting good governance (civil service reform)
- Mitigating short-term adverse effects of adjustment (establishment of social protection funds).

In fiscal 1990 to 2002, the World Bank approved 420 adjustment loans in 102 countries for a total of US$87 billion. The volume of adjustment lending has periodically increased in response to increased external financing needs in developing countries, notably in fiscal 1998 and 1999 during the East Asia financial crisis and in fiscal 2002 following the events of September 11, 2001, and the ensuing global economic downturn. However, the Bank is basically phasing out adjustment lending in the medium term, as it increases devotion to improving infrastructure and fighting poverty.

Cofinancing and Trust Funds

The Bank also helps its member countries obtain financial assistance from cofinancing and trust funds:

- *Cofinancing.* The Bank often cofinances its projects with governments, commercial banks, export credit agencies, multilateral institutions, and private sector investors. Official cofinancing— through either donor government agencies or multilateral financial institutions—constitutes the largest source of cofinancing for Bank-assisted operations.
- *Trust Funds.* These funds enable the Bank, along with bilateral and multilateral donors, to mobilize funds for investment operations as well as for debt relief, emergency reconstruction, and technical assistance. For more on trust funds, see the section on "Trust Funds" above.

Guarantees and risk management

Guarantees promote private financing by covering risks that the private sector is not normally ready to absorb or manage. All Bank guarantees are partial guarantees of private debt, so that risks are shared by the Bank and private lenders. The Bank's objective is to cover risks that it is in a unique position to bear, given its experience in developing countries and its relationships with governments.

IBRD also offers hedging products, which can transform the risk characteristics of a borrower's IBRD obligations even though the negotiated terms of particular loan contracts themselves may be fixed. These products give borrowers improved risk management capability in the context of projects, lending programs, or sovereign asset-liability management. IBRD hedging products include interest rate swaps, interest rate caps and collars, currency swaps, and—on a case-by-case basis—commodity swaps.

Additional information on guarantees and risk management services follows in the sections on IFC and MIGA products and services.

Grants

A limited number of grants are available through the Bank, funded either directly or through partnerships. Most are designed as seed money for pilot projects with innovative approaches and technologies. They also foster collaboration with other organizations and broader participation in development projects. The Development Grant Facility (DGF) provides overall strategy, allocations, and management of Bank grant-making activities. The DGF has supported programs in such sectors as rural development, environment, health, education, economic policy, and private sector development (see the DGF home page at <http://wbln0018.worldbank.org/dgf/dgf.nsf>).

Knowledge sharing

The Bank Group's development mission has always included analytic and advisory services, as well as relevant training and publishing. Since the mid-1990s, however, the Bank Group has made knowledge sharing an explicit objective and has increased its efforts to organize its knowledge-creating activities in a systematic way, so that information can have the broadest possible impact. Thematic networks have become an important part of the Bank Group's organizational structure, and electronic technologies have expanded the ways of delivering information.

Analytic and advisory services

Research by the Development Economics vice presidency informs the Bank Group's work on issues such as the environment, poverty, trade, and globalization. Country clients benefit from a tailored program of economic and sector work geared to their specific development challenges. Economic and sector work examines a country's economic prospects—including, for example, its banking or financial sectors—and trade, poverty, and social safety net issues. The Bank Group's diagnostic work is shared with clients and partners, and draws on their work. The results often form the basis for assistance strategies, government investment programs, and projects supported by IBRD and IDA lending. Much of this economic research output is available through the World Bank Research Web site at <http://econ.worldbank.org>.

In conjunction with the thematic networks, the Bank Group has established Advisory Services to provide information and knowledge on numerous facets of the Bank's work. Examples include environmentally and socially sustainable development; health, nutrition, and population; the financial sector; and law and justice. Advisory Services serve the Bank Group's clients and staff members, other development organizations, and the general public. The main entry point for the Bank Group's Advisory Services is the "Ask Us" Web page, which provides contacts for numerous specific aspects of the organization's work; see <http://www.worldbank.org/ks/askus>.

Some of the Bank Group's networks, sectors, and thematic groups have also prepared toolkits for development practitioners in their particular aspect of development. Topics of such toolkits have included project design; management and monitoring; legal, financial, and procurement requirements; gender; food and nutrition; and resettlement safeguards.

Learning and capacity building

The Bank Group conducts learning and knowledge-sharing programs to enhance the skills and development of its clients, staff members, and partners. The lead unit in this area is the World Bank Institute (WBI), whose work includes training courses, policy consultations, partnerships with training and research institutions worldwide, and the creation and support of knowledge networks related to international development. WBI places special emphasis on distance learning and other innovative uses of technology. Many of its initiatives are described in chapter 5 ("Topics in Development"). WBI's Web site is at <http://www.worldbank.org/wbi>.

Another key initiative is the Staff Exchange Program, which arranges temporary secondment of Bank Group staff members and staff members of participating companies and organizations. The program enhances the professional and technical skills of participating individuals and promotes cultural exchange, fresh perspectives, and diversity for the institutions involved.

Publications, data, and statistics

In addition to issuing annual reports and providing project information, the Bank Group produces and distributes about 200 formal publications a year, in print and in electronic format. Major annual titles include the *World Development Report, World Development Indicators, African Development Indicators, Global Development Finance, Global Economic Prospects,* and *World Bank Atlas.* All formal publications are distributed to World Bank country offices and a network of depository libraries in developing countries; commercial sales offer significant discounts for customers in developing countries (see box 3.6 or contact a country-specific distributor listed in appendix G).

Box 3.6

Obtaining World Bank Group Publications

World Bank Group Publications

P.O. Box 960
Herndon, VA 20172-0960, USA

Tel: (1-800) 645-7247 or (1-703) 661-1580

Fax: (1-703) 661-1501

E-mail: books@worldbank.org

Web: http://publications.worldbank.org/ecommerce

Working in close cooperation with the official statistical systems organized and financed by national governments, the Bank Group generates comprehensive data and statistics on many aspects of development. It also works to improve the coverage and effectiveness of national systems. Much of this information is available online, some for free and some by subscription. The key resource here is the data and statistics Web site at <http://www.worldbank.org/data>. Many other specific datasets are available on the Bank's Web sites.

Events: Conferences, forums, and summits

The Bank Group sponsors, hosts, or participates in numerous conferences, both on its own and in conjunction with other organizations. Among the best-known series is the Annual Bank Conference on Development Economics, which in fact is two gatherings each year, one usually in Washington, D.C., in April or May and the other in a European capital, usually in June. The central calendar for major World Bank events is at <http://www.worldbank.org/events>. Many of the Web sites of specific Bank units also list upcoming events.

IFC Products and Services

A company or entrepreneur, foreign or domestic, seeking to establish a new venture or to expand an existing enterprise can approach IFC directly. Such investors should read "How to Apply for IFC Financing" (available on IFC's Web site), which describes IFC's investment criteria, before submitting an investment proposal. There is no standard application form for IFC financing.

IFC operates on a commercial basis. It invests exclusively in for-profit projects and charges market rates for its products and services, which cover three broad areas: financial products, advisory services, and resource mobilization.

Financial products

IFC's traditional and largest activity is financing private sector projects in developing countries. It provides loans, equity financing, and quasi equity. It also offers financial risk management products and intermediary financing.

Advisory services

IFC provides fee-based advice and technical assistance to private businesses and governments in developing countries. These services cover a broad spectrum, including privatization, business-related public policy, and industry-specific issues.

Resource mobilization

IFC helps companies in developing countries tap into international capital markets. The cornerstone of the mobilization effort is the loan participation program, which arranges syndicated loans from banks. IFC also mobilizes financing from international financial institutions through investment funds, underwriting, securitization, private placement, and other innovative approaches. By acting as a catalyst, IFC leverages its limited resources to the maximum.

MIGA Products and Services

MIGA's products and services fall into three categories: investment guarantees, investment services, and legal counsel.

Investment guarantees

MIGA provides investment guarantees against certain noncommercial risks (that is, political risk insurance) to eligible foreign investors for qualified investments in developing member countries. MIGA's investment guarantees cover the following risks: transfer restriction, expropriation, breach of contract, and war and civil disturbance. MIGA makes a preliminary application for guarantee available on its Web site.

Investment services

MIGA's Investment Marketing Services Department works to equip investment promotion intermediaries with leading-edge knowledge, tools, and techniques to strengthen their capacity to attract and retain foreign direct investment. To this end, MIGA provides both hands-on operational assistance to promotion intermediaries and a range of investment information services to member countries and firms that are contemplating direct investments in the developing world. These core services and products fall into three broad areas: capacity building, information dissemination, and investment facilitation.

Legal counsel

MIGA also provides a broad range of legal support, both internally and for client countries. Its activities include supporting other MIGA departments and the Board of Directors with legal advice, advising countries on membership in MIGA, negotiating agreements with developing member countries in support of underwriting and salvage, providing technical assistance and advice to member countries on issues affecting the attraction of foreign investment, researching and disseminating information, mediating investment disputes, administering claims, and advising on increasing guarantee capacity. MIGA also cooperates with the World Bank Group and with other international and national agencies or institutions on legal aspects of investment protection and guarantee.

ICSID Products and Services

ICSID provides facilities and coordination for the conciliation and arbitration of investment disputes between contracting states and nationals of other contracting states. ICSID's objective in making such facilities available is to promote an atmosphere of mutual confidence between states and foreign investors—an atmosphere that is conducive to increasing the flow of private international investment.

World Bank Project Cycle

World Bank projects are far-ranging operations in client countries and regions. They are managed through sector or regional departments. They range from the administration and management of loans to the implementation of projects within country or region development strategies. Bank activities also support clients through financing and advice that is targeted toward general reform not connected with specific outputs or investments.

This section covers typical phases of the project cycle, including the documentation that is created during each phase. Most of this information is specific to the projects of the World Bank; information about IFC's project cycle follows in the next section. Information on how to access information about World Bank Group projects appears at the end of this section.

Projects go through specific stages in their life cycle (see figure 3.3).

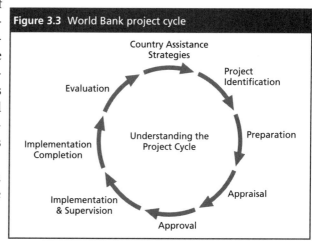

Figure 3.3 World Bank project cycle

Country Assistance Strategies

Project Identification

Evaluation

Understanding the Project Cycle

Preparation

Implementation Completion

Preparation

Appraisal

Implementation & Supervision

Approval

Project Identification

During project identification, both the borrower and the Bank are involved in analyzing development strategies (such as the PRSP and CAS) for the country and in identifying projects that support those strategies. Ideas for projects often emerge from these strategies as well as from the Bank's economic and sector research, the borrower's feasibility studies, and prior projects. Projects should be financially, economically, socially, and environmentally sound. At this point, the project undergoes an environmental screening to determine whether an environmental assessment is required.

The following project documentation is required at this stage:

- Initial Project Information Document
- Integrated Safeguards Data Sheets

Preparation

The borrower is responsible for project preparation, which normally lasts one to two years. The Bank often provides technical and financial assistance. During preparation, a country's project team has to determine all the technical, institutional, economic, environmental, and financial conditions required for the project to succeed. The team must also compare possible alternative methods for achieving the project's objectives. If required, an EA is undertaken. The project is reviewed and, if it is approved for a loan, negotiations ensue to define the terms and conditions of the loan.

Environmental categories A and B projects must disclose the EA. If required, the following documents would be disclosed with the EA:

- Resettlement Action Plan
- Indigenous Peoples Development Plan
- Environmental Management Plan

Appraisal

The Bank is solely responsible for project appraisal, which is usually conducted by Bank staff. The appraisal team reviews all the work conducted during identification and preparation and prepares a Project Appraisal Document (PAD) for investment projects and a Program Document (PGD) for structural operations. Those documents are carefully reviewed and redrafted as necessary for submission to Bank management.

Other project documentation is as follows:

- Revised Project Information Document
- Development Business
- Monthly Operational Summary

Approval

The PAD or the PGD, along with the Memorandum of the President and loan documents, are submitted to the Bank's Board of Executive Directors for approval. If the loan or credit is approved, the loan is signed by the Bank and the borrower.

Along with the PAD and PGD, project documentation includes

- Staff Appraisal Report (for projects approved through 1998)
- Technical Annex

Effectiveness

Following approval, the loan or credit agreement is submitted to whatever final process is required by the borrowing government. For example, agreements may need to be ratified by a country's legislature. The process may last for several months. If the outcome is positive, the loan or credit is declared effective or ready for disbursement, and the agreement is made available to the public.

Implementation and Supervision

Implementation is the responsibility of the borrower, with technical assistance from the Bank as agreed on. Supervision of the project is the responsibility of the Bank. The borrower prepares the specifications and evaluates bids for the procurement of goods and services related to the project. After the Bank reviews this work and determines that its procurement guidelines have been followed, funds will be disbursed.

After funds have been disbursed, Bank supervision entails monitoring, evaluating, and reporting on project progress. At the end of the disbursement period (up to 10 years), a completion report identifying accomplishments, problems, and lessons learned is submitted to the Bank's Board of Executive Directors for approval.

Project documentation at this stage is the Implementation Completion Report.

Evaluation

Following completion of a project, the Bank's Operations Evaluation Department (OED) conducts an audit of the project, in which its outcome is measured against its original objectives. The audit entails a review of the project completion report and preparation of a separate report. Both reports are then submitted to the Board of Executive Directors and to the borrower. These reports are not available to the public; however, OED periodically prepares impact evaluations on sets of projects on the basis of these reports.

OED Impact Evaluation Reports are necessary at this stage.

Other Monitoring

The Quality Assurance Group monitors the quality of the Bank's activities during implementation to facilitate better management. It examines project quality both for loans (shortly after project approval by the Board) and for advisory services (after delivery to country clients). It also monitors the quality of supervision of projects and reports to the Board of Executive Directors on the overall health of the portfolio of ongoing projects through the Annual Report on Portfolio Performance.

Another independent body within the World Bank, the Inspection Panel, provides a forum for citizens who believe they have been or could be harmed by a Bank-financed project.

Project Information

These are several major resources for project documents, which are also called operational documents, and for other project information (see box 3.7 for additional Web links):

- *Projects database.* Available online at <http://www4.worldbank.org/sprojects>, this database enables users to search the entire World Bank project portfolio, from the founding of IBRD to the present. Users can search in the projects database or in project documents, contract awards, or country economic and sector work. The search can be defined by any combination of the following: keyword, region, country or area, theme, sector, project status, product line, lending instrument, year approved, and environmental category. Results show the basic project information, with links to available project documents.

- *Recent loans and credits.* The World Bank also posts information on the loans and credits most recently approved by the Board of Executive Directors: this listing appears under "News" on the Bank's Web site, <http://www.worldbank.org/loansandcredits>. Here the user can view information by data, by topic (sector), by region, or by country. The listings generally include names of contacts who can provide additional information.

- *Documents and reports.* This feature of the World Bank's Web site, available at <http://www-wds.worldbank.org>, provides more than 14,000 World Bank documents—the full range of material that is made available to the public under the disclosure policy. This approach in reaching project documents is an alternative to searching the projects database. This site also includes documents created through the Bank's country economic and sector work, as well as various working papers and informal series from departments around the Bank. Users of the site can access documents in both text and downloadable portable document format (PDF). Printed copies can be ordered from the InfoShop.

- *InfoShop.* The InfoShop is the World Bank Group's development bookstore, located at Bank headquarters. It provides printed copies of project documents. For more information, see "How to Order," at

Web Links for Project Information, Disclosure, and Evaluation

World Bank

Loans and credits: http://www.worldbank.org/loansandcredits

Projects, policies, and strategies: http://www4.worldbank.org/sprojects

Project cycle: http://www.worldbank.org/infoshop/projectcycle.htm

Operational procedures: http://www.worldbank.org.opmanual

Country Assistance Strategies: http://www.worldbank.org/cas

Operational documents: http://www.worldbank.org/infoshop/projinfo.htm

Poverty Reduction Strategy Papers: http://www.worldbank.org/poverty/strategies

Public Information Centers: http://www.worldbank.org/pics

World Bank policy on disclosure of information: http://www.worldbank.org/disclosure

Operations Evaluation Department: http://www.worldbank.org/oed

Inspection Panel: http://www.worldbank.org/inspectionpanel

IFC

Projects: http://www.ifc.org/projects

Project cycle: http://www.ifc.org/proserv/apply/cycle/cycle.html

Policy on disclosure of information: http://www.ifc.org/enviro/enviro/Disclosure_Policy/disclosure.htm

Environment and social review (monitoring of projects): http://www.ifc.org/enviro/EnvSoc

Operations Evaluation Group: http://www.ifc.org/oeg

IFC and MIGA

Office of the Compliance Advisor/Ombudsman: http://www.cao-ombudsman.org/ev.php

MIGA

Projects insured by MIGA: http://www.miga.org/screens/projects/projects.htm

Disclosure policies: http://www.miga.org/screens/policies/disclose/disclose.htm

ICSID

Cases: http://www.worldbank.org/icsid/cases/cases.htm

<http://www-wds.worldbank.org/order.jsp>. The InfoShop also sells the Bank Group's formal publications, books on development topics by other publishers, souvenirs, and gifts.

- *Public Information Centers.* Public Information Centers, or PICs, maintained at the World Bank country offices, make Bank information available to the public and disseminate its work to the widest possible audience. PIC Europe, in Paris, and PIC Tokyo offer the complete range of project documents for all member countries and maintain libraries of recent World Bank publications. Other country office PICs and libraries worldwide have project documents specific to the country in which the office is located and often offer a library of recent Bank publications. Each PIC serves as the central contact in the country for people seeking to obtain Bank documents and information on the Bank's operations. The InfoShop coordinates with all PICs to ensure broad dissemination of information in compliance with the Bank's disclosure policy. For a list of PICs, see appendix A.

IFC Project Cycle

IFC offers a wide variety of financial products to private sector projects in developing countries. The project cycle, outlined below, illustrates the stages a business idea goes through as it becomes an IFC-financed project.

Application for IFC Financing

There is no standard application form for IFC financing. A company or entrepreneur, foreign or domestic, seeking to establish a new venture or to expand an existing enterprise can approach IFC directly. This is best done by reading "How to Apply for IFC Financing" (available on IFC's Web site) and by submitting an investment proposal. After these initial contacts and a preliminary review, IFC may proceed by requesting a detailed feasibility study or business plan to determine whether to appraise the project.

Project Appraisal

Typically, an appraisal team consists of an investment officer with financial expertise and knowledge of the country in which the project is located, an engineer with relevant technical expertise, and an environmental specialist. The team is responsible for evaluating the technical, financial, economic, and environmental aspects of the project. This process entails visits to the proposed site of the project and extensive discussions with the project sponsors. After returning to headquarters, the team submits its recommendations to the senior management of the relevant IFC department.

If financing of the project is approved at the department level, IFC's legal department drafts appropriate documents, with assistance from outside counsel as appropriate. Outstanding issues are negotiated with the company and other involved parties such as governments or financial institutions.

Public Notification

Before the proposed investment is submitted to IFC's Board of Directors for review, the public is notified of the main elements of the project. Environmental review documents are also made available to the public.

Board Review and Approval

The project is submitted to IFC's Board of Directors, which reviews the proposed investment and approves it if it sees fit.

Resource Mobilization

After Board approval, IFC seeks to mobilize additional financing by encouraging other institutions to make investments in the project.

Legal Commitment

If the investment is approved by the Board—and if stipulations from earlier negotiations are fulfilled—IFC and the company will sign the deal, making a legal commitment.

Disbursement of Funds

Funds are disbursed under the terms of the legal commitment signed by all parties.

Project Supervision and Evaluation

After funds have been disbursed, IFC monitors its investments closely. It consults periodically with project managers, and it sends field missions to visit the enterprise. It also requires quarterly progress reports and information on factors that might materially affect the enterprise in which it has invested, including annual financial statements audited by independent public accountants.

The basic instrument of evaluation in IFC is the Expanded Project Supervision Report. These self-evaluative reports (numbering about 70 a year) are prepared by IFC's investment departments on a randomly selected, representative sample of investment operations that have reached early operating maturity (generally five years after board approval). IFC's Operations Evaluation Group reviews each of these reports.

Closing

When an investment is repaid in full—or when IFC exits an investment by selling its equity stake—IFC closes its books on the project.

Project Information

IFC produces a Summary of Project Information for each project it undertakes; it also publishes its environmental documents for each project. All project information is posted on the Web at <http://www.ifc.org/projects>; users can narrow the search by document type, project country, sector, IFC region, environmental category, or keywords.

Partnerships

The World Bank Group has a large array of partners in the global fight against poverty (see box 3.8 for institution-specific Web links). As discussed under "Strategies" earlier in this chapter, the most important partnership is with the developing countries themselves—not only with many government agencies, but also with the whole range of civil society, especially the poor people who are most affected by Bank Group activities.

There are three main types of partnerships: institutional, trust fund, and programmatic. In addition, many partnerships are established with the stakeholders themselves at the country level as part of specific projects.

The Bank Group's connection to the U.N. and to the IMF is covered in chapter 2 ("How the World Bank Group Is Organized"). Partnerships for financing, such as trust funds and cofinancing arrangements, are described in the section on the Bank Group's finances, above. Additional areas of partnership are described in the following subsections.

Box 3.8

Web Links for Partnerships

World Bank Partners:
http://web.worldbank.org/
WBSITE/EXTERNAL/EXTABOUTUS/
0,,contentMDK:20040606~
menuPK:34639~pagePK:
34542~piPK:36600~theSitePK:
29708,00.html

IFC Private Enterprise Partnership: http://www1.ifc.org/pep

MIGA Partnerships:
http://www.miga.org/screens/
partnerships/partnerships.htm

Institutional Partnerships

In addition to the IMF, the U.N., and the U.N.'s many agencies and programs, the Bank Group works with many other organizations whose membership is made up of country governments. Major examples include the following:

- European Union
- World Trade Organization
- Multilateral development banks (MDBs) and other multilateral financial institutions. These institutions provide financial support and professional advice for economic and social development activities in developing countries. The term MDBs typically refers to the World Bank Group and four regional development banks: the African Development Bank Group, the Asian Development Bank, the European Bank for Reconstruction and Development, and the

Inter-American Development Bank Group. Several additional banks and funds that lend to developing countries but have a narrower membership and focus are also identified as other multilateral development institutions. There are also subregional banks in such areas as the Caribbean, Central America, and parts of Africa.

Bilateral Development Agencies

The World Bank Group works with the development agencies of individual countries to coordinate aid and achieve development goals, sometimes formally through trust funds (described earlier). Countries that have such agencies include Australia, Canada, Japan, New Zealand, the United States, and numerous countries in Europe. Work is coordinated by various committees and through consultations that take place throughout the year.

Programmatic Partnerships

The World Bank hosts at its headquarters the secretariats of several closely affiliated organizations, including

- *Consultative Group on International Agricultural Research (CGIAR).* The CGIAR is an association of 62 members that supports agricultural research and related activities carried out by 16 autonomous research centers. Priorities include increasing productivity, protecting the environment, saving biodiversity, improving policies, and strengthening research at the national level. Members of the CGIAR include industrial and developing countries, foundations, and international and regional organizations. CGIAR's Web site is at <http://www.cgiar.org>.
- *Consultative Group to Assist the Poorest (CGAP).* CGAP is a consortium of 29 bilateral and multilateral donor agencies that seeks to improve the capacity of microfinance institutions (specialized institutions that provide financial services to very poor people). CGAP supports the development of these institutions and works to increase their commercial viability and the legal and regulatory framework for them in poor countries. CGAP's Web site is at <http://www.cgap.org>.
- *Development Gateway.* The Development Gateway is an Internet portal for information and knowledge sharing on sustainable development and poverty reduction. Features include AiDA, a comprehensive database of development projects; dgMarket, an international procurement marketplace; and Country Gateways, a network of 41 locally owned and managed public–private partnerships, each of which promotes innovative and

effective use of the Internet and other information and communication technologies in the country to reduce poverty and promote sustainable development. The Web site is at <http://www.developmentgateway.org>.

- *Global Environment Facility (GEF)*. GEF provides grants and concessional loans to help developing countries meet the costs of measures designed to achieve global environmental benefits. The focus is on climate change, biological diversity, international waters, and ozone layer depletion. The World Bank, U.N. Development Programme, and U.N. Environment Programme are the three implementing agencies of GEF, which is supported administratively by the World Bank but remains functionally independent. Each agency finances GEF activities within its respective areas of competence. GEF's Web site is at <http://www/worldbank.org/gef>.

Nongovernmental Organizations and Civil Society

Most development projects approved by the Bank Group today involve the active participation of nongovernmental organizations (NGOs) in their implementation, and most of the Bank Group's country strategies benefit from consultations with civil society organizations. The Bank Group uses the term "civil society organizations" to refer to the wide array of nongovernmental and not-for-profit organizations that have a presence in public life, expressing interests and values of their members or others that are based on ethical, cultural, political, scientific, religious, or philanthropic considerations.

The Bank Group's outreach in this area takes in trade unions, community-based organizations, social movements, faith-based institutions, charitable organizations, research centers, foundations, student organizations, professional associations, and many other entities. Staff members working in 70 country offices around the world reach out to and collaborate with NGOs in a variety of areas, ranging from education and AIDS to the environment. The home pages of the Bank Group's civil society efforts are at <http://www.worldbank.org/civilsociety> (for the World Bank), and <http://www.ifc.org/ngo> (for IFC). MIGA posts its NGO correspondence at <http://www.miga.org/screens/news/news.htm>.

Staff, Consultants, and Vendors

World Bank Group Staff

The institutions of the World Bank Group together have a staff of about 10,000 professionals and support personnel—8,000 at headquarters in Washington, D.C., and 2,000 in the field. The proportion of field personnel has grown rapidly in recent years, reflecting the Bank Group's commitment to operating in close partnership with its clients. Staff members are drawn from most member countries and typically have strong academic backgrounds, a broad understanding of development issues, and international work experience. Most have specializations appropriate to their particular unit.

Staff salaries and benefits are intended to be competitive and are based on data from comparable organizations in the public sector as well as from the private industrial and financial sectors. According to a treaty signed by the U.S. government when the Bank's headquarters was established in Washington, D.C., in 1945, foreign nationals are exempt from federal and state taxes on World Bank Group income. However, U.S. citizens working at the Bank Group are required to pay both federal and state income taxes on their salaries. Hence, in order to keep after-tax income in line for all staff members, the Bank Group handles salaries on a net-of-tax basis and gives an additional allowance to staff members who are liable for income taxes. All staff members also pay local property, sales, and other taxes. These tax arrangements are comparable to those of other international organizations.

Job Openings, Internships, and Scholarships

The Bank Group provides information on its job openings, special job opportunities for younger professionals, and internships through a careers Web site maintained by Human Resources. The Web address is at <http://www.worldbank.org/careers>. There is also information specific to MIGA at <http://www.miga.org/screens/careers/careers.htm>.

In addition, the Bank Group offers scholarship and fellowship programs; information is available online at <http://www.worldbank.org/wbi/scholarships>. Specific programs include the following:

- The *Young Professionals Program* is for highly qualified and motivated people younger than 32 years old who are skilled in areas relevant to the World Bank's operations. Candidates must hold the equivalent of a master's degree and have significant work experience or continued academic study at the doctoral level. Initial appointments are for two years and often lead to a full career in the Bank.

- The *Junior Professional Associates Program* is for recent graduates younger than 29 years old who have superior academic records and an interest in international work. Candidates must hold the equivalent of a bachelor's or master's degree or must be a doctoral candidate. This is a two-year, entry-level program; associates are not eligible for employment with the World Bank for two years following the end of their appointment.

- The *Bank Internship Program* is for nationals of a World Bank member country who are enrolled full time in a master's or doctoral program. Interns work either in the winter (November–January) or the summer (May–September), although dates may vary according to university schedules. Interns in this program receive a salary.
- The *Knowledge Internship Program* is a year-round program open to full-time students in undergraduate and graduate programs. Interns in this program typically earn course credits for their work and do not receive financial compensation.
- The *Joint Japan–World Bank Graduate Scholarship Program* covers up to two years of study toward a master's degree. The candidate must be a national of a World Bank member country, must have been accepted at a university outside their country, must study in a field related to development, must be younger than 45 years old, and must have at least two years of professional experience. The program is funded by the Japanese government, but it does not require study in Japan.
- The *Robert S. McNamara Fellowships Program* is part of the Woodrow Wilson School of Public Affairs at Princeton University. This program provides a full-tuition scholarship, travel allowance, and a stipend for living expenses. The student must be a national of a World Bank member country and have at least seven years of professional experience. Candidates apply directly to the Master's in Public Policy program at Princeton, indicating that they are applying for admission as a McNamara Fellow.

Procurement Opportunities in Projects Financed by IBRD and IDA

Every year, investment projects financed by the World Bank generate billions of dollars in opportunities for suppliers of goods and services. Government agencies from the Bank's borrowing countries are responsible for the purchase of goods and services to support these projects. Bank procedures have been established to ensure that procurement is conducted efficiently and in an open, competitive, and transparent manner.

The procurement policies and procedures in Bank-financed projects are explained in the *Guidelines: Procurement under IBRD Loans and IDA Credits* and the *Guidelines: Selection and Employment of Consultants by World Bank Borrowers* available at <http://www.worldbank.org/procure>. On the same page, under the "Bidding and Consulting Opportunities" tab, the *Resource Guide to Consulting, Supply and Contracting Opportunities in Projects Financed by the World Bank* provides detailed guidance on how to identify and track business opportunities.

Supplying Directly to the World Bank Group

The Bank regularly seeks qualified vendors for assistance in running its operations in Washington and its offices all over the world. Opportunities range from supplying printer toner cartridges to managing complex communications systems. For information on how to sell goods and services to the Bank Group, including vendor registration, the key Web site is the vendor kiosk at <https://info.worldbank.org/vendorkiosk/>. There is also a Web site that lists current business opportunities with the Bank Group; the home page is at: <http://www.worldbank.org/html/extdr/business/rfps.htm>.

A classroom in Timor-Leste

CHAPTER 4

World Bank Group Countries and Regions

This chapter provides information on the countries of the Bank Group: the mechanics of membership, the ways that countries are classified, and the initiatives focusing on groups of countries with shared characteristics or concerns. It then provides a review of each of the regions into which the Bank Group organizes its member countries as it provides development assistance.

Middle East &
North Africa

Africa

Latin America
& the Caribbean

Map 4.1 World Bank Countries and Regions

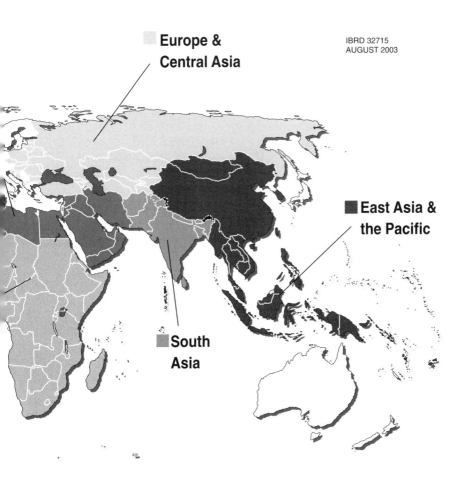

Europe &
Central Asia

IBRD 32715
AUGUST 2003

East Asia &
the Pacific

South
Asia

Member Countries

Membership

The five institutions of the Bank Group are owned by their member countries (see box 4.1 for Web links). To become a member of the International Bank for Reconstruction and Development (IBRD), a country must first join the International Monetary Fund (IMF). Membership in the International Development Association (IDA), the International Finance Corporation (IFC), and the Multilateral Investment Guarantee Agency (MIGA) further requires membership in IBRD. In each of these cases, member countries buy shares in the institution, helping build its capital and borrowing power; this arrangement is called "capital subscriptions." Member countries also sign the founding document of each institution: the Articles of Agreement for IBRD, IDA, and IFC and the MIGA Convention. Membership in the International Centre for the Settlement of Investment Disputes (ICSID) entails signing and ratifying the ICSID Convention and also involves capital subscriptions. Links to these founding documents can be found at <http://www.worldbank.org/articles>.

As of July 2003, IBRD had 184 members, IDA had 164, IFC had 175, MIGA had 163, and ICSID had 139. The up-to-date lists of membership, official country names used by the Bank Group, and communications regarding membership status and capital subscriptions are handled by the Bank Group's Corporate Secretariat. For more information, consult the member countries Web page at <http://www.worldbank.org/members>. In its maps and publications, the Bank Group sometimes indicates contested boundaries or territorial claims between member countries, but it does not endorse any member country's position where such disputes exist.

As covered in chapter 2 ("How the World Bank Group Is Organized"), member countries govern the Bank Group through their representatives, the Board of Governors, and the Board of Executive Directors. The voting power of each executive director is determined by the value of capital subscriptions for the countries that he or she represents. For each of the four

---

Box 4.1

Web Links for Country Membership Information

IBRD/IDA member countries:
http://web.worldbank.org/WBSITE/EXTERNAL/EXTABOUTUS/0,,contentMDK:20040581~
menuPK:34589~pagePK:34542~piPK:36600~theSitePK:29708,00.html

IFC member countries: http://www.ifc.org/about/members/members.html

MIGA member countries: http://www.miga.org/screens/about/members/members.htm

ICSID contracting states: http://www.worldbank.org/icsid/constate/constate.htm

---

shareholding institutions—IBRD, IDA, IFC, and MIGA—the executive director for the United States has the greatest voting power, followed by the executive director for Japan.

Member countries can withdraw from Bank Group institutions at any time by giving notice. A member may also be suspended, and after a year may be expelled if it fails to fulfill any of its obligations to a Bank Group institution. A country that ceases to be a member of the IMF automatically ceases to be a member of the Bank Group unless, within three months, the Bank Group decides by a special majority to allow the country to remain a member. When a country ceases to be a member, it continues to be liable for its contractual obligations, such as servicing its loans. It also continues to be liable for calls on its unpaid subscription resulting from losses sustained by a Bank Group institution on guarantees or loans outstanding on the date of withdrawal.

Member countries are listed by geographic region later in this chapter. A master list—with dates of membership, amounts borrowed, and other data—appears in appendix D. A full list of Bank Group offices appears in appendix G.

Ways of Classifying Countries

Several important distinctions among member countries are commonly used at the Bank Group. Although the meanings of the terms overlap—and all of them make distinctions in terms of wealth—it is important to note that they are not interchangeable.

Low-income, middle-income, and high-income countries

In its analytical and operational work, the Bank Group characterizes country economies as low-income, middle-income (subdivided into lower-middle and upper-middle), and high-income (see table 4.1). It makes these classifications for most nonsovereign territories as well as for independent countries. Low-income and middle-income economies are sometimes referred to as developing economies. On the basis of 2001 gross national income, low-income countries are those with average annual per capita incomes of US$745 or less. For lower-middle-income countries, the figures are US$746 to US$2,975; for upper-middle-income countries, US$2,976 to US$9,205; and for high-income countries, US$9,206 or more. Classification by income does not necessarily reflect development status.

Developing and industrial countries

In general usage at the Bank Group, the term "developing" refers to countries whose economies are classified as low-income or middle-income. The terms "industrial" or "developed" refer to countries whose economies are high-income. The use of these terms is not intended to imply that all

Table 4.1 Classification of Countries by Region and Level of Income

Income group	Subgroup	Sub-Saharan Africa		Asia		Europe and Central Asia		Middle East and North Africa		Americas
		East and Southern Africa	West Africa	East Asia and Pacific	South Asia	Eastern Europe and Central Asia	Rest of Europe	Middle East	North Africa	
Low-income		Angola	Benin	Cambodia	Afghanistan	Armenia		Yemen, Rep. of		Haiti
		Burundi	Burkina Faso	Indonesia	Bangladesh	Azerbaijan				Nicaragua
		Comoros	Cameroon	Korea, Dem. Rep. of	Bhutan	Georgia				
		Congo, Dem. Rep. of	Central African Republic	Lao PDR	India	Kyrgyz Republic				
		Eritrea	Chad	Mongolia	Nepal	Moldova				
		Ethiopia	Congo, Rep. of	Myanmar	Pakistan	Tajikistan				
		Kenya	Côte d'Ivoire	Papua New Guinea		Ukraine				
		Lesotho	Equatorial Guinea	Solomon Islands		Uzbekistan				
		Madagascar	Gambia, The	Timor-Leste						
		Malawi	Ghana	Vietnam						
		Mozambique	Guinea							
		Rwanda	Guinea-Bissau							
		Somalia	Liberia							
		Sudan	Mali							
		Tanzania	Mauritania							
		Uganda	Niger							
		Zambia	Nigeria							
		Zimbabwe	São Tomé and Príncipe							
			Senegal							
			Sierra Leone							
			Togo							

Middle-income									
Lower-middle	Namibia South Africa Swaziland	Cape Verde	China Fiji Kiribati Marshall Islands Micronesia, Federated States of Philippines Samoa Thailand Tonga Vanuatu	Maldives Sri Lanka	Albania Belarus Bosnia and Herzegovina Bulgaria Kazakhstan Macedonia, FYR[a] Romania Russian Federation Turkmenistan Yugoslavia, Fed. Rep. (Serbia and Montenegro)	Turkey	Iran, Islamic Rep. of Iraq Jordan Syrian Arab Republic West Bank and Gaza	Algeria Djibouti Egypt, Arab Rep. of Morocco Tunisia	Belize Bolivia Colombia Cuba Dominican Republic Ecuador El Salvador Guatemala Guyana Honduras Jamaica Paraguay Peru St. Vincent and the Grenadines Suriname
Upper-middle	Botswana Mauritius Mayotte Seychelles	Gabon	American Samoa Malaysia Palau		Croatia Czech Republic Estonia Hungary Latvia Lithuania Poland Slovak Republic	Isle of Man	Lebanon Oman Saudi Arabia	Libya Malta	Antigua and Barbuda Argentina Barbados Brazil Chile Costa Rica Dominica Grenada Mexico Panama Puerto Rico St. Kitts and Nevis St. Lucia Trinidad and Tobago Uruguay Venezuela, R.B. de

(continued)

Table 4.1 Classification of Countries by Region and Level of Income (continued)

Income group	Subgroup	Sub-Saharan Africa		Asia		Europe and Central Asia		Middle East and North Africa		Americas
		East and Southern Africa	West Africa	East Asia and Pacific	South Asia	Eastern Europe and Central Asia	Rest of Europe	Middle East	North Africa	
High-income	*OECD*			Australia Japan Korea, Rep. of New Zealand			Austria Belgium Denmark Finland France[b] Germany Greece Iceland Ireland Italy Luxembourg Netherlands Norway Portugal Spain Sweden Switzerland United Kingdom			Canada United States
	Non-OECD			Brunei French Polynesia Guam Hong Kong, China[c] Macao, China[d] New Caledonia N. Mariana Islands Singapore Taiwan, China		Slovenia	Andorra Channel Islands Cyprus Faeroe Islands Greenland Liechtenstein Monaco San Marino	Bahrain Israel Kuwait Qatar United Arab Emirates		Aruba Bahamas, The Bermuda Cayman Islands Netherlands Antilles Virgin Islands (U.S.)

aFormer Yugoslav Republic of Macedonia.
bThe French overseas departments of French Guiana, Guadeloupe, Martinique, and Réunion are included in France.
cOn 1 July 1997 China resumed its exercise of sovereignty over Hong Kong.
dOn 20 December 1999 China resumed its exercise of sovereignty over Macao.

economies in the group are experiencing similar development or that other economies have reached a preferred or final stage of development.

Part I and Part II
Countries choose whether they are Part I or Part II primarily on the basis of their economic standing. Part I countries are almost all industrial countries and donors to IDA, and they pay their contributions in freely convertible currency. Part II countries are almost all developing countries, some of which are donors to IDA. Part II countries are entitled to pay most of their contributions to IDA in local currency.

MIGA makes a similar distinction between Category I and Category II member countries. The breakdown of countries into these categories differs slightly from the breakdown within IDA.

Donors and borrowers
In general, the term "donor" refers to a country that makes contributions to IDA. A borrower country, however, can be one that borrows from IDA, from IBRD, or in some cases from both. Note, however, that all member countries pay capital subscriptions into IBRD, IDA, IFC, and MIGA—this payment is distinct from a given country's lending and borrowing.

IDA, IBRD, and blend countries—and graduates
The distinctions between IBRD and IDA borrowers—and the circumstances in which a country may be eligible to receive a blend of IBRD and IDA credits—are based on per capita income and the country's creditworthiness. These distinctions are discussed in detail in chapter 2 ("How the World Bank Is Organized"); see also "Country Eligibility for Borrowing" in *The World Bank Annual Report*. Note that as a country's per capita income increases, it can graduate out of eligibility for IDA credits and, in turn, out of eligibility for IBRD loans (see box 4.2). However, wealthier countries remain members of Bank Group organizations, even if they or the enterprises operating within their borders do not draw upon Bank Group services.

Country Activities and Operations
As indicated in chapter 3 ("How the World Bank Operates"), the Bank Group's project databases enable users to search for information on the institutions' activities in a given country. The Bank Group's key resource for comparative data on countries is *World Development Indicators,* published each year in April. In addition, the World Bank maintains numerous country-specific Web sites; some of these are maintained by the regional vice presidencies, and some by the country offices themselves. The portal Web page to World Bank information on countries, as well as regions, is at <http://www.worldbank.org/countries>. Country information for IFC is

accessible through the Web sites of the investment regions; links to these sites are at <http://www.ifc.org/sitemap>.

The appendixes provide a number of resources covering both borrower and donor countries:

- A list of country groupings that form the constituencies of the 24 executive directors, with the total voting power that each director represents (appendix E).
- A comprehensive table of member countries, including their memberships in the various Bank Group institutions, the years they joined, and their individual voting power (appendix D).
- A list of additional country resources, including Bank Group country offices and Web sites (appendix G). Offices that serve as Public Information Centers (PICs) are identified. Also included, where applicable, are depository libraries and distributors of World Bank publications.

Initiatives for Groups of Countries

Some Bank Group initiatives target groups of countries with key features in common; for example, their income level, their degree of indebtedness, or the strength of their institutions.

Heavily Indebted Poor Countries initiative

Established by the World Bank, the IMF, and member countries in 1996, and significantly expanded in 1999, the Heavily Indebted Poor Countries (HIPC) initiative is a comprehensive approach to reducing the external debt of the world's poorest, most heavily indebted countries. Its goals are to help countries move from endless restructuring of debt to lasting debt relief, to reduce multilateral debt, and to free up resources for countries that pursue economic and social reform targeted at measurable poverty reduction.

The HIPC initiative assists countries that are eligible only for IDA credits and for comparable assistance from the IMF's Poverty Reduction and Growth Facility. Other qualifying countries are those that face an unsustainable debt situation, determined on the basis of a joint Bank–IMF assessment, even after traditional debt relief mechanisms are applied. The Web site of the initiative is at <http://www.worldbank.org/hipc>.

Low-income countries under stress initiative

In November 2001, a task force was set up to review the World Bank Group's assistance to poorly performing countries. The task force examined the reasons for the lack of success of the Bank's (and other donors') assistance programs. A summary of the findings of the task force was issued and discussed by the Board of Executive Directors in March and July 2002. Improving effectiveness of external assistance to countries with very weak policies and institutions has become a priority for the World Bank Group. For more information, see <http://www.worldbank.org/licus>.

Fast-Track countries

In November 2001, the Bank established the Fast-Track Initiative as a central element in the plan to accelerate progress toward the achievement of the Millennium Development Goals for education. In June 2002, the criteria were announced for inviting countries to seek support under this initiative. Eighteen countries met the eligibility requirements (involving a sectorwide plan for education nested within a broader development strategy involving a Poverty Reduction Strategy Paper (PRSP) in place): Albania, Bolivia, Burkina Faso, Ethiopia, The Gambia, Ghana, Guinea, Guyana, Honduras, Mauritania, Mozambique, Nicaragua, Niger, Tanzania, Uganda, Vietnam, the Republic of Yemen, and Zambia. Additionally, five other countries were identified as having the largest numbers of children out of school (Bangladesh, the Democratic Republic of Congo, India, Nigeria, and Pakistan). The Bank pledged to increase support for these countries so that they can become eligible for fast-track support as soon as possible.

Middle-income countries

Faced with a distinct set of development challenges, middle-income countries continue to seek Bank Group services to enhance their debt and risk management flexibility and to improve their institutional capacity for designing and implementing economic and sector reforms. Following the recommendation of the 2001 middle-income country task force, the Bank Group now emphasizes the complementary role of advisory services and has improved its lending instruments to meet the dynamic needs of middle-income countries. For example, a deferred drawdown option for adjustment loans was approved by the Board of Executive Directors, and the corresponding instrument is now available to clients. The Bank has also introduced new financial products, including variable-spread single currency loans, fixed-spread loans, and local currency loans, which provide more flexible options for both low- and middle-income clients.

Small states

"Small states" is a term applied to a diverse group of sovereign developing countries—some quite wealthy, some very poor; some islands or groups of islands; some landlocked; and many with populations of 1.5 million or less. Forty-five developing countries have populations of 1.5 million or less, and 41 of these are members of the World Bank.

The recent report of the Commonwealth Secretariat–World Bank Joint Task Force on Small States identified a number of characteristics that developing small states share and that shape their developmental challenges. For instance, many are especially vulnerable to external events, including natural disasters that cause high volatility in national incomes; many suffer from limited capacity in the public and private sectors; and many currently face an uncertain and difficult economic transition under a changing world trade regime.

Regional Groupings

Most Bank Group institutions approach their work by grouping developing countries into geographic regions. As discussed in chapter 2 ("How the World Bank Group Is Organized"), these regions are one dimension of an organizational matrix, the other dimension being the thematic network aspects of development that cut across regions. The sections below provide a brief overview of Bank Group regions: which countries they include, a few essential facts, and some information on the Bank Group's activities and priorities. They also offer information on major regional initiatives, which in most cases are partnership initiatives between the Bank Group and other organizations or governments.

The portal Web page to information on World Bank regions, as well as countries, is at <http://www.worldbank.org/countries>. Additional issue briefs for world regions can be found at <http://www.worldbank.org/issuebriefs>. Links to the Web sites of IFC investment regions can be found at <http://www.ifc.org/sitemap>. More comprehensive information on regions can be found in the annual reports of the Bank Group institutions, as well as on the Web sites listed.

The regional sections hereafter follow the organization of the World Bank in regional vice presidencies (see figure 4.1 for the relative size of lending to these regions). IFC's regional departments correspond to this arrangement, except that there are two separate but closely coordinated departments within Europe and Central Asia, and a few countries are assigned to different regions from those assigned at the Bank. In its annual report, MIGA reports on East Asia and the Pacific and South Asia as a single region. ICSID does not organize its work by regions.

Note that, strictly speaking, Bank Group regions refer only to the countries that are eligible for borrowing or other services. Wealthier member countries that lie within these geographic areas—for example, Singapore, Oman, and Barbados—are not normally included in lists of countries within these regions. The Bank Group gathers economic information on all countries, however, and operates offices in a number of donor countries.

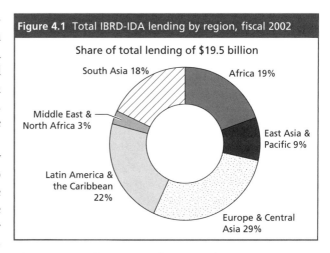

Figure 4.1 Total IBRD-IDA lending by region, fiscal 2002

Share of total lending of $19.5 billion

South Asia 18%
Africa 19%
Middle East & North Africa 3%
East Asia & Pacific 9%
Latin America & the Caribbean 22%
Europe & Central Asia 29%

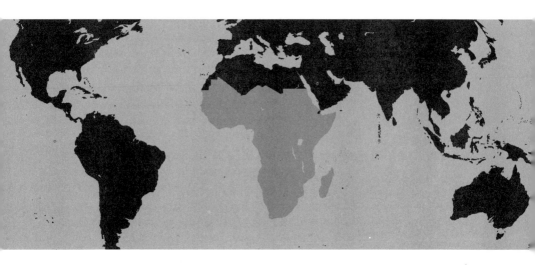

Africa (Sub-Saharan)

This World Bank region includes the following countries that are eligible for borrowing:

Angola	Ethiopia	Niger
Benin	Gabon	Nigeria
Botswana	The Gambia	Rwanda
Burkina Faso	Ghana	São Tomé and Principe
Burundi	Guinea	Senegal
Cameroon	Guinea-Bissau	Seychelles
Cape Verde	Kenya	Sierra Leone
Central African Republic	Lesotho	Somalia
Chad	Liberia	South Africa
Comoros	Madagascar	Sudan
Democratic Republic of Congo	Malawi	Swaziland
	Mali	Tanzania
Republic of Congo	Mauritania	Togo
Côte d'Ivoire	Mauritius	Uganda
Equatorial Guinea	Mozambique	Zambia
Eritrea	Namibia	Zimbabwe

All of these countries are members of IBRD. As for the other institutions:

- Namibia and Seychelles are not members of IDA.
- Djibouti is included in IFC's Africa region. São Tomé and Principe is not a member of IFC.
- Comoros, Gabon, Guinea-Bissau, Liberia, Niger, São Tomé and Principe, and Somalia are not members of MIGA.

- Angola, Cape Verde, Equatorial Guinea, Eritrea, Ethiopia, Guinea-Bissau, Namibia, São Tomé and Principe, and South Africa are not members of ICSID.

The World Bank in Sub-Saharan Africa

Meeting the Millennium Development Goals by 2015 raises difficult challenges in many African countries. Approximately 300 million Africans—nearly half the region's population—still live in extreme poverty. The spread of HIV/AIDS threatens to wipe out important gains in life expectancy. The lack of political and economic progress in some of the key countries of the continent is eroding their ability to attract investment. For much of the region, inequality is still high and growth remains insufficient to prevent an increase in the number of poor. Many people still have no access to basic services and cannot effectively participate in the modern economy. See box 4.3 for regional key facts.

The Bank's strategy in Africa is to accelerate progress toward reaching the Millennium Development Goals. The strategic objectives are consistent with those outlined by African heads of state in the New Partnership for Africa's Development (NEPAD) initiative and are based on the analysis of the seminal study *Can Africa Claim the 21st Century?* Major areas of focus have been identified, including improving governance and resolving conflict; developing Africa's enormous human resource potential; diversifying production and increasing competitiveness; and reducing aid dependence and debt, in part by strengthening the partnership with the donor community. To maximize the impact of assistance, the recent allocation of IDA resources across countries has mirrored the quality of policies and institutions. Several countries have, as a result, received increased assistance.

> **Box 4.3**
>
> **Key Facts for IBRD Countries in Sub-Saharan Africa, 2002**
>
> Total population: 0.7 billion
>
> Population growth: 2.3 percent
>
> Life expectancy at birth: 47 years
>
> Infant mortality per 1,000 births: 91
>
> Female youth illiteracy: 27 percent
>
> 2001 gross national income per capita: US$470
>
> Number of persons living with HIV/AIDS: 28.5 million

The World Bank continues to focus on some important regional priorities, including providing further debt relief, offering postconflict support, assisting with efforts on HIV/AIDS and other communicable diseases, assisting with regional integration, capacity building, and increasing access to global markets for African products (see figures 4.2 and 4.3 for thematic and sectoral breakdowns of lending). The region's portal Web site is at <http://www.worldbank.org/afr>.

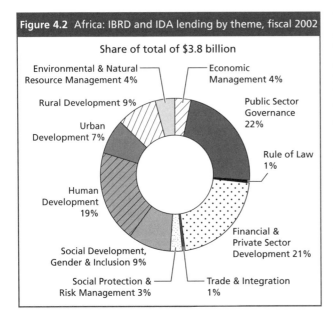

Figure 4.2 Africa: IBRD and IDA lending by theme, fiscal 2002

Share of total of $3.8 billion

- Environmental & Natural Resource Management 4%
- Economic Management 4%
- Rural Development 9%
- Public Sector Governance 22%
- Urban Development 7%
- Rule of Law 1%
- Human Development 19%
- Financial & Private Sector Development 21%
- Social Development, Gender & Inclusion 9%
- Social Protection & Risk Management 3%
- Trade & Integration 1%

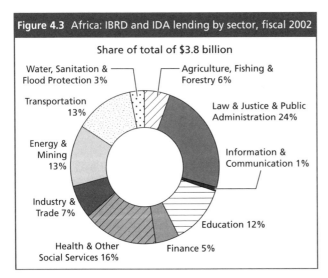

Figure 4.3 Africa: IBRD and IDA lending by sector, fiscal 2002

Share of total of $3.8 billion

- Water, Sanitation & Flood Protection 3%
- Agriculture, Fishing & Forestry 6%
- Transportation 13%
- Law & Justice & Public Administration 24%
- Energy & Mining 13%
- Information & Communication 1%
- Industry & Trade 7%
- Education 12%
- Health & Other Social Services 16%
- Finance 5%

IFC in Sub-Saharan Africa

The environment for private sector investment remains difficult in Sub-Saharan Africa. Under such circumstances, IFC is finding innovative ways to support the private sector's contribution to development. The core of IFC strategy in Sub-Saharan Africa mirrors overall IFC corporate strategy, in which investment priority is given to private provision of physical infrastructure, development of dynamic private financial institutions, expanded telecommunications and information technology, and support for small and medium enterprises and tourism businesses.

The Africa department's Web site is at <http://www.ifc.org/africa>.

MIGA in Sub-Saharan Africa

The Sub-Saharan Africa region is a priority area for MIGA; the agency works to attract new investment and build greater institutional capacity in the region. MIGA has established a regional field office in Johannesburg; it also works through some 30 field missions and mobile offices. The agency pursues new investment project guarantees and undertakes numerous technical assistance activities in the region. Its efforts are focused on the need for infrastructure investment in southern Africa and on how best to support privatization efforts involving public–private partnerships.

Regional Initiatives
Regional initiatives in Sub-Saharan Africa include the following:

- The *Africa Project Development Facility (APDF)* supplies experienced managers and technical personnel to small and medium private companies in Africa. APDF offers customized training services to local managers and staff members to upgrade their skills and improve performance and productivity of their company. The program is a joint initiative of IFC, the United Nations Development Programme (UNDP), and the African Development Bank. The Web site is at <http://apdf.ifc.org/index.htm>.

- The *African Management Services Company (AMSCO)* provides business advice and enterprise support services to small and medium enterprises in Africa, as well as financial institutions and consultants who serve such enterprises. AMSCO is sponsored by the African Development Bank and IFC, with IFC as the executing agency. The Web site is at <http://www.amsco.org>.

- The *Global Partnership for Eliminating Riverblindness* is an initiative to eliminate onchocerciasis in Sub-Saharan Africa, and to help affected countries maintain control of the disease. The program is a joint initiative of the UNDP, the Food and Agriculture Organization, the World Bank, and the World Health Organization. The Web site is at <http://www.worldbank.org/gper/right.htm>.

- The *Indigenous Knowledge Program* documents local or traditional knowledge in developing countries and applies this knowledge to issues of development. The program is a partnership between the World Bank and various U.N. agencies, bilateral development agencies, and nongovernmental organizations (NGOs). The Web site is at <http://www.worldbank.org/afr/ik/index.htm>.

- The *Multi-Country HIV/AIDS Program (MAP)* is a World Bank initiative that is making US$1 billion in flexible and rapid funding available to African countries as they increase their efforts to combat HIV/AIDS. The Web site is at <http://www.worldbank.org/afr/aids/map.htm>.

- The *New Partnership for Africa's Development (NEPAD)* is a development initiative owned and led by Africans, with support from the World Bank, the U.N., and a wide range of development agencies and NGOs. The Web site is at <http://www.nepad.org>.

- The *Nile Basin Initiative* is a regional partnership of the 10 countries in the Nile basin, to fight poverty, promote economic development, and coordinate management of Nile basin water resources. The Web site is at <http://www.nilebasin.org>.

- The *Transport Policy Program for Africa* is a partnership between the World Bank and numerous bilateral and multilateral agencies. This program is aimed at facilitating policy development and related capacity building in the transport sector of Sub-Saharan Africa. The Web site is at <http://www.worldbank.org/afr/ssatp>.

Key Publications

The following publications address issues in Sub-Saharan Africa:

- *Administrative Barriers to Foreign Investment: Reducing Red Tape in Africa*
- *African Development Indicators*
- *African Poverty at the Millennium: Causes, Complexities, and Challenges*
- *Africa's International Rivers: An Economic Perspective*
- *Aid and Reform in Africa*
- *Can Africa Claim the 21st Century?*
- *A Chance to Learn: Knowledge and Finance for Education in Sub-Saharan Africa*
- *Education and Health and Sub-Saharan Africa: A Review of Sector-Wide Approaches*
- *Faith in Development: Partnership between the World Bank and the Churches of Africa*
- *The Future of African Cities: Challenges and Priorities in Urban Development*
- *Intensifying Action against HIV/AIDS in Africa*
- *The Legal and Regulatory Framework for Environmental Impact Assessments: A Study of Selected Countries in Sub-Saharan Africa*
- *Reforming Business-Related Laws to Promote Private Sector Development: The World Bank Experience in Africa*

East Asia and the Pacific

This World Bank region includes the following countries that are eligible for borrowing:

Cambodia	Malaysia	Philippines
China	Marshall Islands	Samoa
Fiji	Federated States of Micronesia	Solomon Islands
Indonesia		Thailand
Kiribati	Mongolia	Timor-Leste
Republic of Korea	Myanmar	Tonga
Lao People's Democratic Republic	Palau	Vanuatu
	Papua New Guinea	Vietnam

All of these countries are members of IBRD and IDA. As for the other institutions:

- Timor-Leste is not a member of IFC.
- Kiribati, the Marshall Islands, Myanmar, the Solomon Islands, and Tonga are not members of MIGA.
- Cambodia, Kiribati, the Lao PDR, the Marshall Islands, Myanmar, Palau, Thailand, Vanuatu, and Vietnam are not members of ICSID.

The World Bank in East Asia and the Pacific

From 1965 to 2000, East Asian economics grew faster than all others in the world. The top eight economies have grown twice as fast as the rest of East Asia, three times as fast as Latin America and South Asia, and 25 times as fast as Sub-Saharan Africa. As a result of this growth, human welfare improved dramatically. Life expectancy increased from almost 40 years in 1960 to 69 years in 1999, and the number of people living in absolute poverty, measured at US$1 per day, was cut nearly in half, dropping from 452 million in 1990 to 250 million in 2000. A host of other social indicators, from education to appliance ownership, also improved rapidly. See box 4.4 for regional key facts.

Progress on structural and institutional reforms remains a key focus for the World Bank in the region. These reforms include accelerating financial and corporate restructuring; improving competitiveness; tackling impediments that undermine the investment climate; ensuring adequate social protection; pursuing public sector–governance reforms in such areas as public expenditure management, public financial accountability and transparency, civil service reform, and decentralization; and preventing countries from retreating into environmental neglect.

To reduce vulnerability and to ensure that poor people benefit from growth, Bank strategy has evolved from supporting safety nets and crisis assessment to focusing on the policies and institutions that help households manage social risks, that build an effective social policy framework, and that enable the poor to participate in the benefits of growth. Social programs have increasingly emphasized community empowerment and demand-driven approaches to promote efficiency, transparency, and effectiveness. See figures 4.4 and 4.5 for thematic and sectoral breakdowns of lending. The region's portal Web site is at <http://www.worldbank.org/eap>.

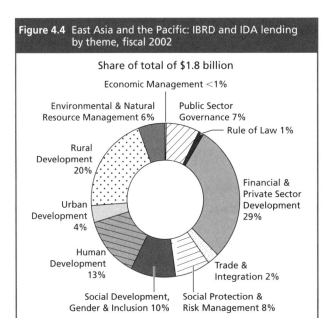

Figure 4.4 East Asia and the Pacific: IBRD and IDA lending by theme, fiscal 2002

Share of total of $1.8 billion

Economic Management <1%

Environmental & Natural Resource Management 6%

Public Sector Governance 7%

Rule of Law 1%

Rural Development 20%

Financial & Private Sector Development 29%

Urban Development 4%

Human Development 13%

Trade & Integration 2%

Social Development, Gender & Inclusion 10%

Social Protection & Risk Management 8%

IFC in East Asia and the Pacific

In East Asia, IFC focuses on supporting the restructuring of banks and companies, strengthening the financial sector, raising corporate governance standards, and investing in projects at the frontier of private sector development. The East Asia crisis and the recent impact of the global downturn revealed the extent of structural vulnerabilities in Asia's economies. In this context, IFC's strategic focus is on strengthening the sustainability of private sector devel-

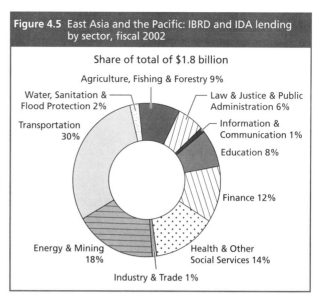

Figure 4.5 East Asia and the Pacific: IBRD and IDA lending by sector, fiscal 2002

Share of total of $1.8 billion

Agriculture, Fishing & Forestry 9%

Water, Sanitation & Flood Protection 2%

Law & Justice & Public Administration 6%

Transportation 30%

Information & Communication 1%

Education 8%

Finance 12%

Energy & Mining 18%

Health & Other Social Services 14%

Industry & Trade 1%

opment by building financial sector institutions; by developing model transactions that will catalyze further private investment in a variety of sectors; and by setting standards for corporate governance, international accounting, environmental technologies, best practices, and efficiency of operations.

In fiscal 2002, IFC widened its support for the development of financial markets; enhanced its regional strategy by fostering links between the housing and financial markets; strengthened small and medium enterprises; and helped local firms improve corporate governance. The East Asia department's Web site is at <http://www.ifc.org/asia>.

MIGA in East Asia and the Pacific

MIGA supports projects in East Asia through its guarantee program as well as through technical assistance activities in the region. Technical assistance goals for East Asia include developing and implementing targeting strategies to mobilize and promote investment opportunities; identifying and fostering sectors with solid potential for investment promotion; and devising targeted work programs. Other key objectives involve assisting in the development and implementation of information technology tools and promotional materials.

Regional Initiatives

The following initiatives are in place in East Asia and the Pacific:

- The *Asia Alternative Energy Program* is a partnership between the World Bank and key bilateral donors to incorporate alternative energy options into the design of energy sector strategies and lending operations for all of the Bank's client countries in Asia. The Web site is at <http://www.worldbank.org/astae>.

- The *Asia Development Forum* is a regional forum to strengthen links and policy dialogues within the development community of the Asia and Pacific region. It is sponsored by the Asian Development Bank, the Korea Development Institute, the Korea Institute for International Economic Policy, and the World Bank. The Web site is at <http://www.adb.org/Documents/Events/2002/ADF>.

- The *China Project Development Facility* helps support the development of private small and medium enterprises in the interior of China. It is funded by IFC and donor countries.

- The *Mekong Private Sector Development Facility* supports the development of private, domestically owned, small and medium enterprises in Cambodia, Lao PDR, and Vietnam. It is managed by IFC and funded by the Asian Development Bank and donor countries. The Web site is at <http://www.mpdf.org>.

- The *South Pacific Project Facility* provides financial and business advisory services to the region's small and medium businesses; it also supports sectoral and regional programs that meet private sector needs. It is managed by IFC and funded by the Asian Development Bank and donor countries. The Web site is at <http://sppf.ifc.org>.

Key Publications

The following publications deal with regional issues:

- *Asian Corporate Recovery: Findings from Firm-Level Surveys in Five Countries*
- *Can East Asia Compete? Innovation for Global Markets*
- *China and the Knowledge Economy: Seizing the 21st Century*
- *China 2020: Development Challenges in the New Century*
- *China's Emerging Private Enterprises: Prospects for the New Century*
- *Corporate Governance and Enterprise Reform in China: Building the Institutions of Modern Markets*
- *Democracy, Market Economics, and Development: An Asian Perspective*
- *East Asia: Recovery and Beyond*
- *East Asian Labor Markets and the Economic Crisis: Impacts, Responses, and Lessons*
- *Free Trade Area Membership as a Stepping Stone to Development: The Case of ASEAN*
- *Innovative East Asia*
- *Pacific Island Economies: Building a Resilient Economic Base for the 21st Century*
- *Private Infrastructure in East Asia: Lessons Learned in the Aftermath of the Crisis*
- *Rethinking the East Asian Miracle*
- *Social Cohesion and Conflict Prevention in Asia: Managing Diversity through Development*
- *World Development Report 1996: From Plan to Market*

South Asia

This World Bank region includes the following countries that are eligible for borrowing:

Afghanistan	India	Pakistan
Bangladesh	Maldives	Sri Lanka
Bhutan	Nepal	

All of these countries are members of IBRD and IDA. As for the other institutions:

- Afghanistan and Pakistan are included in IFC's Middle East and North Africa region. Bhutan is not a member of IFC.
- Afghanistan, Bhutan, and Maldives are not members of MIGA.
- Bhutan, India, and Maldives are not members of ICSID.

The World Bank in South Asia

South Asia entered the 21st century after a decade of rapid economic and social development. Growth rates for the region averaged 5.9 percent annually during the 1990s. In recent years, many nations in the region have reduced tariffs, removed trade barriers, dismantled restrictions on domestic and foreign private investment, and reformed their financial systems. However, South Asia still attracts the lowest rate of foreign direct investment in the world, at just 0.5 percent of gross domestic product (GDP). Economies are still highly protected, and intraregional trade is still far below its potential. See box 4.5 for regional key facts.

Despite recent gains, the region remains one of the most disadvantaged in the world—more than one-third of its 1.4 billion people live on less than

US$1 a day, making South Asia home to nearly half of the world's poor. This pervasive poverty is both a cause and consequence of its low level of human development and, in particular, the low status afforded to women. Despite improvements in education and health services, the region still has the world's highest youth illiteracy rate and one-third of the world's maternal deaths. Nearly half of the children under five years of age are malnourished. Environmental degradation, inadequate infrastructure, and social exclusion are among many other obstacles to growth and poverty reduction. If the Millennium Development Goal of halving poverty by 2015 is to be realized, South Asia's performance will be critical.

South Asia's long-term economic prospects will also hinge on much-needed reforms in the key sectors of banking, power, and infrastructure, as well as on commitments to improve public spending and reform state enterprises. Improved governance—including stronger regulatory reforms and increased transparency—is a critical challenge for the region.

The World Bank's focus in South Asia is on the following goals: reducing poverty and vulnerability by promoting country and community ownership of development efforts; responding quickly to crises, such as war or natural disaster; supporting increased investment in human development, especially for marginalized groups; encouraging private sector–led and equitably shared economic growth; supporting client government efforts to improve governance through institutional and policy reforms; building development partnerships between governments, donors, civil society, and communities; and protecting the natural resources that sustain livelihoods (see figures 4.6 and 4.7 for thematic and sectoral breakdowns of lending). The region's portal Web site is at <http://www.worldbank.org/sar>.

IFC in South Asia

Economic growth in South Asia is rapid by world standards, but the economies are still not vigorous enough to address the needs of the poor who live in the region. The unstable political environment, uncertain fiscal and regulatory conditions, inadequate infrastructure, and slow pace of reform impede growth. Despite historically high domestic savings, financing for private investment remains scarce throughout South Asia.

IFC's strategy in South Asia is to support four areas:

- The financial sector, by building strong domestic institutions that expand the range of services and deepen markets, especially for poorly served small and medium enterprises
- Infrastructure, including privatization of public utilities and private provision of new infrastructure
- Manufacturing and service companies, by promoting restructuring and modernization to help meet the challenges of globalization
- Private sector provision of health and education, by making selective investments to improve quality and access.

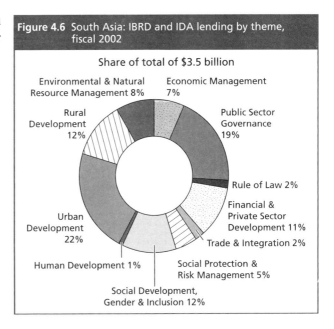

Figure 4.6 South Asia: IBRD and IDA lending by theme, fiscal 2002

Share of total of $3.5 billion

Environmental & Natural Resource Management 8%
Economic Management 7%
Rural Development 12%
Public Sector Governance 19%
Rule of Law 2%
Financial & Private Sector Development 11%
Urban Development 22%
Trade & Integration 2%
Human Development 1%
Social Protection & Risk Management 5%
Social Development, Gender & Inclusion 12%

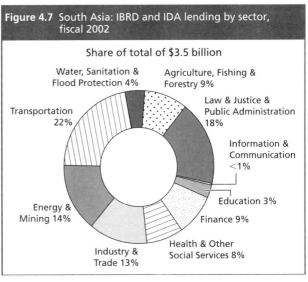

Figure 4.7 South Asia: IBRD and IDA lending by sector, fiscal 2002

Share of total of $3.5 billion

Water, Sanitation & Flood Protection 4%
Agriculture, Fishing & Forestry 9%
Transportation 22%
Law & Justice & Public Administration 18%
Information & Communication <1%
Energy & Mining 14%
Education 3%
Finance 9%
Industry & Trade 13%
Health & Other Social Services 8%

investments to improve quality and access.

The South Asia department's Web site is at <http://www.ifc.org/asia>.

MIGA in South Asia

MIGA supports projects in South Asia through guarantees and technical assistance. Recent guarantee activity has occurred in the power sector in Nepal and the software and telecommunications industries in Pakistan.

Regional Initiatives

South Asia initiatives include the following:

- Immunization efforts in India and South Asia are a collaboration between the World Bank and governments in the region. These efforts are a major focus of the Global Alliance for Vaccines and Immunization, a coalition of public and private institutions. The Web site is at <http://lnweb18.worldbank.org/sar/sa.nsf/2991b676f98842f0852567d7005d2cba/2ffee22cd5749ce5852569d90057e4ed?OpenDocument>.

- South Asia Urban Air Quality Management is a regional program. The World Bank, with support from the UNDP, is identifying where more data are needed to arrive at viable policy recommendations and is assisting governments, civil society, and the media as they work to improve urban air quality. The Web site is at <http://www.worldbank.org/sarurbanair>.

Key Publications

The following publications deal with South Asia:

- *Better Health Systems for India's Poor: Findings, Analysis, and Options*
- *Building Local Bond Markets: An Asian Perspective*
- *Conflict and Cooperation on South Asia's International Rivers: A Legal Perspective*
- *Forging Subregional Links in Transportation and Logistics in South Asia*
- *India: The Challenges of Development*
- *Leapfrogging? India's Information Technology Industry and the Internet*
- *The Next Ascent: An Evaluation of the Aga Khan Rural Support Program, Pakistan*
- *Poverty Reduction in South Asia: Promoting Participation of the Poor*

Europe and Central Asia

This World Bank region includes the following countries that are eligible for borrowing:

Albania	Hungary	Russian Federation
Armenia	Kazakhstan	Serbia and Montenegro
Azerbaijan	Kyrgyz Republic	Slovak Republic
Belarus	Latvia	Slovenia
Bosnia and Herzegovina	Lithuania	Tajikistan
Bulgaria	Former Yugoslav Republic	Turkey
Croatia	of Macedonia	Turkmenistan
Czech Republic	Moldova	Ukraine
Estonia	Poland	Uzbekistan
Georgia	Romania	

All of these countries are members of IBRD, IFC, and MIGA. As for the other institutions:

- Belarus, Bulgaria, Estonia, Lithuania, Romania, Serbia and Montenegro, and Turkmenistan are not members of IDA.
- Kyrgyz Republic, Moldova, Poland, the Russian Federation, Serbia and Montenegro, and Tajikistan are not members of ICSID.

The World Bank in Europe and Central Asia

Notwithstanding broad-based growth, Europe and Central Asia remain highly diverse, in terms of both per capita income and global integration. Per capita income ranges from US$10,070 in Slovenia to US$170 in Tajikistan. The prevalence of poverty ranges from less than 5 percent to more than 50 percent of the population—although it is now generally declining as a result of the region's continuing growth. Although many countries, especially those in Central Europe and the Baltics, are firmly headed toward European and global integration and graduation from Bank borrowing, others still struggle with long-simmering tensions and the constraints of geography. Europe and Central Asia's diversity is reflected in the broad and evolving nature of the Bank's assistance program. See box 4.6 for regional key facts.

The regional efforts of the World Bank focus on:

- Building a stable climate for investment through systemic reforms, which include maintaining macroeconomic stability, legal reform, and improved corporate governance; sectoral reforms such as utility regulation and pricing, and better-functioning labor and financial markets; and selective investments in industrial restructuring and infrastructure

- Improving public sector governance through reforms to encourage transparency, participation, improved public service, decentralization, anticorruption capabilities, and overall accountability of government

- Empowering poor people where traditions and institutions of voice and accountability are still nascent

- Fighting communicable diseases, including HIV/AIDS and tuberculosis

- Protecting the environment through reforestation, phase-out of ozone-depleting substances, improved practices, and major environmental clean-up programs

- Improving countries' international competitiveness through more-effective use of knowledge and technology in the public and private sectors

- Enhancing financial institutions by assessing and improving standards and codes and by establishing a legal and institutional framework for dealing with money laundering and terrorist financing.

See figures 4.8 and 4.9 for thematic and sectoral breakdowns of lending. The region's portal Web site is at <http://www.worldbank.org/eca>.

IFC in Europe and Central Asia

IFC divides its Europe and Central Asia work into two regional departments: (a) Central and Eastern Europe and (b) Southern Europe and Central Asia. IFC's assistance strategy is shaped by the dual nature of the region. At one end of the spectrum, some countries are preparing to join the European Union, which will reinforce their transition to market and solidify their integration with Western private capital. Other countries, such as Armenia, Belarus, Georgia, Russia, and Ukraine continue to struggle in their transition. The business environment remains difficult, flows of foreign direct investment are still low, and capital flight continues to drain economic resources. Nonetheless, the potential business opportunities in these countries are enormous.

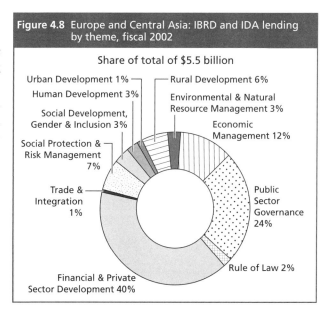

Figure 4.8 Europe and Central Asia: IBRD and IDA lending by theme, fiscal 2002

Share of total of $5.5 billion

- Urban Development 1%
- Human Development 3%
- Social Development, Gender & Inclusion 3%
- Social Protection & Risk Management 7%
- Trade & Integration 1%
- Financial & Private Sector Development 40%
- Rural Development 6%
- Environmental & Natural Resource Management 3%
- Economic Management 12%
- Public Sector Governance 24%
- Rule of Law 2%

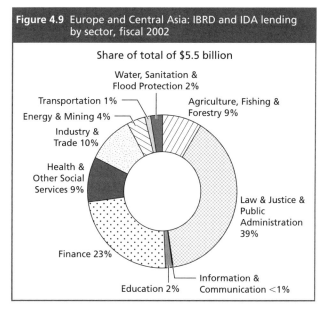

Figure 4.9 Europe and Central Asia: IBRD and IDA lending by sector, fiscal 2002

Share of total of $5.5 billion

- Water, Sanitation & Flood Protection 2%
- Transportation 1%
- Energy & Mining 4%
- Industry & Trade 10%
- Health & Other Social Services 9%
- Finance 23%
- Education 2%
- Agriculture, Fishing & Forestry 9%
- Law & Justice & Public Administration 39%
- Information & Communication <1%

IFC's strategy is tailored to fit the considerable challenges the region presents. In Central Europe, although private capital is becoming more accessible, there are significant differences within countries and among segments of the economy in the ability to attract investment. IFC works on sectors and regions that private financing has not yet reached, emphasizing its catalytic role with potential investors.

Central Asian countries have yet to develop the free market institutions to allow small business growth and attract foreign direct investment. The difficult business environment, the absence of experienced managers, the intraregional rivalries, and the distance from major export markets all combine to discourage private sector–led growth. Small and medium-size enterprises dominate the private sector. Here, IFC activities center on building intermediaries to help channel funds to the small and medium-size enterprises.

IFC has also developed partnerships with other governments to establish direct technical assistance to local companies and local governments, as well as to provide other types of financing and business development assistance. The Europe department's Web site is at <http://www.ifc.org/europe>.

MIGA in Europe and Central Asia
Guarantees in the energy, agribusiness, manufacturing, and finance sectors, as well as strong capacity building assistance, highlight MIGA's current efforts in Europe and Central Asia.

Regional Initiatives
Regional initiatives include the following:

- The *CIS 7 Initiative* is an international initiative to reduce poverty and promote growth and debt sustainability in low-income countries that were formerly part of the Soviet Union: Armenia, Azerbaijan, Georgia, Kyrgyz Republic, Moldova, Uzbekistan, and Tajikistan. Partners include the countries' governments and multilateral and bilateral donors. The Web site is at <http://www.worldbank.org/cis7>.
- The *Global Environment Facility Strategic Partnership on the Black Sea–Danube Basin* works to reduce water pollution in the Black Sea–Danube Basin. The partnership requires the cooperation of all stakeholders, including country governments, the Black Sea and Danube Commissions, NGOs, the private sector, and multilateral and bilateral financiers. The Web site is at <http://www.worldbank.org/blacksea-danube>.
- The *Private Enterprise Partnership* is the technical assistance arm of IFC in the former Soviet Union. It works with donors, investors, local businesses, and governments to attract private direct investment, to stimulate the growth of small and medium enterprises, and to improve the business climate. The Web site is at <http://www1.ifc.org/pep>.
- The *Social Development Initiative for South East Europe* aims to provide the governments of South East Europe, the donor community involved in the region, and the World Bank with the capacity to carry out social

analyses, promote institution building, and launch pilot projects to address inter-ethnic tensions and social cohesion issues in southeast Europe. The Web site is at <http://www.worldbank.org/sdisee>.

- *Southeast Europe Enterprise Development* is a multidonor initiative managed by IFC to strengthen small and medium enterprises in Albania, Bosnia and Herzegovina, FYR Macedonia, and Serbia and Montenegro. The Web site is at <http://www.ifc.org/test/seed>.

Key Publications

The following publications deal with regional issues:

- *Decentralizing Education in Transition Societies: Case Studies from Central and Eastern Europe*
- *Financial Transition in Europe and Central Asia: Challenges of the New Decade*
- *Labor, Employment, and Social Policies in the EU Enlargement Process: Changing Perspectives and Policy Options*
- *Making Transition Work for Everyone: Poverty and Inequality in Europe and Central Asia*
- *Prospects for Improving Nutrition in Eastern Europe and Central Asia*
- *The Road to Stability and Prosperity in South Eastern Europe: A Regional Strategy Paper*
- *Trade Performance and Policy in the New Independent States*
- *Transition—The First Ten Years: Analysis and Lessons for Eastern Europe and the Former Soviet Union*
- *World Development Report 1996: From Plan to Market*

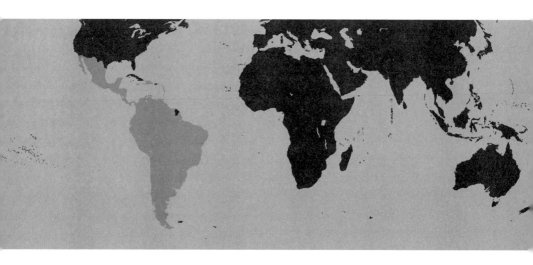

Latin America and the Caribbean

This World Bank region includes the following countries that are eligible for borrowing:

Antigua and Barbuda	El Salvador	Peru
Argentina	Grenada	St. Kitts and Nevis
Belize	Guatemala	St. Lucia
Bolivia	Guyana	St. Vincent and the
Brazil	Haiti	Grenadines
Chile	Honduras	Suriname
Colombia	Jamaica	Trinidad and Tobago
Costa Rica	Mexico	Uruguay
Dominica	Nicaragua	República Bolivariana
Dominican Republic	Panama	de Venezuela
Ecuador	Paraguay	

All of these countries are members of IBRD. As for the other institutions:

- Jamaica, Suriname, Trinidad and Tobago, and the República Bolivariana de Venezuela are not members of IDA.
- The Bahamas and Barbados are included in IFC's Latin America and the Caribbean region. St. Vincent and the Grenadines and Suriname are not members of IFC.
- Antigua and Barbuda, Mexico, and Suriname are not members of MIGA.
- Antigua and Barbuda, Belize, Brazil, Dominica, the Dominican Republic, Guatemala, Haiti, Mexico, and Suriname are not members of ICSID.

The World Bank in Latin America and the Caribbean

Latin America and the Caribbean is a region of staggering diversity, with people who speak Spanish, Portuguese, English, French, and some 400 indigenous languages. Its topography and ecosystems range from tropical islands to high sierras and altiplanos, rainforests, deserts, and sprawling plains. It is the most-urbanized region in the developing world, with three-quarters of its people living in and around cities, but natural resources and agriculture are important to many of its economies, which include some of the developing world's largest, such as Brazil and Mexico, and some of the smallest. Despite immense resources and dynamic societies, deep inequalities of wealth persist in most countries. Almost one-third— 168 million—of the region's people live in poverty (defined as living on less than US$2 a day); of these, 77 million are extremely poor (living on less than US$1 a day). See box 4.7 for regional key facts.

> **Box 4.7**
>
> **Key Facts for IBRD Countries in Latin America and the Caribbean, 2002**
>
> Total population: 0.5 billion
>
> Population growth: 1.5 percent
>
> Life expectancy at birth: 70 years
>
> Infant mortality per 1,000 births: 29
>
> Female youth illiteracy: 6 percent
>
> 2001 gross national income per capita: $3,560
>
> Number of persons living with HIV/AIDS: 1.9 million

The World Bank's assistance follows a strategy of six priorities:

- Education, emphasizing quality and bridging the digital divide in the Americas
- Financial sector support, which includes managing volatility and channeling resources for investment and economic development
- Distribution and social protection aspects of economywide policies, which include addressing the social impact of adjustment, the distribution and quality of public spending, safety nets, and self-protection and market insurance instruments, as well as strengthening links between economic growth and poverty reduction
- Institutional reform and governance, which cover improving public sector, judicial, legal, and regulatory systems; improving delivery of services to the poor; empowering civil society; increasing transparency and accountability; supporting decentralization; and promoting results-oriented public sector management
- Empowerment and inclusion of marginalized groups, including indigenous peoples, Latin Americans of African ancestry, women, and the rural and urban poor, through community-driven development programs and support for sustainable natural resource management

- Environmental sustainability, emphasizing pollution control (and the urban services and pollution control initiatives needed to achieve it), as well as measures to combat irreversible environmental degradation.

See figures 4.10 and 4.11 for thematic and sectoral breakdowns of lending. The region's portal Web site is at <http://www.worldbank.org/lac>.

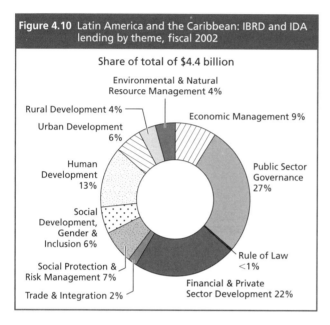

Figure 4.10 Latin America and the Caribbean: IBRD and IDA lending by theme, fiscal 2002

Share of total of $4.4 billion

Environmental & Natural Resource Management 4%
Rural Development 4%
Urban Development 6%
Economic Management 9%
Human Development 13%
Public Sector Governance 27%
Social Development, Gender & Inclusion 6%
Social Protection & Risk Management 7%
Trade & Integration 2%
Financial & Private Sector Development 22%
Rule of Law <1%

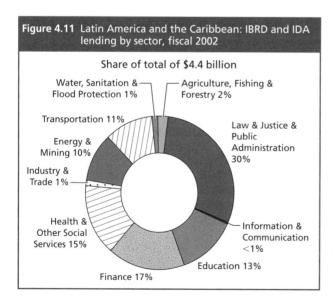

Figure 4.11 Latin America and the Caribbean: IBRD and IDA lending by sector, fiscal 2002

Share of total of $4.4 billion

Water, Sanitation & Flood Protection 1%
Agriculture, Fishing & Forestry 2%
Transportation 11%
Energy & Mining 10%
Law & Justice & Public Administration 30%
Industry & Trade 1%
Health & Other Social Services 15%
Information & Communication <1%
Education 13%
Finance 17%

IFC in Latin America and the Caribbean

Stronger growth through higher investment and savings as well as a better distribution of the benefits of that growth are critical to the region's development. IFC carries out carefully selected transactions in sectors and companies that demonstrate both a sustainable impact and especially strong financial prospects. The intention is to catalyze broader development.

IFC will also work to improve the investment climate. In countries where the private sector enjoys better prospects, IFC intends to form a partnership with companies taking the lead in sustainability and governance practices. On a sectoral level, IFC emphasizes building physical infrastructure, deepening financial systems, reaching smaller firms through financial intermediaries, targeting frontier countries and sectors, and supporting private participation in the social sector businesses. The Latin America and the Caribbean department's Web site is at <http://www.ifc.org/lac>.

MIGA in Latin America and the Caribbean

MIGA supports projects in the Latin America and Caribbean region through its guarantee program. MIGA also undertakes technical assistance activities in the region, focusing on investment promotion in countries that have not been recipients of substantial foreign direct investment in the past.

Regional Initiatives

The following initiatives are in place in Latin America and the Caribbean:

- The *Clean Air Initiative for Latin American Cities* focuses on reversing the deterioration of urban air quality caused by rapid urbanization, increased vehicular transport, and industrial production. It is a partnership of city governments, private sector companies, international development agencies and foundations, NGOs, and academic institutions, with a technical secretariat at the World Bank. The Web site is at <http://www.worldbank.org/cleanair>.
- The *Multi-Country HIV/AIDS Prevention and Control Lending Program for the Caribbean* provides loans or credits to help individual countries finance their national HIV/AIDS prevention and control projects. The Web site is at <http://www.worldbank.org/lachealth>.

Key Publications

Publications about Latin America and the Caribbean include the following:

- *Accounting for Poverty in Infrastructure Reform: Learning from Latin America's Experience*
- *Colombia: The Economic Foundation of Peace*
- *Closing the Gap in Education and Technology*
- *From Natural Resources to the Knowledge Economy: Trade and Job Quality*
- *Gender-Related Dimensions of Alcoholism*
- *The Health of Women in Latin America and the Caribbean*
- *Labor Market Reform and Job Creation: The Unfinished Agenda in Latin American and Caribbean Countries*
- *Mexico: A Comprehensive Development Agenda for the New Era*
- *Poverty and Policy in Latin America and the Caribbean*
- *Poverty Reduction and Human Development in the Caribbean: A Cross-Country Study*
- *Securing Our Future in a Global Economy*
- *Sustainable Amazon: Limitations and Opportunities for Rural Development*
- *Turmoil in Latin America*

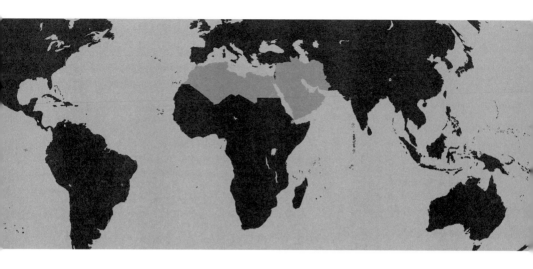

Middle East and North Africa

This World Bank region includes the following countries that are eligible for borrowing:

Algeria	Iraq	Syrian Arab Republic
Djibouti	Jordan	Tunisia
Arab Republic of Egypt	Lebanon	Republic of Yemen
Islamic Republic of Iran	Morocco	

All of these countries are members of IBRD. There are also World Bank activities in the West Bank and Gaza. As for the other institutions:

- Afghanistan, Bahrain, Kuwait, Oman, Pakistan, Saudi Arabia, and the United Arab Emirates, are also included in IFC's Middle East and North Africa region, which also covers the West Bank and Gaza. Djibouti is included in IFC's Africa region.
- Djibouti, the Islamic Republic of Iran, and Iraq are not members of MIGA.
- Djibouti, the Islamic Republic of Iran, Iraq, Lebanon, the Syrian Arab Republic, and the Republic of Yemen are not members of ICSID.

The World Bank in the Middle East and North Africa

The Middle East and North Africa is a region of 20 countries with a population of 300 million people. It includes both the oil-rich economies of the Persian Gulf and countries that have scant resources relative to their populations, such as Egypt, Morocco, and the Republic of Yemen. The region's economic fortunes over much of the past quarter century have been heavily influenced by two factors: the price of oil and a legacy of economic policies and structures that had emphasized a leading role for the state. See box 4.8 for regional key facts.

Beginning in the 1980s, many of the region's economies implemented far-reaching economic reforms to restore macroeconomic balances and promote private sector–led development. But the region continues to face important economic and social challenges. Unemployment rates average close to 20 percent, and the public sector's share of the region's economy is the highest in the world. Basic infrastructure and services vital for private sector growth remain inadequate, and integration with the global economy lags behind that of other developing economies. Although measured poverty rates are lower than in any other developing region, nearly 30 percent of the population lives on less than US$2 a day. Impediments to private sector expansion include cumbersome regulatory regimes, poorly functioning legal and judicial systems, still substantially unmodernized and state-dominated banking sectors, and relatively underdeveloped capital markets.

The World Bank's objectives in the region are to strengthen the momentum for building a climate for investment, job creation, and sustainable growth; and to empower the poor to become assets in the development process. The Bank encourages inflows of private investment into the region by actively using World Bank guarantees, which help reduce investors' perceptions of risk and help lower borrowers' costs. The Bank's focus includes public sector efficiency and governance, education, gender, and sustainable water resource management (see figures 4.12 and 4.13 for

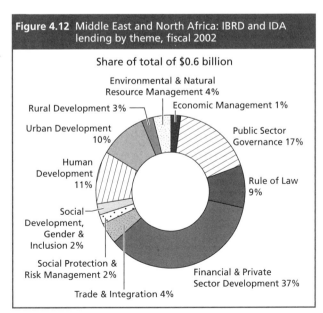

Figure 4.12 Middle East and North Africa: IBRD and IDA lending by theme, fiscal 2002

Share of total of $0.6 billion

Environmental & Natural Resource Management 4%
Economic Management 1%
Rural Development 3%
Public Sector Governance 17%
Urban Development 10%
Human Development 11%
Rule of Law 9%
Social Development, Gender & Inclusion 2%
Social Protection & Risk Management 2%
Trade & Integration 4%
Financial & Private Sector Development 37%

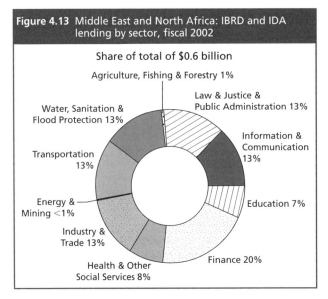

Figure 4.13 Middle East and North Africa: IBRD and IDA lending by sector, fiscal 2002

Share of total of $0.6 billion

Agriculture, Fishing & Forestry 1%
Law & Justice & Public Administration 13%
Water, Sanitation & Flood Protection 13%
Information & Communication 13%
Transportation 13%
Energy & Mining <1%
Education 7%
Industry & Trade 13%
Finance 20%
Health & Other Social Services 8%

a thematic and sectoral breakdown of lending). The region's portal Web site is at <http://www.worldbank.org/mena>.

IFC in the Middle East and North Africa

IFC strategy targets investments where development potential is greatest. Because many economies in the Middle East and North Africa region are dominated by small or medium enterprises, supporting them is critical to development. As a result, IFC investments in financial markets are ultimately structured to support smaller businesses. IFC continued to work this year with sponsors to develop projects in power, water, transport, and telecommunications. The department's Web site is at <http://www.ifc.org/mena>.

MIGA in the Middle East and North Africa

MIGA offers guarantee services in the region and provides support to regional investors making investments outside the region. It undertakes technical assistance initiatives and participates in a broader World Bank Group outreach effort, which is aimed at promoting use of a wider array of the World Bank Group's tools for developing the private sector.

Regional Initiatives

Regional initiatives in the Middle East and North Africa include the following:

- The *Governance in the Middle East and North Africa* initiative seeks to improve governance institutions and processes, the weaknesses of which may lead to disappointing economic performance. It is a partnership of individual researchers from the region, local think tanks, and donor agencies. The Web site is at <http://www1.worldbank.org/mena/governance>.
- The *Mediterranean Development Forum* is a biennial conference, with participation by the World Bank Institute, the Bank's Middle East and North Africa region, the UNDP, and think tanks. Its goals include

empowering civil society to participate in shaping public policy, making a contribution to the policy debate in key areas of regional interest, improving the extent and quality of research on economic and social policy issues, and improving networks to promote development in the region. The Web site is at <http://www.worldbank.org/wbi/mdf>.

- The *North African Enterprise Development* facility is a multidonor initiative managed by IFC; it works to support small and medium enterprises in the countries of North Africa.

Key Publications

The following publications deal with the Middle East and North Africa:

- *Cultural Heritage and Development: A Framework for Action in the Middle East and North Africa*
- *Globalization and Firm Competitiveness in the Middle East and North Africa Region*
- *Partners for Development: New Roles for Government and Private Sector in the Middle East and North Africa*
- *Reducing Vulnerability and Increasing Opportunity: Social Protection in the Middle East and North Africa*
- *Reproductive Health in the Middle East and North Africa: Well-Being for All*
- *Trade Policy Developments in the Middle East and North Africa*

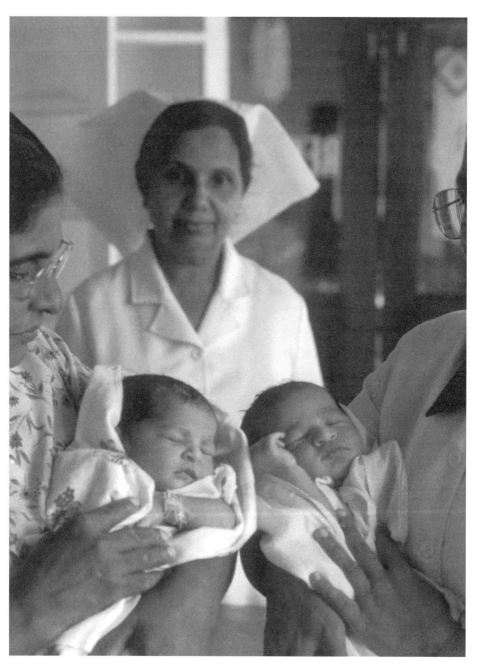

Infant health care is a focus in Sri Lanka

CHAPTER 5

Topics in Development

This chapter provides an overview of major aspects of development in which the World Bank Group is involved. These topics are listed alphabetically, with attention to key initiatives, Web sites, and publications. Because of space constraints, the listing of topics is not intended to be comprehensive.

The broad themes in Bank Group work are covered under "Strategies" in chapter 3 ("How the World Bank Group Operates"). As discussed in that section, the Bank Group has an increasing emphasis on social aspects of development. A key organizing principle in its work is the Millennium Development Goals as defined by the United Nations.

Another key aspect of Bank Group activities, as explained in chapter 2 ("How the World Bank Group Is Organized"), is the matrix that provides for thematic networks in addition to units focusing on world regions. These networks are made up of development sectors; many sectors correspond to the topics covered in this chapter. For a full list of sectors, see appendix F.

Topics covered in this chapter are as follows:

- Agriculture and rural development
- Aid effectiveness
- Combating corruption
- Conflict prevention and reconstruction
- Debt relief
- Economic research and data
- Education
- Empowerment and participation
- Energy and mining
- Environment
- Financial sector
- Gender
- Globalization
- Governance and the public sector
- Health, nutrition, and population
- Indigenous peoples
- Information and communication technologies
- Infrastructure
- Labor and social protection
- Law and justice
- Poverty
- Private sector development
- Social development
- Sustainable development
- Trade
- Transportation
- Urban development
- Water

Agriculture and Rural Development

Some 75 percent of the world's poor live in rural areas. The Bank Group pursues its work in agriculture and rural development through the units and programs discussed below.

Agribusiness Department (IFC)

The technical, financial, and market expertise necessary for evaluation of agribusiness projects is centralized in the Agribusiness Department of the International Finance Corporation (IFC). Its staff comprises investment officers, engineers, and economists, all with specialized international experience. IFC supports projects involving primary agricultural production, aquaculture, and fishing, as well as marketing (for example, silos, cold and controlled atmosphere storage facilities, and wholesale markets), food processing, and distribution. As a rule, preference is given to investment projects that have the largest demonstrated benefits to the overall efficiency and competitiveness of the supply chain and that have the highest overall contribution to economic development. For more on IFC and agribusiness, see <http://www.ifc.org/agribusiness>.

Agriculture and Rural Development Department (World Bank)

Agriculture and Rural Development is one of the departments that make up the Environmentally and Socially Sustainable Development (ESSD) network. The department prepares and implements the World Bank's corporate strategy on rural development, monitors the Bank's portfolio of agriculture and rural projects, and promotes knowledge-sharing among agriculture and rural development practitioners, inside and outside the Bank. The unit is responsible for formulating the Bank's rural development strategy and for providing analytical and advisory services to the Bank's regions. The department's focus includes gender and rural development, rural producer organizations, sustainable agriculture, water resources management, and forests and forestry. The unit's Web site is at <http://www.worldbank.org/rural>. Additional information appears on the Sustainable Development Web site at <http://www.worldbank.org/sustainabledevelopment>.

Other Resources

Other resources include the following:

- The *ESSD Advisory Service,* whose focus includes agriculture and rural development, has a Web site at <http://www.worldbank.org/essdadvisoryservice>. The e-mail address is <eadvisor@worldbank.org>.
- The *Consultative Group on International Agricultural Research (CGIAR)* is a Bank Group affiliate whose secretariat is at Bank headquarters. Its Web site is at <http://www.cgiar.org>.
- *World Bank Research* provides information on agriculture and rural development. Click "Topics" at <http://econ.worldbank.org>, and select "Agriculture" or "Rural Development."

Key Publications

Several publications address agriculture and rural development:

- *Agricultural Trade Liberalization in a New Trade Round: Perspectives of Developing Countries and Transition Economies*
- *Agriculture and the Environment: Perspectives on Sustainable Rural Development*
- *Agriculture, Trade, and the WTO: Creating a Trading Environment for Development*
- *Global Environmental Benefits of Land Degradation Control on Agricultural Land*
- *Intellectual Property Rights in Agriculture: The World Bank's Role in Assisting Borrower and Member Countries*
- *Land Policy for Growth and Poverty Reduction*
- *Rural Development, Natural Resources, and the Environment: Lessons of Experience in Eastern Europe and Central Asia*

Aid Effectiveness

The effectiveness of aid in reducing poverty, improving lives, and stimulating economic growth has always been a central concern of the Bank Group. The broad acceptance of the Millennium Development Goals by the international community makes measuring progress an even more critical focus.

Operations Evaluation

The effectiveness of specific programs and projects for the people and countries participating in them is assessed by the World Bank's independent Operations Evaluation Department (OED) and by equivalent units for IFC and the Multilateral Investment Guarantee Agency (MIGA). These units provide advice to the Board of Executive Directors, which is based on evaluations at the project, country, and sector levels. Each year, evidence from those evaluations is marshaled to produce a summary report on the Bank's development effectiveness. As covered in chapter 3 ("How the World Bank Group Operates"), evaluation is an integral part of the life cycle of every project, as is monitoring for quality while a project is under way. The Web site for OED is at <http://www.worldbank.org/oed>.

Quality Assurance Group

As part of the Bank's goal of fighting poverty with passion and professionalism while decreasing defects in workmanship, the Quality Assurance Group (QAG) conducts real-time assessments of the Bank's performance in its major product lines. QAG systematically assesses quality in each of the Bank's three areas of operation: new lending, portfolio management, and advisory services. These examinations cover economic, financial, technical, environmental, social, and institutional aspects of operations and assess the degree to which operations align with the Country Assessment Strategy and client participation.

Other Resources

The following Web sites are also useful:

- The *OED Help Desk* has a Web site at <http://www.worldbank.org/oed>. Its e-mail address is <eline@worldbank.org>.
- *World Bank Research* has a program on aid effectiveness research. See <http://www.worldbank.org/research/aid>.

Key Publications

Publications on aid effectiveness include the following:

- *Aid and Reform in Africa*
- *Annual Review of Development Effectiveness*
- *Assessing Aid: What Works, What Doesn't, and Why*
- *A Case for Aid: Building a Consensus for Development Assistance*

Combating Corruption

The Bank Group has identified corruption as the single greatest obstacle to economic and social development. Through bribery, fraud, and the misappropriation of economic privileges, corruption taxes poor people by diverting resources from those who need them most. Since the mid-1990s, the Bank Group has launched more than 600 anticorruption programs and governance initiatives in nearly 100 client countries. The goals include increasing political accountability, strengthening civil society participation, creating a competitive private sector, establishing institutional restraints on power, and improving public sector management.

Initiatives include encouraging disclosure of assets by public officials, training judges, teaching investigative reporting to journalists, and supporting strong corporate governance through educational outreach by IFC. Nearly one-quarter of new projects now include public expenditure and financial reform components. Even more important, the Bank Group's commitment to eliminating corruption has helped inspire a truly global response to the problem. The Bank Group is working to integrate governance and anticorruption measures into all of its planning and operational work.

The Bank Group is also committed to ensuring that the projects it finances are free from corruption. The Bank Group has stringent procurement and anticorruption guidelines and an anonymous hotline for corruption complaints. It maintains a list of firms and individuals ineligible to be awarded Bank Group–financed contracts. The Web portal for anticorruption issues is at <http://www1.worldbank.org/publicsector/anticorrupt>.

Other Resources

A fraud and corruption hotline is available at <http://www.worldbank.org/investigations>.

Key Publications

The following publications address corruption issues:

- *Combating Corruption: A Comparative Review of Selected Legal Aspects of State Practice and International Initiatives*
- *Corrupt Cities: A Practical Guide to Cure and Prevention*
- *Curbing Corruption: Toward a Model for Building National Integrity*

Conflict Prevention and Reconstruction

The Bank Group works in countries afflicted by conflict, supporting international efforts to assist war-torn populations in resuming peaceful development. It also seeks to understand the causes of conflict and to determine ways that conflict can be prevented. The Conflict Prevention and Reconstruction Unit of the World Bank takes the lead in this area; it conducts research and provides analysis on conflict and development to support country units working in conflict-affected countries. The Bank also supports the disarmament, demobilization, and reintegration of excombatants, as well as mine survey and awareness initiatives. It has established the Post-Conflict Fund, which provides financing for physical and social reconstruction initiatives in postwar societies. The portal Web site is at <http://www.worldbank.org/conflict>.

Other Resources

World Bank Research has a program on the economics of civil war, crime, and violence. For more information, see <http://econ.worldbank.org/programs/3102>.

Key Publications

Publications dealing with conflict prevention and reconstruction include the following:

- *Post-Conflict Reconstruction: The Role of the World Bank*
- *Social Cohesion and Conflict Prevention in Asia: Managing Diversity through Development*
- *Violent Conflict and the Transformation of Social Capital: Lessons from Cambodia, Rwanda, Guatemala, and Somalia*
- *The World Bank's Experience with Post-Conflict Reconstruction*

Debt Relief

In 1996, the World Bank and the International Monetary Fund (IMF) launched the Heavily Indebted Poor Countries (HIPC) initiative—the first comprehensive approach to reducing the external debt of the world's poorest, most-indebted countries. Through the HIPC initiative, external debt servicing will be cut by approximately US$50 billion. When completed, the initiative will cut by more than two-thirds the outstanding debt of more than 30 countries, lowering their indebtedness to levels well below the average for developing countries overall. (The World Bank itself will reduce its debt claims by nearly US$11 billion, and the IMF by approximately US$4 billion.) As part of the initiative, these countries are reorienting their budgetary priorities toward key social and human development sectors. For more on the HIPC initiative, see its Web site at <http://www.worldbank.org/hipc>. The e-mail address for comments on HIPC is <hipc@worldbank.org>.

Other Resources

Many Bank Group countries also participate in the Paris Club, an informal group of official creditors—industrial countries in most cases—that seek solutions for debtor nations facing payment difficulties. Paris Club creditors agree to reschedule debts due to them. Although the Paris Club has no legal basis, its members agree to a set of rules and principles designed to reach a coordinated agreement on debt rescheduling quickly and efficiently. This voluntary gathering dates back to 1956, when Argentina agreed to meet its public creditors in Paris. Since then, the Paris Club and related ad hoc groups have reached more than 300 agreements covering 76 debtor countries. The Paris Club has extensive contact with the IMF and the Bank Group because the Paris Club normally requires countries to have an active IMF-supported program in order to qualify for a rescheduling agreement. The Web site is at <http://www.clubdeparis.org>.

The Paris Club is paralleled by the London Club, an informal organization of commercial creditors. Officials of the Bank Group have been invited to meetings of the London Club in an effort to coordinate debt relief and repayment efforts with economic policy advice.

Economic Research and Data

The Bank Group conducts extensive economic research and, with the help of country governments and other partners, assembles a wide range of economic data.

Data and Statistics

The Bank Group is a leading publisher of economic data and statistics on all aspects of development, both in print and online (see box 5.1 for Web links). Some information is free, and some is available with a subscription. Major titles appear under "Key Publications" at the end of this section. The Development Data Group is the lead unit in this area; the portal Web site is at <http://www.worldbank.org/data>. The Development Data Group can also be reached by phone at (1-202) 473-7824 or (1-800) 590-1906, fax at (1-202) 522-1498, or e-mail at <data@worldbank.org>.

Commercial sales of print and electronic publications are handled by the Office of the Publisher. This unit can be contacted through its Web site at <http://publications.worldbank.org/ecommerce>, or by phone at

---

Box 5.1

Web Links for Data and Statistics

World Bank Group Data and Statistics: http://www.worldbank.org/data

Online databases: http://www.worldbank.org/data/onlinedatabases/onlinedatabases.html

Financial sector databases: http://www.worldbank.org/finance

Financial sector statistics: http://www.worldbank.org/finance

Living standards measurement study: http://www.worldbank.org/lsms

PovertyNet—data on poverty: http://www.worldbank.org/poverty/data

Research on domestic financial systems databases: http://www.econ.worldbank.org/topic.php?topic=9

Statistical capacity building: http://www.worldbank.org/data/tas

World Bank–Global Environment Facility projects database: http://www.worldbank.org/gef

World Bank research datasets: http://econ.worldbank.org/resource.php?type=18

(1-703) 661-1580 or (1-800) 645-7247, fax at (1-703) 661-1501, or e-mail at <books@worldbank.org>.

Research

The Bank Group's economic analysis provides a big picture of economic trends, the cumulative effectiveness of development programs, specific indicators of development, and other factors that affect economic progress. The portal Web site for World Bank Research is at <http://econ.worldbank.org>; the e-mail for general queries is <research@worldbank.org>. Specific research programs or topical Web pages are as follows:

- Economic growth research covers macroeconomic stabilization, monetary policy, fiscal policy, fiscal decentralization, industrial restructuring, currency crises, financial intermediation, and public expenditure. The Web site is at <http://www.worldbank.org/research/growth>.
- International capital flows are covered at <http://www.worldbank.org/research/projects/capflows.htm>.
- International economics research covers trade and capital flows, such as studies of foreign direct investment, commodity risk management, and microeconomic evidence on trade and growth. The Web site is at <http://econ.worldbank.org/topic.php?topic=16>.
- The Living Standards Measurement Study can be found at <http://www.worldbank.org/lsms>
- Macroeconomic and growth research is discussed at <http://econ.worldbank.org/topic.php?topic=18>.
- Transition economies research focuses on current and former socialist economies and covers topics such as the household impact of market-oriented reforms in China, the consequences of large-scale privatization in Mongolia, and the targeting of social assistance in Eastern Europe and the former Soviet Union. The Web site is at <http://econ.worldbank.org/topic.php?topic=24>.

IFC maintains its own research database at <http://www.ifc.org/research>. The Web site for IFC's Economics Department is at <http://www.ifc.org/economics>.

Other Resources

Various resources are available on the Internet:

- The *Policy Research Bulletin* is published quarterly to inform the development community of the Bank's policy and research. The Web site is at <http://www.worldbank.org/html/dec/Publications/Bulletins/home.html>.
- *Policy Research Working Papers* are available at <http://www.worldbank.org/research/workingpapers>.

- The *PREM Advisory Service* focuses on economic policy, gender, governance and public sector reform, and poverty, among other issues. It publishes *PREM Notes*, which summarizes good practice and key policy findings on those topics. Its Web site is at <http://www1.worldbank.org/prem>. The e-mail address is <premadvisory@worldbank.org>.
- The *World Bank Institute* has a macroeconomics and policy assessment skills program. Its Web site is at <http://www.worldbank.org/wbi/macroeconomics>.
- The *World Bank Research Observer* and the *World Bank Economic Review* are journals published by the World Bank. Current issues are available by subscription. The archive database is searchable on the home page, but back issues must be ordered from Oxford Journals. The Web site is at <http://www.worldbank.org/research/journals>.

Key Publications

The following are research publications:

- *Annual Bank Conference on Development Economics*
- *Economic Analysis of Investment Operations: Analytical Tools and Practical Applications*
- *Frontiers of Development Economics*
- *Global Development Finance*
- *Global Economic Prospects*
- *Little Data Book*
- *Little Green Data Book*
- *A Strategy for Development*
- *World Bank Atlas*
- *World Bank Economists' Forum*
- *World Bank Research Program: Abstracts of Current Studies*
- *World Development Indicators*
- *World Development Report*

Education

The Bank Group recognizes that universal, high-quality education reduces poverty and inequality and sustains economic growth. Such education is also fundamental for the construction of democratic societies and globally competitive economies. It improves people's skills, which, in turn, improve their income. Consequently, achieving universal primary education for all is one of the eight Millennium Development Goals. The portal Web site for education issues is at <http://www1.worldbank.org/education>.

The Bank Group pursues its work in education and training through the following units and programs.

Education Department (World Bank)

The Education Department is part of the Human Development network. Major education initiatives include the following. Education activities, programs, and projects at the region or country level can also be accessed through the Web sites of the Bank's regions.

- *Education for the Knowledge Economy (EKE)* is an analytical program for understanding how education and training systems need to change in order to meet the challenges of the knowledge economy. EKE offers practical and sustainable policy options for developing countries.
- *Education for All (EFA)* is a commitment by the international community to achieve education for "every citizen in every society." The EFA partnership believes that education is key to sustainable development, to peace and stability within and among countries, and to people's full participation in the societies and economies of the 21st century. EFA is committed to ensuring that by 2015 all children—especially girls and disadvantaged children—are enrolled in and able to complete a primary education.
- *Early Child Development (ECD)* is a knowledge source that assists policymakers, program managers, and practitioners in their efforts to promote the healthy growth and development of young children. Visit ECD at <http://www.worldbank.org/children>.

World Bank Institute

World Bank Institute (WBI) is the main training and educational unit of the Bank Group. WBI conducts training sessions and policy consultations, and creates and supports knowledge networks related to international economic and social development. The focus includes distance learning and other emerging technologies for education and training. WBI serves member countries, Bank Group staff members and clients, and other people working in the areas of poverty reduction and sustainable development. WBI has programs focusing on AIDS, poverty reduction, community empowerment and social inclusion, education, the financial sector, governance and the public sector, health and population, infrastructure, knowledge for development, macroeconomics and policy assessment, the private sector and corporate governance, social protection, sustainable development, trade and investment, and urban and city management. Visit <http://www.worldbank.org/wbi>.

WBI's Education Program focuses on education reform and on two initiatives for teacher training and classroom learning: World Links for Development (WorLD) and the Development Education Program.

IFC Investments in Private Education

IFC supports private education in four key ways:

- Through *postsecondary vocational and technical training in developing countries.* Given a growing demand for access to technical and vocational training in developing countries, IFC works with private investors and provides advice or technical assistance to help establish sustainable education business projects.

- Through *universities.* IFC supports the development of private universities in developing countries and campus-based initiatives such as distance learning and e-learning.
- Through *information technology in education.* IFC also assists projects that introduce or support new information and communications technologies for education in developing economies. Projects include the development of curriculum-related content for distribution by CD-ROM or through the Internet.
- Through *schools.* IFC considers proposals from private sector sponsors that target large-scale school projects in developing countries. Projects may include construction or education services that are cross-sectoral and that can demonstrate improved access to quality educational opportunities.

Other Resources

The following resources are also useful:

- *Education Advisory Service.* The Web site is at <http://www.worldbank.org/education>. The service may be contacted by e-mail at <eservice@worldbank.org>.
- *World Bank Research.* To visit the Web site, click "Topics" at <http://econ.worldbank.org>, and select "Education."

Key Publications

Publications addressing education issues include the following:

- *Decentralizing Education in Transition Societies: Case Studies from Central and Eastern Europe*
- *Education and HIV/AIDS: A Window of Hope*
- *From Early Child Development to Human Development: Investing in Our Children's Future*
- *Higher Education in Developing Countries: Peril and Promise*

Empowerment and Participation

Broader participation in the development process and empowerment of poor people to play a role are key objectives of the Bank Group, as reflected in the Comprehensive Development Framework, the Poverty Reduction Strategy Papers, and the Bank Group's partnerships with civil society. The Bank Group also has conducted conversations with 60,000 poor people in 60 countries and has worked to incorporate poor people's perspectives in its day-to-day work.

The philosophy resulting from the Bank Group's experience is that poverty is about more than inadequate income or even low human development. It is also about lack of voice and lack of representation. It is about vulnerability to abuse and corruption. It is about lack of fundamental freedom of action, choice, and opportunity. The Bank Group believes that people who live in poverty should not be treated as a liability, but rather as a creative asset—a group that will contribute more than anyone else to the eradication of poverty. An empowering approach to poverty reduction puts poor people at the center of development and creates the conditions that enable poor men and women to gain increased control over their lives through access to information, inclusion and participation, accountability, and local organizational capacity.

Initiatives related to empowerment and participation include the following:

- The *Participation and Civic Engagement Group* promotes methods and approaches that encourage stakeholders, especially the poor, to influence and share control over development priorities, policymaking, resource allocations, and access to public goods and services. The Web site is at <http://www.worldbank.org/participation>.
- The *Development Marketplace* is a program that promotes innovative development ideas through early-stage seed funding. The program links social entrepreneurs with poverty-fighting ideas to partners with resources to help implement their vision. Since 1998, the Development Marketplace has awarded over US$14 million to more than 200 groundbreaking projects through global competitions and country innovation days.
- IFC supports public participation and community empowerment through extensive *civil society outreach efforts* with local nongovernmental organizations, community leaders, media representatives, and all other stakeholders. IFC believes that early engagement with the community, along with maximum public disclosure, is the best business model in the developing world and emerging markets.

Other Resources

Further resources include the following:

- The *World Bank Institute* has a community empowerment and social inclusion learning program. The Web site is at <http://www.worldbank.org/wbi/communityempowerment>.
- *World Bank Research* has a program on inequity around the world. See <http://www.worldbank.org/research/inequality>.
- The *Community Empowerment and Social Inclusion Learning Program* of WBI works to help create the conditions that enable the poor and the excluded to shape their own development. The Web site is at <http://www.worldbank.org/wbi/communityempowerment>.

Key Publications

These publications also address empowerment and participation issues:

- *Doing Better Business through Effective Public Consultation and Disclosure*
- *Investing in People: Sustaining Communities through Good Business Practice*
- *Voices of the Poor*

Energy and Mining

The Bank Group sees energy as a fundamental driver of economic development and believes that countries must develop their own energy programs in careful and sustainable ways. The Bank Group's objectives in the energy sector include helping the poor directly, improving macroeconomic and fiscal balances, promoting good governance and private sector development, and protecting the environment. The Bank Group's energy program includes some joint units of the World Bank and IFC. The portal Web site for energy issues is at <http://www.worldbank.org/energy>.

The Bank Group also works to help countries ensure environmentally and socially responsible development of their mineral resources. The Bank Group pursues its work in this area through the Oil, Gas, Mining, and Chemicals Department, a joint unit of the World Bank and IFC. The department aims to improve coordination between work on public sector policy and activities in private sector investment. Its Web page is at <http://www.worldbank.org/mining> or <http://www.ifc.org/mining>.

Other Resources

These resources are also useful:

- The *Energy Help Desk* can be contacted at <energyhelpdesk@worldbank.org>.
- The *Extractive Industries Review* is a recent evaluation of Bank Group involvement in this sector. The Web site is at <http://www.eireview.org>.
- The *IFC Power Department* has information on its Web site at <http://www.ifc.org/power>. In 2003, this department is merging with IFC's Infrastructure Department.
- The *Mining Help Desk* can be contacted at <mining@worldbank.org>.
- The *Renewable Energy and Energy Efficiency Fund (REEF)* is an investment fund that targets projects in environmentally friendly technologies run by the private sector in developing countries. REEF is an initiative of IFC and partners. The Web site is at <http://www.ifc.org/reef>.
- The *Oil, Gas, Mining, and Chemicals Department* is a joint department of the World Bank and IFC. Its Web site is at <http://www.worldbank.org/mining> or <http://www.ifc.org/mining>.

Key Publications

These publications also cover energy and mining issues:

- *Energy from Biomass: A Review of Combustion and Gasification Technologies*
- *Energy Services for the World's Poor*

- *Fuel for Thought: An Environmental Strategy for the Energy Sector*
- *Large Mines and the Community: Socioeconomic and Environmental Effects in Latin America, Canada, and Spain*
- *Natural Gas: Private Sector Participation and Market Development*
- *Rural Energy and Development: Improving Energy Supplies for Two Billion People*

Environment

The Bank Group supports environmental protection and improvement in the developing world. It conducts research and advocacy on environmental issues and ensures environmental protection in its own work through careful adherence to safeguards it has established.

Environment Department (World Bank)

Part of the Environmentally and Socially Sustainable Development (ESSD) network, this department is responsible for the World Bank's environment strategy for developing countries. This strategy has these priorities: improving quality-of-life aspects (people's health, livelihood, and vulnerability) that are affected by environmental conditions; improving the quality of growth by supporting policy, regulatory, and institutional frameworks for sustainable environmental management and by promoting sustainable private development; and protecting the quality of the regional and global commons such as climate change, forests, water resources, and biodiversity. The unit also maintains the Bank Group's portal Web site for environmental issues at <http://www.worldbank.org/environment>.

Environment and Social Development Department (IFC)

IFC places heavy emphasis on environmental due diligence in its project investments. Each investment must be examined for its attention to environmental issues by IFC's team of environment finance professionals. The Environment and Social Development Department works to meld the concerns of the environment with the needs of the private sector. The key Web site is at <http://www.ifc.org/enviro/index.html>.

Some of the links under "Other Resources" below describe IFC's policies and outlook on private investment and the environment in more detail.

Other Resources

For information on the Bank Group's environmental safeguards, see chapter 3 ("How the World Bank Group Operates"), as well as the following resources:

- The *IFC Environment and Social Review* monitors projects. The Web site is at <http://www.ifc.org/EnvSoc>.
- The *IFC Environmental, Health, and Safety Guidelines* are available at <http://www.ifc.org/env_guidelines>.

- MIGA's *Environment and Disclosure Policies* are available at <http://www.miga.org/policies>.
- The *Operational Manual* includes safeguard policies. The Web site is at <http://www.worldbank.org/opmanual>.
- The *ESSD Advisory Service* Web site is at <http://lnweb18.worldbank.org/ESSD/essdext.nsf/5ByDocName/ESSDAdvisoryService>. The e-mail address is <eadvisor@worldbank.org>.
- The *Global Environment Facility* is a Bank Group affiliate whose secretariat is at Bank headquarters. For more information, see "Programmatic Partnerships" under "Partnerships" in chapter 3 or see <http://www.worldbank.org/gef>.
- The *Prototype Carbon Fund* seeks to mitigate climate change through reductions in greenhouse gases, and encourages public–private partnerships. An initiative of the Bank Group, donor governments, and private industry, the fund has a help desk at <http://prototypecarbonfund.org/router.cfm?Page=HelpDesk>. The Web site is at <http://prototypecarbonfund.org>.
- *World Bank Research* has environmental resources. Click "Topics" at <http://econ.worldbank.org>, and select "Environment." For the program on Infrastructure and the Environment, see <http://econ.worldbank.org/programs/2328>.

Key Publications

Many publications address environmental issues:

- *Environment Matters*
- *The Environmental and Social Challenges of Private Sector Projects: IFC's Experience*
- *Environmental Economics for Sustainable Growth: A Handbook for Practitioners*
- *The Environmental Implications of Privatization: Lessons for Developing Countries*
- *Greening Industry: New Roles for Communities, Markets, and Governments*
- *The Legal and Regulatory Framework for Environmental Impact Assessments: A Study of Selected Countries in Sub-Saharan Africa*
- *Little Green Data Book*
- *Making Sustainable Commitments: An Environment Strategy for the World Bank*
- *Protecting the Global Environment: Initiatives by Japanese Business*
- *Trade, Global Policy, and the Environment*
- *World Development Report 1992: Development and the Environment*
- *World Development Report 2002: Sustainable Development in a Dynamic World*

Financial Sector

A healthy, trustworthy financial system is fundamental to economic development. The Bank Group helps countries strengthen their financial systems, grow their economies, restructure and modernize institutions, and respond to the savings and financing needs of all people. Major initiatives are as follows.

Financial Sector Network (World Bank Group)

The Bank Group formed the Financial Sector network to provide clients with policy research, advice, and technical support on financing issues. The network focuses on banking systems, capital markets, credit systems, financing of housing, insurance and contractual savings, payments systems, rural financing, microfinance, and small and medium enterprises. The network's Web site is at <http://www1.worldbank.org/finance>.

Global Financial Markets Group (IFC)

IFC considers support for financial markets to be a cornerstone of its investment policies and a critical tool for private sector development. IFC's Global Financial Markets Group is the lead unit in financial sector matters. Visit <http://www.ifc.org/financialmarkets>. IFC also seeks innovative ways to finance microentrepreneurs, who play a key role in the private sector of many economies in the developing world; the lead unit in this area is the Small and Medium Enterprise Department; for more information see "Small and Medium Enterprise Department (World Bank Group)" below under "Private Sector Development."

Other Resources

More resources are listed below:

- The *Consultative Group to Assist the Poorest (CGAP)* is a Bank Group affiliate focusing on microfinance, whose secretariat is at Bank headquarters. For more information, see "Programmatic Partnerships" under "Partnerships" in chapter 3, or see <http://www.cgap.org>.
- The *Financial Sector Advisory Service* answers questions about the financial sector. The e-mail address is <askfinancialsector@worldbank.org>.
- The *Interest Bearing Notes Newsletter* is a periodical publication of the World Bank's Financial Sector. The Web site is at <http://econ.worldbank.org/programs/finance/topic/IBN>.
- The *World Bank Institute* has a banking and finance program. The Web site is at <http://www.worldbank.org/wbi/banking>.
- *World Bank Research* has financial sector resources. Click "Topics" at <http://econ.worldbank.org>, and select "Domestic Finance." There are also specific programs on credit reporting systems, finance research, and policies and institutions that promote savings.

Key Publications

Publications about financial matters include these:

- *Analyzing Banking Risk: A Framework for Assessing Corporate Governance and Financial Risk Management*
- *Building Trust: Developing the Russian Financial Sector*
- *Developing Government Bond Markets: A Handbook*
- *Development and Regulation of Non-Bank Financial Institutions*
- *Financial Risk Management*
- *Finance for Growth: Policy Choices in a Volatile World*
- *Financial Sector Policy for Developing Countries: A Reader*
- *Financial Sector Reform: A Review of World Bank Assistance*
- *Microfinance Handbook*
- *The Microfinance Revolution*

Gender

The Bank Group seeks to reduce gender disparities and to enhance women's participation in economic development through its programs and projects. It summarizes knowledge and experience, provides gender statistics, and promotes discussion on issues of gender and development. The Gender and Development group within the Poverty Reduction and Economic Management (PREM) network is the lead unit in this area. The key gender-related goal is the Millennium Development Goal to eliminate gender-related disparities at all levels of education by 2015. See the Web site at <http://www.worldbank.org/gender>.

Other Resources

Other resources include the PREM Advisory Service, which deals with many issues, including gender. The service publishes *PREM Notes,* which summarizes good practice and key policy findings. The Web site is at <http://www1.worldbank.org/prem>. The e-mail address is <premadvisory@worldbank.org>.

Key Publications

Many publications address gender issues:

- *The Economics of Gender in Mexico: Work, Family, State, and Market*
- *Ecuador Gender Review: Issues and Recommendations*
- *Engendering Development: Through Gender Equality in Rights, Resources, and Voice*
- *Gender and Law: Eastern Africa Speaks*
- *Mainstreaming Gender and Development in the World Bank: Progress and Recommendations*
- *Toward Gender Equality: The Role of Public Policy*

Globalization

Globalization of trade, finance, investment, and industry has created both progress and problems. The Bank Group believes that globalization has helped reduce poverty in a large number of developing countries, but that it must be harnessed better to help the world's poorest, most-marginalized countries improve the lives of their citizens. The Bank Group's portal Web site on globalization issues is at <http://www1.worldbank.org/economicpolicy/globalization>.

Other Resources

World Bank Research provides more information about globalization. Click "Topics" at <http://econ.worldbank.org>, and select "Globalization."

Key Publications

Globalization is also the subject of these publications:

- *Facets of Globalization: International and Local Dimensions of Development*
- *Globalization and Firm Competitiveness in the Middle East and North Africa Region*
- *Globalization and National Financial Systems*
- *Globalization, Growth, and Poverty: Building an Inclusive World Economy*
- *The International Finance Corporation and Its Role in Globalization*
- *Local Dynamics in an Era of Globalization: 21st Century Catalysts for Development*
- *World Development Report 1999/2000: Entering the 21st Century*

Governance and the Public Sector

A fundamental role of the Bank Group is to help the governments of client countries function better. Although this goal is simple to define, it is both complex and difficult to accomplish. The Bank Group has a number of initiatives dealing with governance issues, including public sector group activities, public services research, and World Bank Institute (WBI) governance and knowledge-sharing programs.

The Public Sector Group is the lead unit in this area and is responsible for the World Bank's governance and public sector strategy. The unit focuses on building efficient and accountable public sector institutions, rather than simply providing policy advice. Its work reflects the understanding that good policies are not enough—that the Bank Group cannot afford to look the other way when a country has deeply dysfunctional public institutions that limit accountability, set perverse rules of the game, and cannot sustain development. The unit also maintains the portal Web site on governance and public sector reform at <http://www1.worldbank.org/publicsector>.

Other Resources

Various resources are available on the Internet:

- The *PREM Advisory Service* deals with many issues, including governance and public sector reform. The service publishes *PREM Notes*, which summarizes good practice and key policy findings. The Web site is at <http://www1.worldbank. org/prem>. The e-mail address is <premadvisory@worldbank.org>.
- The *World Bank Institute* has programs on governance and on public finance, decentralization, and poverty reduction. The Web site is at <http://www. worldbank.org/wbi>.
- *World Bank Research* provides information about governance and the public sector. Click "Topics" at <http://econ.worldbank.org>, and select "Governance" or "Public Sector Management." There are also programs on public sector downsizing and public services research. See also the section on "Infrastructure" below.

Key Publications

Publications in this area include the following:

- *Generating Public Sector Resources to Finance Sustainable Development: Revenue and Incentive Effects*

- *Government at Risk: Contingent Liabilities and Fiscal Risk*
- *How Businesses See Government: Responses from Private Sector Surveys in 69 Countries*
- *Information Systems for Government Fiscal Management*
- *International Accounting Standards: A Practical Guide*
- *Managing the Regulatory Process: Design, Concepts, Issues, and the Latin America and Caribbean Story*
- *Public Expenditure Management Handbook*
- *Reforming Public Institutions and Strengthening Governance: A World Bank Strategy*
- *Taxation of Financial Intermediation*
- *World Development Report 1997: The State in a Changing World*
- *World Development Report 2002: Building Institutions for Markets*

Health, Nutrition, and Population

World Bank and Health

The World Bank commits an average of US$1 billion in new lending each year for health, nutrition, and population projects in the developing world. It seeks to focus its assistance where the impact will be greatest—directly on people. The lead unit is Health, Nutrition, and Population (often abbreviated HNP), a sector unit of the Human Development network. HNP organizes its work into the broad categories of nutrition, population and reproductive health, poverty and health, health systems development, and public health. Public health is further broken down into categories including HIV/AIDS, other communicable diseases, tobacco, and mental health.

HNP's portal Web site is at <http://www1.worldbank.org/hnp>. Specific resources include the following:

- The *Health and Population Advisory Service* handles queries to HNP in all areas except nutrition, which has its own advisory service (see below). The service may be contacted by phone at (1-202) 473-2256, fax at (1-202) 522-3234, or e-mail at <healthpop@worldbank.org>.
- The *Health and Poverty* Web site focuses on how developments in health affect efforts to reduce poverty in developing countries. Visit <http://www.worldbank.org/poverty/health>.
- The *Health Systems Development* Web site examines all aspects of health systems, including market demand, financing, human resources, and service delivery. Go to <http://www1.worldbank.org/hnp/hsd>.
- The *HIV/AIDS* Web site emphasizes that HIV/AIDS is not only a health problem, it is also a development problem that threatens human welfare, socioeconomic advances, productivity, social cohesion, and even national security. The World Bank is a key source

of funding to combat HIV/AIDS. For information and resources, visit <http://www1.worldbank.org/hiv_aids>. The Bank also participates in partnerships such as UNAIDS and the Multi-Country HIV/AIDS Program in Africa.

- The *Integrated Management of Childhood Illness* Web site is at <http://www.worldbank.org/imci>.

- The *Malaria* Web site addresses this devastating illness. The World Bank provides some US$200 million in direct financing for malaria control activities in more than 25 countries. Most deaths are in Africa, but malaria is also on the rise in many countries where it had once been sharply reduced or even eradicated. See <http://www1.worldbank.org/Malaria>. The Bank also participates in Roll Back Malaria, a global partnership with malaria-affected countries, multilateral and bilateral development agencies, nongovernmental organizations (NGOs), the research community, the private sector, and the media.

- The *Mental Health* Web site provides information about this issue. It is at <http://www.worldbank.org/mentalhealth>.

- The *Nutrition Advisory Service* provides information about nutrition. Nearly half of child mortality in low-income countries can be linked to malnutrition. The World Bank's approach to nutrition targets poor people, especially young children and their mothers, with emphasis on community- and school-based nutrition programs, food fortification programs, and food policy reforms. To date, the World Bank has committed nearly US$2 billion to support nutrition programs. The Web site is at <http://www.worldbank.org/nutrition>. Contact Nutrition Advisory Service by phone at (1-202) 473-2255, fax at (1-202) 522-3234, or e-mail at <nutrition@worldbank.org>.

- The *Population and Reproductive Health* Web site describes Bank activities and resources in this area. Problems such as early and unwanted childbearing, sexually transmitted infections, and pregnancy-related illness and death account for much of the burden of disease in developing countries, especially among the poor who often lack access to minimal health care. The Web site is at <http://www.worldbank.org/population>.

- The *Tobacco* Web site provides information on tobacco policies and control measures. The World Bank has a formal policy of not lending for tobacco production or processing, directly or indirectly, and of encouraging tobacco control in developing countries. Visit <http://www1.worldbank.org/tobacco>.

- The *Tuberculosis* Web site details the World Bank's effort to fight tuberculosis. The World Bank combats tuberculosis by providing policy dialogue and advice, by lending to countries to strengthen health systems and control the disease, by doing analytic work, and by becoming involved in global partnerships. The Web site is at <http://www.worldbank.org/tuberculosis>.

- The *Vaccines and Immunization* Web site provides a summary of key facts, priority interventions, indicators, useful implementation lessons, and links to additional resources and information. The Bank Group supports immunization worldwide because it saves lives and is one of the most cost-effective, equitable health interventions available. Vaccine-preventable diseases disproportionately affect the poorest people in developing countries. Visit <http://www.worldbank.org/vaccines>.

IFC and Health

As public health care facilities face mounting capacity strains in the developing world, the private health care market is stepping in to absorb some of the demand. IFC seeks to boost the private health care infrastructure in developing countries and emerging markets through investments in ancillary services; pharmaceutical devices; education and training; and e-health, insurance, and medical facilities. For more information, see <http://www.ifc.org/che/health.htm>.

With respect to AIDS, IFC has prepared "Good Practice Note: HIV/AIDS in the Workplace" as part of the IFC Against AIDS program. Its purpose is to help clients and others in the private sector to understand and manage the risks associated with the impact of HIV/AIDS on their work forces and the communities in which they operate. See <http://www.ifc.org/enviro/Publications/HIV/hiv.htm>.

Other Resources

Other health resources include the following:

- The *Global Partnership for Eliminating Riverblindness* is discussed under "Regional Initiatives" under "Africa (Sub-Saharan) in chapter 4 or at <http://www.worldbank.org/gper>.
- *HNP Advisory Services,* at <http://www1.worldbank.org/hnp/advisory>, includes the Health and Population Advisory Service at <healthpop@worldbank.org>, and the Nutrition Advisory Service at <nutrition@worldbank.org>.
- The *Multi-Country HIV-AIDS Program* is described under "Regional Initiatives" under "Africa (Sub-Saharan)" in chapter 4 or at <http://www.worldbank.org/afr/aids/map.htm>.
- *UNAIDS* has information on its Web site at <http://www.unaids.org>.
- The *World Bank Institute* has a program on health and population and a leadership program on AIDS. See <http://www.worldbank.org/wbi>.
- *World Bank Research* offers information about health and population. Click "Topics" at <http://econ.worldbank.org>, and select "Health and Population."

Key Publications

Numerous publications address health and population issues:

- *Confronting AIDS*
- *Curbing the Epidemic*
- *Education and HIV/AIDS: A Window of Hope*
- *Environmental Health: Bridging the Gaps*
- *HIV/AIDS in the Caribbean: Issues and Options*
- *HIV/AIDS in the Workplace*
- *Innovations in Health Service Delivery: The Corporatization of Public Hospitals*
- *Intensifying Action against HIV/AIDS in Africa*
- *An International Assessment of Health Care Financing: Lessons for Developing Countries*
- *Investing in Health: Development Effectiveness in the Health, Nutrition, and Population Sectors*
- *Population and the World Bank: Adapting to Change (revised edition)*
- *Principles of Health Economics for Developing Countries*
- *Private Participation in Health Services*
- *Prospects for Improving Nutrition in Eastern Europe and Central Asia*
- *The TB and HIV/AIDS Epidemics in the Russian Federation*
- *Social Reinsurance: A New Approach to Sustainable Community Health Financing*
- *World Development Report 1993: Investing in Health*

Indigenous Peoples

The Bank Group seeks to promote indigenous peoples' development and to ensure that the development process fosters respect for the dignity, human rights, and uniqueness of indigenous peoples. The lead unit in this area is the Bank's Indigenous Peoples Group, which is responsible for policies and guidelines to promote greater understanding within the Bank Group and its member countries of the value of cultural diversity in poverty reduction, sustainable development, and effective nation building. The Bank Group also works in this area through partnerships with indigenous organizations, other donor agencies, and governments. The portal Web site is at <http://www.worldbank.org/indigenous>.

IFC and Indigenous Peoples

IFC takes seriously the potentially disruptive nature of some private investments that involve the resettling of indigenous peoples. IFC has established policies regarding resettlement, as set forth in its *Resettlement Handbook*. See <http://www.ifc.org/enviro/Publications/ResettlementHandbook/resettlementhandbook.htm>.

Other Resources

The *Indigenous Knowledge Program* documents the local or traditional knowledge in developing countries and applies this knowledge to the issues of development. This program is a partnership of the World Bank's Africa region with various U.N. agencies, bilateral development agencies, and NGOs. The Web site is at <http://www.worldbank.org/afr/ik>.

Key Publications

The following publications deal with involuntary resettlement of indigenous peoples:

- *The Economics of Involuntary Resettlement: Questions and Challenges*
- *Handbook for Preparing a Resettlement Action Plan*

Information and Communication Technologies

Information and communication technologies have the potential to speed development and improve a variety of social services. The World Bank has two programs that focus on the best ways to support technology implementation: the Global Information and Communication Technologies (GICT) Department and the Development Communication Division (DEVCOMM).

Global Information and Communication Technologies Department

A joint department of the World Bank and IFC, GICT helps develop and promote access to information and communication technologies in developing countries. GICT provides governments, private companies, and community organizations with the capital and expertise needed to develop and exploit such technologies to reduce poverty and foster development. The Web site is at <http://info.worldbank.org/ict>.

Development Communication Division (World Bank)

DEVCOMM provides clients with strategic communication advice and tools to develop and implement successful projects and pro-poor reform efforts. DEVCOMM works to create mechanisms to broaden public access to information on reforms; strengthen clients' abilities to listen to their constituencies and negotiate with stakeholders, empower grassroots organizations; and support communications activities that are grounded in public opinion research. The Web site is at <http://www.worldbank.org/developmentcommunications>.

Other Resources

Other resources include the following:

- The Development Gateway is an interactive portal for information- and knowledge-sharing on sustainable development and poverty reduction, offering, for example, a comprehensive database of development projects, an international procurement marketplace, and knowledge-sharing on key development topics. It is operated by the Development Gateway Foundation, a not-for-profit organization based in Washington, D.C. The foundation is governed by a board of directors, representing major donors and partners from international organizations, the public and private sector, and civil society. The Development Gateway connects to Country Gateways, a network of 44 locally owned and managed public–private partnerships with the mission of facilitating country-level innovative and effective use of the Internet and other information and communication technologies. The Web site is <http://www.developmentgateway.org>.

- The Global Development Learning Network (GDLN) is a fully interactive, multichannel network that harnesses video, Internet, and satellite communications to build local capacity, learning, and knowledge in the developing world and to develop a global community dedicated to fighting poverty. Its vision is for decisionmakers to have affordable and regular access to a global network of peers, experts, and practitioners with whom they may share ideas and experiences regarding the fight against poverty. The network operates through the facilities of GDLN partners around the world. The Web site is <http://www.gdln.org>.

Key Publications

Publications addressing information and communication technologies include these:

- *The Diffusion of Information Technology: Experience of Industrial Countries and Lessons for Developing Countries*
- *Information and Communication Technologies: A World Bank Group Strategy*
- *Information Infrastructure: The World Bank Group's Experience*
- *Information Systems for Government Fiscal Management*
- *Telecommunications and Information Services for the Poor: Toward a Strategy for Universal Access*
- *Telecommunications Legislation in Transitional and Developing Economies*

Infrastructure

Infrastructure development remains a fundamental focus of the Bank Group, and poor people are acutely aware that infrastructure could significantly improve the quality of their lives. The Bank Group's infrastructure work is organized by departments, which focus on energy; information and communication technologies; mining; oil, gas, and chemicals; transport; urban development; and water supply and sanitation. Some of these departments are joint World Bank–IFC units. The portal Web site for infrastructure issues is at <http://www.worldbank.org/infrastructure>.

IFC and Infrastructure

Infrastructure is a significant part of IFC's work of assisting the development of private sector business opportunities in emerging economies. IFC's Infrastructure Department offers expertise in helping private sector sponsors finance infrastructure projects in member countries. The Department is subdivided into the practice areas of power (formerly a separate department), transport, and utilities. Some sectors (including oil and gas, as well as telecommunications) are handled by other departments. IFC has also established a Municipal Finance Department to make direct investments in municipalities and other subsovereign governments that bear much of the responsibility for infrastructure. For a link to IFC's infrastructure activities, see <http://www.ifc.org/infrastructure>.

Other Resources

The following resources are also useful:

- The *Infrastructure Help Desk* has a Web site at <http://www.worldbank.org/infrastructure/helpdesk.htm>. The e-mail address is <InfraHelp@worldbank.org>.
- The *Public–Private Infrastructure Advisory Facility* (PPIAF) is a multidonor technical assistance facility aimed at helping developing countries improve the quality of their infrastructure through private sector involvement. Launched in July 1999, PPIAF was developed as a joint initiative of the governments of Japan and the United Kingdom, working closely with the World Bank. The Web site is at <http://www.ppiaf.org>.
- The *World Bank Institute* has infrastructure programs. The Web site is at <http://www.worldbank.org/wbi/themes.html>.
- *World Bank Research* provides information about infrastructure. Click "Topics" at <http://econ.worldbank.org>, and select "Infrastructure." There are also programs on infrastructure and environment and on public services research.

Key Publications

Much has been published about infrastructure:

- *Accounting for Poverty in Infrastructure Reform: Learning from Latin America's Experience*
- *Attracting Foreign Direct Investment into Infrastructure: Why Is It So Difficult?*
- *Concessions for Infrastructure: A Guide to Their Design and Award*
- *Contracting for Public Services: Output-Based Aid and Its Applications*
- *Dealing with Public Risk in Private Infrastructure*
- *Infrastructure for Poor People*
- *Private Infrastructure in East Asia: Lessons Learned in the Aftermath of the Crisis*
- *World Development Report 1994: Infrastructure for Development*
- *World Development Report 2004: Making Services Work for Poor People*

Labor and Social Protection

The Bank Group studies and generally supports measures that seek to improve or protect human capital, such as labor market interventions, publicly mandated unemployment, old-age insurance, and targeted income support. Those interventions help individuals, households, and communities better manage the income risks that leave people vulnerable; they also contribute to the solidarity, social cohesion, and social stability of a country. Topics on which the Bank Group provides information and resources through its Human Development network include child labor, children and youth, disability, labor markets, pensions, safety nets, and social funds. The Web portal for social protection issues is at <http://www1.worldbank.org/sp>. The World Bank also maintains a Social Protection Advisory Service: fax queries to (1-202) 614-0471 or e-mail <socialprotection@worldbank.org>.

IFC and Social Protection

IFC will not support projects that use forced or harmful child labor. Projects should comply with the national laws of the host countries, including those that protect core labor standards, and with related treaties ratified by the host countries.

Forced labor consists of all work or service, not voluntarily performed, which is exacted from an individual under threat of force or penalty. Harmful child labor consists of the employment of children that is (a) economically exploitative; (b) likely to be hazardous to, or to interfere with, the child's education; or (c) likely to be harmful to the child's health or physical, mental, spiritual, moral, or social development.

Other Resources

Other resources include the following:

- The *Social Protection Help Desk* can provide useful information. Contact the help desk by e-mail at <socialprotection@worldbank.org>.
- The *World Bank Institute* has a social protection learning program. The Web site is at <http://www.worldbank.org/wbi/socialprotection>.
- *World Bank Research* provides labor information. Click "Topics" at <http://econ.worldbank.org>, and select "Labor and Employment."

Key Publications

Some publications about social protection follow:

- *Addressing Harmful Child Labor in the Workplace and Supply Chain*
- *Balancing Protection and Opportunity: A Strategy for Social Protection in Transition Economies*
- *Crafting Labor Policy: Techniques and Lessons from Latin America*
- *Labor, Employment, and Social Policies in the EU Enlargement Process: Changing Perspectives and Policy Options*
- *Labor Market Reform and Job Creation: The Unfinished Agenda in Latin American and Caribbean Countries*
- *New Ideas about Old Age Security: Toward Sustainable Pension Systems in the 21st Century*
- *Pension Reform in Europe: Process and Progress*
- *Safety Net Programs and Poverty Reduction: Lessons from Cross-Country Experience*
- *Social Funds: Assessing Effectiveness*
- *World Development Report 1995: Workers in an Integrating World*

Law and Justice

The Bank Group is an active supporter of legal and judicial reforms that address the needs of the poor and the most vulnerable in developing countries. The lead unit in this area, the Legal and Judicial Reform Practice Group of the World Bank, works with governments, judges, lawyers, scholars, civil society representatives, and other organizations to build better legal institutions and judicial systems. Other areas of activity for the Bank include environmental and international law, and the role of legal systems in private sector development, finance, and infrastructure. The Bank's Law and Justice Web site at <http://www4.worldbank.org/legal>, provides information on all of these activities, with links to several legal databases.

Other Resources

Other legal resources are as follows:

- The *Bank Documents* Web resource has links to key Bank Group documents, including articles of agreement, manuals and guidelines, and other materials. See <http://www4.worldbank.org/lawlibrary>.
- The *Legal Help Desk* has a Web site at <http://www4.worldbank.org/legal/help.html>. The e-mail address is <legalhelpdesk@worldbank.org>.

Key Publications

These publications deal with law and justice:

- *A Framework for the Design and Implementation of Competition Law and Policy*
- *Comprehensive Legal and Judicial Development: Towards an Agenda for a Just and Equitable Society in the 21st Century*
- *Intellectual Property Rights and Economic Development*
- *Legislating for Sustainable Fisheries: A Guide to Implementing the 1993 FAO Compliance Agreement and 1995 U.N. Fish Stocks Agreement*
- *Reforming Business-Related Laws to Promote Private Sector Development: The World Bank Experience in Africa*
- *Resolution of Financial Distress: An International Perspective on the Design of Bankruptcy Laws*

Poverty

Fighting poverty is central to the Bank Group's mission. The Bank Group considers a comprehensive understanding of poverty and its possible solutions to be fundamental for everyone involved in development. This understanding involves defining poverty, studying trends over time, setting goals to reduce poverty, and measuring results. The Bank Group's portal Web site on this topic is PovertyNet, which provides resources and support for people working to alleviate poverty. Visit <http://www.worldbank.org/poverty>.

IFC on Poverty

IFC assists in the fight against poverty by focusing many of its investments in sectors that have the most direct effect on living standards. Those include the financial sector, infrastructure, information and communication technologies, small and medium enterprises, health, and education.

Other Resources

Other resources include the following:

- *PREM Advisory Service,* whose focus includes poverty, among other issues, publishes *PREM Notes,* which summarizes good practice and key policy findings. The Web site is at <http://www1.worldbank.org/prem>. The e-mail address is <premadvisory@worldbank.org>.
- The *World Bank Institute* has a program on attacking poverty. The Web site is at <http://www.worldbank.org/wbi/attackingpoverty>.
- *World Bank Research* provides poverty information. Click "Topics" at <http://econ.worldbank.org>, and select "Poverty." There is also a program on poverty research and a Living Standards Measurement Study.

Key Publications

These publications address poverty:

- *African Poverty at the Millennium: Causes, Complexities, and Challenges*
- *Can the Poor Influence Policy? Participatory Poverty Assessments in the Developing World*
- *The City Poverty Assessment: A Primer*
- *Evaluating the Impact of Development Projects on Poverty: A Handbook for Practitioners*
- *IDA's Partnership for Poverty Reduction: An Independent Evaluation of Fiscal Years 1994–2000*
- *Implementing the Millennium Development Goals*
- *Poverty and Policy in Latin America and the Caribbean*
- *Poverty Reduction and the World Bank: Progress in Operationalizing the WDR 2000/2001*
- *Poverty Reduction in the 1990s: An Evaluation of Strategy and Performance*
- *A Sourcebook for Poverty Reduction Strategies*
- *Voices of the Poor*
- *World Development Report 2000/2001: Attacking Poverty*

Private Sector Development

The Bank Group places a major emphasis on the private sector in spurring economic growth and reducing poverty. Working with the private sector is central to the mission of IFC and important to the World Bank and MIGA as well. The focus of Bank Group efforts includes private sector advisory services, corporate governance, corporate social responsibility practice, investment climate, private participation in infrastructure, and privatization transactions. The Private Sector Department takes the lead in this area, along with the Small and Medium Enterprise Department; both are joint World Bank–IFC units. IFC has also established the Global Manufacturing and Services Department, which places special emphasis on the manufacturing sector. Private sector development is also the focus of many partnerships with other organizations. The portal Web sites include <http://www.worldbank.org/privatesector> for private sector development and <http://www.ifc.org/proserv/services/advisory/advisory.html> for IFC advisory services.

Corporate social responsibility (CSR) recently has come into strong focus as a crucial element in fostering sustainable and equitable development worldwide. The Private Sector Advisory Services Department's CSR Practice unit advises developing-country governments about public policy instruments that can be used to encourage CSR in a cost-effective manner. The CSR and Sustainable Competitiveness program of the WBI includes courses and dialogues designed to help participants better understand this issue.

Small and Medium Enterprise Department (World Bank Group)

This joint department of the World Bank and IFC helps develop financing projects for small and medium enterprises (SMEs). Its Web site is at <http://www.ifc.org/sme>.

Programs of the department include the following:

- *Topics in SME Finance* focuses on topics of special relevance to SME finance in developing countries, including credit lines, risk sharing, leasing, credit scoring and credit bureaus, risk capital and equity funds, SME strategy development, financial technologies, and specialized financing (micro and rural, housing, and energy).
- World Bank Group *SME finance activities* provide current information on IFC's SME finance investment portfolio, the joint World Bank–IFC Small and Medium Enterprise Department's Capacity Building Facility and Project Development Facilities, as well as SME projects of the World Bank and MIGA.
- *SME Project Development Facilities* support enterprises in specific countries and regions. These are locally based; see individual listings in the regional sections of chapter 4 ("World Bank Group Countries and Regions"). The Web site for the facilities is at <http://ifcnet.ifc.org/sme/pdf>.

Other Resources

A number of resources are available in this area:

- The *Committee of Donor Agencies for Small Enterprise Development* works to share information and coordinate the efforts of agencies in this field. The secretariat is housed in the World Bank–IFC Small and Medium Enterprise Department. The Web site is at <http://www.sedonors.org>.

- *Doing Business* is a database that provides indicators of the cost of doing business by identifying specific regulations that enhance or constrain business investment, productivity, and growth. Data cover both developing and industrial economies. Doing Business is an initiative of the World Bank–IFC Private Sector Department and external partners. The Web site is at <http://rru.worldbank.org/DoingBusiness>.

- The *Foreign Investment Advisory Service* helps developing-country governments improve the foreign direct investment environment of their countries. The service is a joint World Bank–IFC initiative. The Web site is at <http://www.fias.net>.

- *Investment Marketing Services* is a unit of MIGA. The Web site is at <http://www.miga.org/screens/services/ims/ims.htm>.

- *Private Sector Advisory Services* has a Web site at <http://www.worldbank.org/privatesector/contactus.htm>.

- *Public Policy for the Private Sector* is an online World Bank Group journal covering public policy innovations for private sector–led and market-based solutions for development. Issues can be viewed and downloaded at <http://www1.worldbank.org/viewpoint>.

- The *Public–Private Infrastructure Advisory Facility* is a multidonor technical assistance facility aimed at helping developing countries improve the quality of their infrastructure through private sector involvement. The facility is a joint initiative of the governments of Japan and the United Kingdom, working closely with the World Bank. The Web site is at <http://www.ppiaf.org>.

- *Rapid Response* provides information and policy advice for developing countries. It focuses on the investment climate, private participation in sectors with complex market design and regulatory issues, privatization transactions and policy, and output-based aid—delivering public services through private contracts. Rapid Response includes free resources and fee-based advisory services. The Web site is at <http://rru.worldbank.org>.

- The *World Bank Institute* has programs on the private sector and corporate governance. They can be accessed at <http://www.worldbank.org/wbi/corpgov>. For microfinance and SMEs see <http://www.worldbank.org/ wbi/banking/microfinance>.

- *World Bank Research* provides information about private sector development. Click "Topics" at <http://econ.worldbank.org>, and select "Industry" or "Private Sector Development."

Key Publications

Publications about private sector development include these:

- *Corporate Governance: A Framework for Implementation*
- *Doing Business*
- *The Environmental and Social Challenges of Private Sector Projects: IFC's Experience*
- *Firm Size and the Business Environment: Worldwide Survey Results*
- *Greening Industry: New Roles for Communities, Markets, and Governments*
- *How Businesses See Government: Responses from Private Sector Surveys in 69 Countries*
- *A Market-Oriented Strategy for Small and Medium Scale Enterprises*
- *The Privatization Challenge: A Strategic, Legal, and Institutional Analysis of International Experience*
- *Promoting Environmentally and Socially Responsible Private Sector Investment*
- *Unleashing Russia's Business Potential: Lessons from the Regions for Building Market Institutions*

Social Development

Currently, the Bank is developing its first Bank-wide Social Development Strategy (due out in 2004). The strategy will focus on two related outcomes: (a) enhancement of people's assets and capabilities, and (b) ensuring that there is an enabling environment in which they can maximize their returns from those assets. Furthermore, in cooperation with other donors, the Bank is developing a more systematic approach to poverty and social impact analysis in order to understand the intended and unintended effects of policy reform on the well-being of various social groups.

The Social Development Group, in the Bank Group's ESSD network, collaborates with a wide range of partners to ensure that the social dimensions of development are taken into account in the Bank Group's work. The Social Development Group's work focuses on empowerment, inclusion, and security for poor people. Areas of activity include participation and civic engagement, social analysis, conflict prevention and reconstruction, community-driven development, and social safeguards. The unit's Web site is at <http://www.worldbank.org/socialdevelopment>. Additional information appears on the Sustainable Development Web site, http://lnweb18.worldbank.org/ESSD/essdext.nsf/43ByDocName/SocialDevelopment>.

See also IFC's Environment and Social Development Department, which is discussed above at "Environment and Social Development Department (IFC)" under "Environment." The Web site is at <http://www.ifc.org/ enviro/index.html>.

Other Resources

More information about social development can be obtained from the following:

- The *ESSD Advisory Service* has a Web site at <http://lnweb18.worldbank.org/ESSD/essdext.nsf/5ByDocName/ESSDAdvisoryService>. The e-mail address is <eadvisor@worldbank.org>.
- *World Bank Research* provides information about social development. Click "Topics" at <http://econ.worldbank.org>, and select "Social Development."

Key Publications

These publications deal with social development:

- *The Environmental and Social Challenges of Private Sector Projects: IFC's Experience*
- *New Social Policy Agendas for Europe and Asia: Challenges, Experience, and Lessons*
- *Social Capital: A Multifaceted Perspective*
- *Understanding and Measuring Social Capital: A Multi-Disciplinary Tool for Practitioners*

Sustainable Development

The ESSD Network was formed to advance sustainable development within the Bank Group, by ensuring that actions taken today to promote development and reduce poverty do not result in environmental degradation or social exclusion tomorrow. That means dealing with the comprehensive nature of development in the implementation of projects and programs by the Bank Group and its partners. Specifically, participation, empowerment, strengthened institutions, environmental protection, conservation, and a focus on the rural poor are all foundations for sustained and inclusive economic growth. The network ensures this broader focus in Bank Group activities. Its Web portal for sustainable development issues is at <http://www.worldbank.org/sustainabledevelopment>.

IFC and Sustainability

IFC makes sustainability a key corporate priority and promotes sustainable business practices in the developing world and emerging markets. IFC has also conducted research that has overturned the conventional wisdom on business practices in emerging markets. Hence it found that paying attention to social aspects of an investment tends to improve the profitability of the investment. The Web site for IFC sustainability resources is at <http://www.ifc.org/sustainability>.

Other Resources

Other resources include the following:

- *ESSD Advisory Service* has a Web site at <http://lnweb18.worldbank.org/ESSD/ essdext.nsf/5ByDocName/ESSDAdvisoryService>. The e-mail address is <eadvisor@worldbank.org>.
- The *World Bank Institute* has a sustainable development program. The Web site is at <http://www.worldbank.org/wbi/sustainabledevelopment>.

Key Publications

These publications address sustainable development:

- *Developing Value: The Business Case for Sustainability*
- *Making Sustainable Commitments: An Environment Strategy for the World Bank*
- *World Development Report 2003: Sustainable Development in a Dynamic World*

Trade

The Bank Group's work on trade has two central objectives. At the global level, the Bank Group aims to promote changes in the world trading system to make it more supportive of development, especially of the poorest countries and of poor people across the developing world. That work entails continued collaboration with the World Trade Organization (WTO), other multilateral agencies, and donor countries, including work to maximize the development impact of regional trading agreements. At the country level, the Bank Group aims to promote integration through trade as a core aspect of development strategies. That effort involves providing strategic assistance to client countries to support trade-related reforms, with special efforts to target the low-income countries that are most in need of Bank support. The Bank Group's Web portal on trade issues, maintained by the WBI, is at <http://www1.worldbank.org/wbiep/trade>.

IFC and Trade

IFC supports banking institutions that provide trade enhancement facilities to local companies, as part of IFC's larger goal of seeking innovative ways to boost the private sector in the developing world and emerging markets.

Other Resources

The following can provide more trade information:

- *World Bank Research* provides information about international economics. Click "Topics" at <http://econ.worldbank.org>, and select "International Economics."
- *International Trade* has a Web site at <http://www.worldbank.org/research/trade/index.htm>.

Key Publications

Trade-related publications include the following:

- *Agricultural Trade Liberalization in a New Trade Round: Perspectives of Developing Countries and Transition Economies*
- *Agriculture, Trade, and the WTO: Creating a Trading Environment for Development*
- *Commodity Market Reforms: Lessons of Two Decades*
- *Development, Trade, and the WTO: A Handbook*
- *Regional Integration and Development*
- *Trade Blocs*
- *Trade, Global Policy, and the Environment*
- *Trade Laws and Institutions: Good Practices and the World Trade Organization*
- *Trade Policy Developments in the Middle East and North Africa*
- *Trade, Technology, and International Competitiveness*

Transportation

Transportation is the key infrastructure asset for the movement of goods, people, and resources; it encompasses roads, rail, seaports, airports, and all manner of vehicles and management systems. More commonly referred to as "transport" within the Bank Group, this sector focuses on access, the role of the public and private sectors, and institutional and financial development. Areas of activity include economics and policy, ports and logistics, railways, roads and highways, and rural and urban transport. Special concerns include globalization of trade, congestion and pollution, operating deficits in public transport systems, and expenditure to maintain and modernize transport infrastructure. The Web portal for transport issues is at <http://www.worldbank.org/transport>.

IFC and Transportation

Sound transport infrastructure and services are crucial to private sector development; with increased government liberalization in the transport industry, the private sector has been able to play a significant role in financing projects, as well as providing managerial and technical expertise. IFC's staff dedicated to transportation is grouped into two units within the Infrastructure Department: the Transportation Infrastructure Unit, which focuses on ports, airports, and roads, and the Transportation Services Unit, which covers shipping, airlines, railroads, and trucking. Visit <http://www.ifc.org/transportation>.

Other Resources

The *Transport Help Desk* has a Web site at <http://www.worldbank.org/helpdesk.htm>. The e-mail address is <transport@worldbank.org>.

Key Publications

The following publications concern transport issues:

- *Design and Appraisal of Rural Transport Infrastructure: Ensuring Basic Access for Rural Communities*
- *Forging Subregional Links in Transportation and Logistics in South Asia*
- *Improving Rural Mobility: Options for Developing Motorized and Nonmotorized Transport in Rural Areas*
- *Integration of Transport and Trade Facilitation: Selected Regional Case Studies*
- *Privatization and Regulation of Transport Infrastructure: Guidelines for Policymakers and Regulators*
- *Trade and Transport Facilitation: An Audit Methodology*
- *Trade and Transport Facilitation: A Toolkit for Audit, Analysis, and Remedial Action*

Urban Development

The Bank Group work in urban development focuses on improving the lives of poor people and promoting equity. That effort includes the creation of city development strategies, an agenda for development modeled roughly on country strategies and created by local people with broad participation. Other areas of activity include disaster management, land and real estate, local economic development, municipal finance, urban community upgrades, urban poverty, and waste management. The main Web site for urban issues is at <http://www.worldbank.org/urban>. IFC has also established a Municipal Finance Department, which will make direct investments in infrastructure and other services that are controlled by municipalities and other subsovereign governments.

Other Resources

Other urban development resources include the following:

- *Cities Alliance* is a global alliance of cities and their development partners committed to improve the living conditions of the urban poor. The secretariat is housed at the World Bank. Visit <http://www.citiesalliance.org>.
- The *Urban Help Desk* offers e-mail advice at <urbanhelp@worldbank.org>.
- *World Bank Institute* has a program on urban and city management. Its Web site is at <http://www.worldbank.org/wbi/urban>.
- *World Bank Research* can provide information about urban development. Click "Topics" at <http://econ.worldbank.org>, and select "Urban Development."

Key Publications

These publications deal with urban development:

- *The Challenge of Urban Government: Policies and Practices*
- *The City Poverty Assessment: A Primer*
- *Corrupt Cities: A Practical Guide to Cure and Prevention*
- *Historic Cities and Sacred Sites: Cultural Roots for Urban Futures*
- *Urban Air Quality Management: Coordinating Transport, Environment, and Energy Policies in Developing Countries*

Water

Water is the focus of Bank Group efforts in two broad areas: (a) water resources management, and (b) water supply and sanitation. Specific issues include coastal and marine management, dams and reservoirs, groundwater, irrigation and drainage, river basin and watershed management, water management across national boundaries, water and the environment, and water economics. Water is also the focus of one of the Millennium Development Goals: the objective for 2015 is to reduce by half the proportion of people without sustainable access to safe drinking water. Portal Web sites include water resources management at <http://www.worldbank.org/water>, and water supply and sanitation at <http://www.worldbank.org/watsan>.

IFC and Water Resources

IFC is represented on the World Bank Group's Water and Urban Sector Board and contributes to the development of ideas and policies in this sector. IFC draws on its experience to provide input from an investor perspective. It often works in collaboration with the World Bank. However, IFC's main role is to support investors who undertake private sector water projects. IFC has invested in water projects in a wide range of countries, including Argentina, Panama, the Philippines, and India.

Other Resources

The *Water Help Desk* has a Web site at <http://www.worldbank.org/html/fpd/water/helpdesk.html>. It also offers e-mail advice at <whelpdesk@worldbank.org>.

Key Publications

Publications on the water sector include these:

- *Groundwater in Rural Development: Facing the Challenges of Supply and Resource Sustainability*
- *Groundwater Quality Protection: A Guide for Water Service Companies, Municipal Authorities, and Environment Agencies*
- *Institutional Frameworks in Successful Water Markets: Brazil, Spain, and Colorado, USA*
- *The Political Economy of Water Pricing Reforms*
- *Salinity Management for Sustainable Irrigation: Integrating Science, Environment, and Economics*
- *Water Quality Modeling: A Guide to Effective Practice*

Appendixes

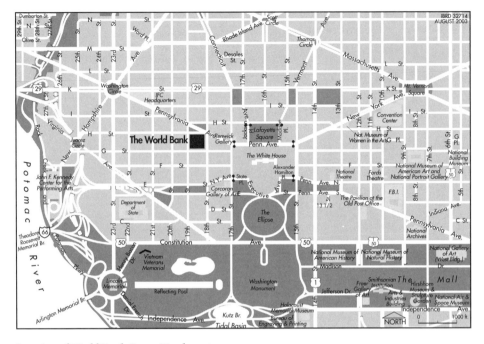

Location of World Bank Group Headquarters

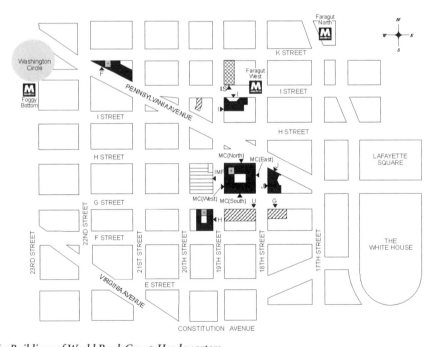

The Buildings of World Bank Group Headquarters

Contacting the World Bank Group

Headquarters and General Inquiries

The offices and Web sites listed below are good sources of general information about the five World Bank Group institutions: the International Bank for Reconstruction and Development (IBRD), the International Development Association (IDA), the International Finance Corporation (IFC), the Multilateral Investment Guarantee Agency (MIGA), and the International Centre for Settlement of Investment Disputes (ICSID).

General contact information

World Bank Group
1818 H Street, NW
Washington, DC 20433, USA
Web: http://www.worldbankgroup.org or http://www.worldbank.org
Tel: (1-202) 473-1000
Fax: (1-202) 477-6391
Weather: (1-202) 458-7669

Staff directory orders

World Bank Publications
Tel: (1-800) 645-7247 or (1-703) 661-1580
Fax: (1-703) 661-1501
Web: http://publications.worldbank.org/ecommerce

IBRD and IDA contact information

Same as for World Bank Group
Contact page: http://www.worldbank.org/contacts

IFC contact information
International Finance Corporation
2121 Pennsylvania Avenue, NW
Washington, DC 20433, USA
Web: http://www.ifc.org
Contact page: http://www.ifc.org/about/contacts/contacts.html

MIGA contact information
Mail: Same as for World Bank Group
Location:
Multilateral Investment Guarantee Agency
1800 G Street, NW, Suite 1200
Washington, DC 20433, USA
Web: http://www.miga.org
Contact page: http://www.miga.org/screens/contacts/contacts.htm

ICSID contact information
Same as for World Bank Group
Web: http://www.worldbank.org/icsid
Contact page: http://www.worldbank.org/icsid/contact.htm

Media Relations, News, and Public Affairs

The External Affairs Department of the World Bank and the Corporate Relations Units of IFC and MIGA are the key resources for media relations, news, press contacts, public affairs, and access to World Bank Group experts and the speakers' bureau. Generally, the Bank Group organizations also feature news stories and major events on their home pages.

IBRD and IDA
- The DevNews Media Center provides press releases, feature stories, reviews of press coverage, speeches and transcripts, issue briefs, and an events calendar. It also provides access to the speakers' bureau, to World Bank experts, and to media contacts. Web: http://www.worldbank.org/mediacontacts
- Electronic newsletters offer a wide range of material by free e-mail subscription, including the daily press review, the World Bank weekly update, and many newsletters from specific sectors, regions, and partnerships of the Bank. Web: http://www.worldbank.org/subscriptions
- The Online Media Briefing Center is a password-protected site available only to accredited journalists. Web: http://media.worldbank.org

IFC
- The IFC Pressroom provides press releases and links to media contacts, country factsheets, general information about IFC, publications, speeches, briefs, and project documents. Web: http://www.ifc.org/about/contacts/contacts.html

MIGA

- MIGA News and Events provides newsletters, press releases, feature stories, an events calendar, and correspondence with nongovernmental organizations. Web: http://www.miga.org/screens/news/news.htm

ICSID

- News from ICSID is a biennial newsletter, with the current issue and archive available online. Web: http://www.worldbank.org/icsid/news/news.htm

Public Information

Various offices within the World Bank provide public information.

Public information centers

InfoShop/Public Information Center (PIC)
1818 H Street, NW Room J1-060
Washington, DC 20433, USA
Tel: (1-202) 458-5454
Fax: (1-202) 522-1500
E-mail: pic@worldbank.org
(For PICs in other countries, see appendix G.)

World Bank publications

To order publications:
Tel: (1-800) 645-7247 or (1-703) 661-1580
Fax: (1-703) 661-1501
Web: http://publications.worldbank.org/ecommerce

World Bank Group feedback service

This service helps Web users locate online information resources, project information, and publications. Although the site does not provide in-depth research, it can guide users to those Web sites most likely to have the replies to their questions. The feedback service also welcomes suggestions on how to make the Web site more useful.

Web: http://www.worldbank.org/feedback

E-mail: feedback@worldbank.org

Projects, policies, strategies, and research

These database portals give access to information on World Bank Group projects, policies, and strategies. They are searchable by sector, region, country, or development theme.

Documents and reports: http://www-wds.worldbank.org

Projects, policies, and strategies: http://www4.worldbank.org/sprojects

IFC projects: http://www.ifc.org/projects

World Bank Operational Manual: http://wbln0018.worldbank.org/Institutional/Manuals/OpManual.nsf

World Bank research: http://econ.worldbank.org

World Bank Group articles of agreement and other basic documents: http://www.worldbank.org/articles

Annual reports

Annual reports of World Bank Group organizations and programs are available online in portable document format (PDF) or hypertext markup language (HTML). The reports are published in multiple languages, and the Web sites include past editions.

World Bank annual report: http://www.worldbank.org/annualreport

IFC annual report: http://www.ifc.org/ar2001

MIGA annual report: http://www.miga.org/annualreport

ICSID annual report: http://www.worldbank.org/icsid/pubs/1998ar/main.htm

Libraries

The Library Network consists of 12 libraries and resource centers, which serve the World Bank Group and International Monetary Fund. The libraries offer the following services, which span the full spectrum of Bank Group and Fund business: research, consultation, procurement of information products, content organization, and document delivery. All of the libraries are located in downtown Washington, D.C., with the exception of the World Bank country office libraries and PICs. Some libraries admit visitors by appointment only.

Distinct from the Library Network, the PovertyNet Library is an online, Web-accessible library of reports and documents devoted to poverty in the developing world. The library contains a variety of poverty-related documents including technical reports and papers, abstracts, speeches, interviews, and press releases.

World Bank Group and IMF Joint Bank–Fund Library: http://jolis.worldbankimflib.org/libraries/e-jl.htm

The Library Network: http://jolis.worldbankimflib.org/external.htm

Sectoral and IT Resource Library: http://jolis.worldbankimflib.org/libraries/e-sitrc.htm

IFC Library: http://jolis.worldbankimflib.org/libraries/e-ifc.htm

Outside visitor access to the Library Network: http://jolis.worldbankimflib.org/e-nlvisit.htm

PovertyNet Library: http://poverty.worldbank.org/library

Timeline of World Bank Group History

1944   The United Nations (U.N.) Monetary and Financial Conference draws up the World Bank (International Bank of Reconstruction and Development—IBRD) Articles of Agreement at Bretton Woods, New Hampshire, with 44 countries represented.

1945   Twenty-eight governments sign the Articles of Agreement in Washington.

1946   The World Bank formally begins operations June 25.

The first loan applications are received (from Chile, Czechoslovakia, Denmark, France, Luxembourg, and Poland).

1947   The Bank makes its first bond offering—US$250 million—in New York City.

The Bank makes its first loan—US$250 million—to France.

1948   The Bank makes its first development loan—US$13.5 million—to Chile.

1950   The first loan is made to a national development bank—US$2 million—to Ethiopia.

1951   Finland and Yugoslavia are the first countries to repay their Bank loans in full.

1952   Japan and the Federal Republic of Germany become members.

1953   The first three loans to Japan, totaling US$40.2 million, are approved.

1955   The Economic Development Institute (now the World Bank Institute) is established to serve as the Bank's staff college.

1956   The International Finance Corporation (IFC) is established as a private sector affiliate of the Bank, with 31 members and authorized capital of US$100 million.

1957   IFC makes its first investment—US$2 million—in Siemens in Brazil to expand manufacturing.

1958   In a wake of deterioration in India's balance of payments, the first meeting of the India Aid Consortium takes place in Washington.

1960   The Indus Water Treaty is signed by Pakistan, India, and the World Bank.

The International Development Association (IDA) is established as part of the World Bank with initial subscriptions of US$912.7 million.

1961   The Bank loans US$80 million to Japan to finance the "bullet train."

IDA extends the first development credit—US$9 million—to Honduras for highway development.

1962   IFC establishes an advisory panel of investment bankers.

The first education loan is made—a US$5 million IDA credit to Tunisia for school construction.

IFC makes its first equity investment, to Fabrica Española Magentos S.A. of Spain.

1963   The Bank launches the Junior Professional recruitment and training program (now the Young Professionals program).

Eighteen newly independent African countries join the Bank.

1966   The International Centre for Settlement of Investment Disputes (ICSID) is established.

1967   Developing countries form the Group of 77 as a convention and a negotiation arm.

France, the Federal Republic of Germany, Japan, the United Kingdom, and the United States form the Group of 5 (G5) to convene meetings of finance ministers and governors of central banks. (The group became G7 in 1976 with the addition of Italy and Canada. This group, with the addition of Russia, is now known as the G8.)

1970   The Bank makes its first loan for population planning—US$2 million—to Jamaica.

The Bank's new commitments exceed US$2 billion for the first time.

1971   Japan becomes one of the five largest shareholders.

The first loan is made for pollution control—US$15 million—to Brazil.

1972   The Bank redeploys projects' and programs' staff members into regional departments to enable the institution to function more effectively.

The World Bank Group Staff Association comes into existence.

1974   The Interim Committee of the International Monetary Fund (IMF) and the Development Committee are established to advise the Boards of Governors.

The Position of Director General of Operations Evaluation is established to ensure independent evaluation of projects and programs.

President Robert S. McNamara delivers a speech at the annual meeting in which, for the first time, poverty is placed at top of the Bank's agenda.

1975   IBRD and IDA commit nearly US$1 billion in one fiscal year for rural development projects.

Shirley Boskey is appointed as the Bank's first female manager at the director level (International Relations Department).

The Project Preparation Facility is created.

IFC's first major commercial loans are syndicated, for projects in Brazil and the Republic of Korea.

1978   The executive directors endorse a Bank policy to assess the environmental impact of Bank-assisted projects.

The first *World Development Report* team, led by E. Stern, publishes a report with the theme of accelerating growth and alleviating poverty.

1979   The Bank's new commitments exceed US$10 billion for the first time.

The Bank begins lending for health projects.

1980   IBRD's authorized capital stock increases by US$44 billion to US$85 billion.

The first structural adjustment loan is approved—US$200 million—for Turkey.

The People's Republic of China assumes representation for China and quickly becomes one of the largest borrowers.

1981   The position of World Bank ombudsman is established.

The term "emerging markets" is coined by IFC. The Emerging Markets Data Base is developed.

1982   Anne Krueger is appointed as first female vice president (Economics and Research).

A Bank loan for the Polonoroeste program in Brazil finances a 90-mile highway across the Amazon rainforest, unintentionally attracting a large influx of settlers and spurring deforestation and international outcry.

1983   The Bank establishes a Small Grants program to fund activities to promote cooperation among nongovernmental organizations (NGOs), governments, academics, and media.

1984   IFC establishes a US$20 billion special fund to stimulate private sector development.

The NGO Working Group is established to build consensus among NGOs worldwide regarding the World Bank, as well as to provide a forum for dialogue about development issues.

The first direct IFC borrowings in international capital markets are made.

1986   The Foreign Investment Advisory Service is formed.

1987 In a major reorganization, all staff members are reselected into positions. New Country Departments combine functions formerly divided between "Programs" and "Projects" staff members. Regional and Central Environment Departments are created.

The Emerging Markets Data Base is launched commercially.

1988 The Multilateral Investment Guarantee Agency (MIGA), the newest affiliate of the Bank Group, is established.

1989 The Bank's Executive Board endorses a directive on disclosure of information.

1990 The Global Environment Facility is launched.

1991 China replaces India as the largest IDA borrower.

1992 The *World Development Report* focuses on the environment.

An independent review of the Sardar Sarovar project in India (Narmada Dam) is conducted. (Bank participation in the project is canceled in 1995.)

A task force proposes steps to improve the Bank's portfolio management.

A 15 percent budget cut results in staff downsizing.

Excellence through Equality recommends an increase in the proportion of women at higher grade levels. Diversity strategy is extended in 1998 to include gender, nationality, race, sexual orientation, culture, and disability.

The Russian Federation and 12 other republics of the former Soviet Union become members of IBRD and IDA.

1993 The Institutional Development Fund is established to support innovative capacity-building initiatives.

An independent Inspection Panel is established to investigate external complaints from individual groups negatively affected by Bank-funded projects.

IFC initiates the first environmental training for financial intermediaries.

1994 The Public Information Center is opened.

The Bank unveils a three-year, US$1.2 billion program to assist Palestinians in the West Bank and Gaza in transition to autonomous rule.

"Dollar budgeting" is introduced.

The World Bank celebrates its 50th anniversary while being widely criticized by NGOs and member governments.

1995 The executive directors select James D. Wolfensohn as ninth president of the World Bank Group.

The importance of girls' education is strongly emphasized.

1996 A trust fund for Bosnia and Herzegovina is created.

The Quality Assurance Group (QAG) is established to provide real-time information on the quality of the Bank's work.

Knowledge Management is launched to connect those who need to know with those who do know, to collect know-how, and to make knowledge accessible.

IMF, World Bank, and donors launch the Heavily Indebted Poor Countries (HIPC) initiative to alleviate debt. (The framework is significantly enhanced in 1999.)

1997   The Governance Action Plan is introduced. After just two years, more than 600 specific governance and clean government initiatives are started in almost 100 borrower countries.

Adaptable lending instruments are introduced.

Bank operations are reorganized into a matrix structure (country departments and networks of related-sector families) and begin to decentralize.

The Bank approves a loan of US$3 billion to Korea and approves other loans to economies affected by the Korean financial crisis to restore investor confidence and minimize social costs of the crisis.

The Board of Executive Directors approves the Strategic Compact—a fundamental organizational renewal program.

The Extending IFC's Reach initiative is launched, thereby targeting countries where difficult environments hamper investments.

1998   The Knowledge Bank initiative is launched.

The Bank approves the Kosovo Special Fund.

The Bank holds the first Development Marketplace to reward innovation in development.

IFC strengthens environmental and social policies.

1999   The Bank's vision for the new millennium is articulated: "Our dream is a world free of poverty."

The Bank Group adopts the Comprehensive Development Framework (CDF), and at their annual meetings the Bank Group and IMF agree to implement country-owned poverty reduction strategies.

IFC and MIGA appoint a Compliance Advisor/Ombudsman to improve accountability to locally affected communities.

The IFC–World Bank rationalization begins by merging some units in the Bank and IFC with similar functions.

The focus on new IFC sectors, such as health and education, is increased.

China graduates from IDA in 1999/2000.

2000   Bank and IMF Spring Meetings in Washington, D.C., and Annual Meetings in Prague draw large protests.

The Bank commits an additional US$500 million to fight HIV/AIDS.

The Inspection Panel reviews the China Western Poverty Project. Chinese authorities decide to use their own resources to implement the controversial component.

The Bank and its partners create the Global Development Gateway, a portal on development, where users can find and contribute information, resources, and tools.

The HIPC initiative delivers on its year 2000 promise: 22 countries receive more than US$34 billion in debt-service relief.

The Bank makes its first Internet bond offer—US$4 billion.

Completed Bank projects with satisfactory outcome ratings reach 75 percent for the first time in nearly 20 years (up from 60 percent in 1996).

The IFC reaches a record for new investment approvals in Sub-Saharan Africa—US$1.2 billion.

The United National Millennium Summit establishes the Millennium Development Goals for Achievement by 2015.

2001   IMF and the Bank Group cancel their Annual Meetings following the attacks of September 11.

The Bank and its partners establish the Global Development Learning Network, a distance-learning initiative in developing countries.

Partners in the Global Partnership to Eliminate Riverblindness pledge US$39 million to eliminate the disease in all of Africa by 2010.

The Federal Republic of Yugoslavia—now Serbia and Montenegro—becomes eligible for new World Bank funding.

The Bank Group participates in calls for decreasing agricultural subsidies in developed countries.

The Bank revises its disclosure policy to promote better transparency and accountability in its development work.

2002   The Bank Group participates in the first U.N. International Conference on Financing for Development, held in Monterrey, Mexico.

The Bank Group resumes normal operations in Afghanistan. Operations had been suspended in 1979 after the invasion by the Soviet Union.

Timor-Leste, formerly East Timor, joins IBRD as its 184th member.

With its partners, the World Bank establishes the Education for All fast-track initiative to help ensure by 2015 that developing countries provide every girl and boy with a complete primary school education.

2003   The Bank lends US$505 million in support of Brazil's accelerated program of human development reforms.

The Bank Group participates in the World Water Forum in Kyoto, Japan, asserting that water is a key driver in growth and poverty reduction.

IFC and its partners launch a program to help local businesses in Azerbaijan benefit from investments in the oil industry.

Ten leading commercial banks adopt the Equator Principles, choosing to follow World Bank and IFC environmental and social guidelines for all of their investment work in developing countries.

The Bank Group participates in U.N. efforts for rebuilding Iraq.

The Bank Group enters the municipal finance market with an investment in a water project in Mexico.

Presidents of the World Bank Group

EUGENE MEYER (1875–1959). Term: June to December 1946. Head of a banking house, Eugene Meyer & Co., and owner of the *Washington Post*.

JOHN J. McCLOY (1896–1989). Term: March 1947 to April 1949. Lawyer whose firm was counsel to Chase National Bank. Held positions in the U.S. government, including assistant secretary of war; resigned from the World Bank to become the U.S. high commissioner to Germany.

EUGENE BLACK (1898–1992). Term: July 1949 to December 1962. Investment banker and senior vice president of Chase Manhattan Bank; previously had been the U.S. executive director to the World Bank and assistant secretary at the U.S. Treasury. Served the longest of any World Bank president.

GEORGE WOODS (1901–1982). Term: January 1963 to March 1968. Investment banker and chairman of First Boston Corp.

ROBERT S. McNAMARA (b. 1916). Term: April 1968 to June 1981. Previously was director and president of Ford Motor Co., and served as secretary of defense in the Kennedy and Johnson administrations.

A. W. CLAUSEN (b. 1923). Term: July 1981 to June 1986. Held positions at Bank of America and BankAmerica Corp. before and after his World Bank tenure; these positions included president, chief executive officer (CEO), and chairman.

BARBER B. CONABLE (b. 1922). Term: July 1986 to August 1991. Member of the U.S. House of Representatives from 1965 to 1985; committee memberships there included the House Ways and Means Committee, the Joint Economic Committee, and the House Budget and Ethics Committees.

LEWIS T. PRESTON (1926–1995). Term: September 1991 to May 1995. Held positions at J. P. Morgan & Co., including president, chairman of the board and CEO, and chairman of the executive committee.

JAMES D. WOLFENSOHN (b. 1933). Term: June 1995 to present. For biography, see box 2.1.

APPENDIX D

Country Membership in World Bank Group Institutions

Once a country has joined the International Monetary Fund (IMF), it may apply for membership in the International Bank for Reconstruction and Development (IBRD). Upon admission, each country makes a capital contribution to IBRD. Only countries belonging to IBRD may apply for membership in the other Bank Group institutions. More information on regions and countries is available in chapter 4 ("World Bank Group Countries and Regions"), including specific ways that International Finance Corporation (IFC) regions differ from those used by IBRD and the International Development Association (IDA). The information in table D.1 is current as of July 15, 2003.

Table D.1 Country Memberships and Voting Shares in Each Institution

Country	IBRD/IDA region	IBRD (founded 1945) Year joined	IBRD Votes	IBRD Percentage of total	IDA (founded 1960) Year joined	IDA Votes	IDA Percentage of total	IFC (founded 1956) Year joined	IFC Votes	IFC Percentage of total	MIGA (founded 1988) Year joined	MIGA Votes	MIGA Percentage of total	ICSID (founded 1966) Year joined
Afghanistan	SA	1955	550	0.03	1961	13,557	0.10	1957	361	0.02	2003	295	0.15	1968
Albania	ECA	1991	1,080	0.07	1991	32,073	0.23	1991	1,552	0.06	1991	279	0.14	1991
Algeria	MENA	1963	9,502	0.59	1963	27,720	0.20	1990	5,871	0.24	1996	1,321	0.69	1996
Angola	AFR	1989	2,926	0.18	1989	48,362	0.35	1989	1,731	0.07	1989	364	0.19	n.m.
Antigua and Barbuda	LAC	1983	770	0.05	n.m.	n.m.	n.m.	1987	263	0.01	n.m.	n.m.	n.m.	n.m.
Argentina	LAC	1956	18,161	1.12	1962	134,439	0.98	1959	38,379	1.60	1992	1,431	0.74	1994
Armenia	ECA	1992	1,389	0.09	1993	2,717	0.02	1995	1,242	0.05	1995	257	0.13	1992
Australia	n.a.	1947	24,714	1.53	1960	180,540	1.31	1956	47,579	1.98	1999	3,196	1.66	1991
Austria	n.a.	1948	11,313	0.70	1961	90,656	0.66	1956	19,991	0.83	1997	1,543	0.80	1971
Azerbaijan	ECA	1992	1,896	0.12	1995	3,803	0.03	1995	2,617	0.11	1992	292	0.15	1992
Bahamas, The	LAC	1973	1,321	0.08	n.m.	n.m.	n.m.	1986	585	0.02	1994	353	0.18	1995
Bahrain	n.a.	1972	1,353	0.08	n.m.	n.m.	n.m.	1995	1,996	0.08	1988	313	0.16	1996
Bangladesh	SA	1972	5,104	0.32	1972	80,183	0.58	1976	9,287	0.39	1988	776	0.40	1980
Barbados	LAC	1974	1,198	0.07	1999	29,714	0.22	1980	611	0.03	1988	297	0.15	1983
Belarus	ECA	1992	3,573	0.22	n.m.	n.m.	n.m.	1992	5,412	0.23	1992	410	0.21	1992
Belgium	n.a.	1945	29,233	1.81	1964	158,185	1.15	1956	50,860	2.12	1992	3,754	1.95	1970
Belize	LAC	1982	836	0.05	1982	4,553	0.03	1982	351	0.01	1992	265	0.14	n.m.
Benin	AFR	1963	1,118	0.07	1963	13,166	0.10	1963	369	0.02	1994	285	0.15	1966
Bhutan	SA	1981	729	0.05	1981	19,583	0.14	n.m.	n.m.	n.m.	n.m.	n.m.	n.m.	n.m.
Bolivia	LAC	1945	2,035	0.13	1961	39,768	0.29	1956	2,152	0.09	1991	397	0.21	1995
Bosnia and Herzegovina	ECA	1993	799	0.05	1993	19,571	0.14	1993	870	0.04	1993	257	0.13	1997
Botswana	AFR	1968	865	0.05	1968	26,854	0.20	1979	363	0.02	1990	265	0.14	1970
Brazil	LAC	1946	33,537	2.07	1963	242,015	1.76	1956	39,729	1.65	1993	2,783	1.44	n.m.
Brunei Darussalam	n.a.	1995	2,623	0.16	n.m.	n.m.	n.m.	n.m.	n.m.	n.m.	n.m.	n.m.	n.m.	2002
Bulgaria	ECA	1990	5,465	0.34	n.m.	n.m.	n.m.	1991	5,117	0.21	1992	820	0.43	2001
Burkina Faso	AFR	1963	1,118	0.07	1963	24,156	0.18	1975	1,086	0.05	1988	238	0.12	1966
Burundi	AFR	1963	966	0.06	1963	25,706	0.19	1979	350	0.01	1998	251	0.13	1969
Cambodia	EAP	1970	464	0.03	1970	13,705	0.10	1997	589	0.02	1999	341	0.18	n.m.

Country	Region	Year	Amount	%	Year	Amount	%	Year	Amount	%	Year	Amount	%	Year
Cameroon	AFR	1963	1,777	0.11	1964	26,050	0.19	1974	1,135	0.05	1988	284	0.15	1967
Canada	n.a.	1945	45,045	2.79	1960	408,597	2.97	1956	81,592	3.39	1988	5,402	2.80	n.m.
Cape Verde	AFR	1978	758	0.05	1978	4,916	0.04	1990	265	0.01	1993	227	0.12	n.m.
Central African Republic	AFR	1963	1,112	0.07	1963	13,620	0.10	1991	369	0.02	2000	237	0.12	1966
Chad	AFR	1963	1,112	0.07	1963	13,980	0.10	1998	1,614	0.07	2002	237	0.12	1966
Chile	LAC	1945	7,181	0.44	1960	31,782	0.23	1957	11,960	0.50	1988	662	0.34	1991
China	EAP	1945	45,049	2.79	1960	273,252	1.98	1969	24,750	1.03	1988	5,707	2.96	1993
Colombia	LAC	1946	6,602	0.41	1961	53,080	0.39	1956	12,856	0.53	1995	947	0.49	1997
Comoros	AFR	1976	532	0.03	1977	13,141	0.10	1992	264	0.01	n.m.	n.m.	n.m.	1978
Congo, Democratic Rep. of	AFR	1963	2,893	0.18	1963	17,041	0.12	1970	2,409	0.10	1989	773	0.40	1970
Congo, Rep. of	AFR	1963	1,177	0.07	1963	11,375	0.08	1980	381	0.02	1991	292	0.15	1966
Costa Rica	LAC	1946	483	0.03	1961	12,480	0.09	1956	1,202	0.05	1994	383	0.20	1993
Côte d'Ivoire	AFR	1963	2,766	0.17	1963	23,069	0.17	1963	3,794	0.16	1988	487	0.25	1966
Croatia	ECA	1993	2,543	0.16	1993	40,374	0.29	1993	3,132	0.13	1993	507	0.26	1998
Cyprus	n.a.	1961	1,711	0.11	1962	37,001	0.27	1962	2,389	0.10	1988	360	0.19	1966
Czech Republic	ECA	1993	6,558	0.41	1993	65,386	0.47	1993	9,163	0.38	1993	961	0.50	1993
Denmark	n.a.	1946	13,701	0.85	1960	143,391	1.04	1956	18,804	0.78	1988	1,442	0.75	1968
Djibouti	MENA	1980	809	0.05	1980	532	0.00	1980	271	0.01	n.m.	n.m.	n.m.	n.m.
Dominica	LAC	1980	754	0.05	1980	16,749	0.12	1980	292	0.01	1991	227	0.12	n.m.
Dominican Republic	LAC	1945	2,342	0.14	1962	27,780	0.20	1956	1,437	0.06	1997	324	0.17	n.m.
Ecuador	LAC	1945	3,021	0.19	1961	35,989	0.26	1956	2,411	0.10	1988	498	0.26	1986
Egypt, Arab Rep.	MENA	1945	7,358	0.45	1960	67,385	0.49	1956	12,610	0.52	1988	986	0.51	1972
El Salvador	LAC	1946	391	0.02	1962	6,244	0.05	1956	279	0.01	1991	299	0.16	1984
Equatorial Guinea	AFR	1970	965	0.06	1972	6,167	0.05	1992	293	0.01	1994	227	0.12	n.m.
Eritrea	AFR	1994	843	0.05	1994	25,295	0.18	1995	1,185	0.05	1996	227	0.12	n.m.
Estonia	ECA	1992	1,173	0.07	n.m.	n.m.	n.m.	1993	1,684	0.07	1992	292	0.15	1992
Ethiopia	AFR	1945	1,228	0.08	1961	26,044	0.19	1956	377	0.02	1991	300	0.16	n.m.
Fiji	EAP	1971	1,237	0.08	1972	9,423	0.07	1979	537	0.02	1990	248	0.13	1977
Finland	n.a.	1948	8,810	0.54	1960	86,168	0.63	1956	15,947	0.66	1988	1,234	0.64	1969
France	n.a.	1945	69,647	4.31	1960	596,483	4.33	1956	121,265	5.04	1989	6,889	3.58	1967
Gabon	AFR	1963	1,237	0.08	1963	2,093	0.02	1970	1,518	0.06	2003	273	0.14	1966
Gambia, The	AFR	1967	793	0.05	1967	19,444	0.14	1983	344	0.01	1992	227	0.12	1975
Georgia	ECA	1992	1,834	0.11	1993	28,859	0.21	1995	1,111	0.05	1992	288	0.15	1992

(continued)

Table D.1 Country Memberships and Voting Shares in Each Institution (continued)

Country	IBRD/IDA region	IBRD (founded 1945) Year joined	Votes	Percentage of total	IDA (founded 1960) Year joined	Votes	Percentage of total	IFC (founded 1956) Year joined	Votes	Percentage of total	MIGA (founded 1988) Year joined	Votes	Percentage of total	ICSID (founded 1966) Year joined
Germany	n.a.	1952	72,649	4.49	1960	966,302	7.02	1956	129,158	5.37	1988	9,113	4.73	1969
Ghana	AFR	1957	1,775	0.11	1960	23,831	0.17	1958	5,321	0.22	1988	609	0.32	1966
Greece	n.a.	1945	1,934	0.12	1962	35,171	0.26	1957	7,148	0.30	1993	670	0.35	1969
Grenada	LAC	1975	781	0.05	1975	20,627	0.15	1975	324	0.01	1988	227	0.12	1991
Guatemala	LAC	1945	2,251	0.14	1961	33,667	0.24	1956	1,334	0.06	1996	317	0.16	2003
Guinea	AFR	1963	1,542	0.10	1969	31,453	0.23	1982	589	0.02	1995	268	0.14	1968
Guinea-Bissau	AFR	1977	790	0.05	1977	6,790	0.05	1977	268	0.01	n.m.	n.m.	n.m.	n.m.
Guyana	LAC	1966	1,308	0.08	1967	24,083	0.17	1967	1,642	0.07	1989	261	0.14	1969
Haiti	LAC	1953	1,317	0.08	1961	25,455	0.18	1956	1,072	0.04	1996	252	0.13	n.m.
Honduras	LAC	1945	891	0.06	1960	27,109	0.20	1956	745	0.03	1992	355	0.18	1989
Hungary	ECA	1982	8,300	0.51	1985	104,883	0.76	1985	11,182	0.47	1988	1,171	0.61	1987
Iceland	n.a.	1945	1,508	0.09	1961	33,116	0.24	1956	292	0.01	1998	267	0.14	1966
India	SA	1945	45,045	2.79	1960	440,609	3.20	1956	81,592	3.39	1994	3,225	1.67	n.m.
Indonesia	EAP	1954	15,231	0.94	1968	126,774	0.92	1956	28,789	1.20	1988	2,026	1.05	1968
Iran, Islamic Rep. of	MENA	1945	23,936	1.48	1960	15,455	0.11	1956	1,694	0.07	n.m.	n.m.	n.m.	n.m.
Iraq	MENA	1945	3,058	0.19	1960	9,407	0.07	1956	397	0.02	n.m.	n.m.	n.m.	n.m.
Ireland	n.a.	1957	5,521	0.34	1960	39,324	0.29	1958	1,540	0.06	1989	827	0.43	1981
Israel	n.a.	1954	5,000	0.31	1960	46,515	0.34	1956	2,385	0.10	1992	1,012	0.53	1983
Italy	n.a.	1947	45,045	2.79	1960	398,415	2.89	1956	81,592	3.39	1988	5,147	2.67	1971
Jamaica	LAC	1963	2,828	0.17	n.m.	n.m.	n.m.	1964	4,532	0.19	1988	358	0.19	1966
Japan	n.a.	1952	127,250	7.87	1960	1,502,886	10.91	1956	141,424	5.88	1988	9,156	4.75	1967
Jordan	MENA	1952	1,638	0.10	1960	24,865	0.18	1956	1,191	0.05	1988	348	0.18	1972
Kazakhstan	ECA	1992	3,235	0.20	1992	806	0.01	1993	4,887	0.20	1993	545	0.28	2000
Kenya	AFR	1964	2,711	0.17	1964	37,753	0.27	1964	4,291	0.18	1988	480	0.25	1967
Kiribati	EAP	1986	715	0.04	1986	11,895	0.09	1986	262	0.01	n.m.	n.m.	n.m.	n.m.
Korea, Republic of	EAP	1955	16,067	0.99	1961	76,922	0.56	1964	16,196	0.67	1988	968	0.50	1967
Kuwait	MENA	1962	13,530	0.84	1962	78,681	0.57	1962	10,197	0.42	1988	1,816	0.94	1979
Kyrgyz Rep.	ECA	1992	1,357	0.08	1992	2,700	0.02	1993	1,970	0.08	1993	254	0.13	n.m.
Lao PDR	EAP	1961	428	0.03	1963	16,957	0.14	1992	528	0.02	2000	237	0.12	n.m.
Latvia	ECA	1992	1,634	0.10	1992	3,659	0.03	1993	2,400	0.10	1998	348	0.18	1997

Country	Region	IBRD Year	IBRD Amount	IBRD %	IDA Year	IDA Amount	IDA %	IFC Year	IFC Amount	IFC %	MIGA Year	MIGA Amount	MIGA %	ICSID Year
Lebanon	MENA	1947	590	0.04	1962	8,562	0.06	1956	385	0.02	1994	427	0.22	2003
Lesotho	AFR	1968	913	0.06	1968	31,414	0.23	1972	321	0.01	1988	265	0.14	1969
Liberia	AFR	1962	713	0.04	1962	22,467	0.16	1962	333	0.01	n.m.	n.m.	n.m.	1970
Libya	AFR	1958	8,090	0.50	1961	7,771	0.06	1958	305	0.01	1993	726	0.38	n.m.
Lithuania	ECA	1992	1,757	0.11	n.m.	n.m.	n.m.	1993	2,591	0.11	1993	364	0.19	1992
Luxembourg	n.a.	1945	1,902	0.12	1964	33,117	0.24	1956	2,389	0.10	1991	381	0.20	1970
Macedonia, FYR	ECA	1993	677	0.04	1993	18,707	0.14	1993	786	0.03	1993	265	0.14	1998
Madagascar	AFR	1963	1,672	0.10	1963	14,966	0.11	1963	682	0.03	1988	353	0.18	1966
Malawi	AFR	1965	1,344	0.08	1965	31,515	0.23	1965	2,072	0.09	1988	254	0.13	1966
Malaysia	EAP	1958	8,494	0.53	1960	53,427	0.39	1958	15,472	0.64	1991	1,197	0.62	1966
Maldives	SA	1978	719	0.04	1978	30,186	0.22	1983	266	0.01	n.m.	n.m.	n.m.	n.m.
Mali	AFR	1963	1,412	0.09	1963	24,808	0.18	1978	701	0.03	1992	320	0.17	1978
Malta	MENA	1983	1,324	0.08	n.m.	n.m.	n.m.	n.m.	n.m.	n.m.	1992	309	0.16	n.m.
Marshall Islands	EAP	1992	719	0.04	1993	4,902	0.04	1992	913	0.04	n.m.	n.m.	n.m.	n.m.
Mauritania	AFR	1963	1,150	0.07	1963	18,275	0.13	1967	464	0.02	1992	288	0.15	1966
Mauritius	AFR	1968	1,492	0.09	1968	37,993	0.28	1968	1,915	0.08	1990	330	0.17	1969
Mexico	LAC	1945	19,054	1.18	1961	102,666	0.75	1956	27,839	1.16	n.m.	n.m.	n.m.	n.m.
Micronesia, Federated States of	EAP	1993	729	0.05	1993	18,424	0.13	1993	994	0.04	1993	227	0.12	1993
Moldova	ECA	1992	1,618	0.10	1994	612	0.00	1995	1,034	0.04	1993	273	0.14	n.m.
Mongolia	ECA	1991	716	0.04	1991	24,389	0.18	1991	394	0.02	1999	235	0.12	1991
Morocco	MENA	1958	5,223	0.32	1960	62,932	0.46	1962	9,287	0.39	1992	790	0.41	1967
Mozambique	AFR	1984	1,180	0.07	1984	15,855	0.12	1984	572	0.02	1994	348	0.18	1995
Myanmar	EAP	1952	2,734	0.17	1962	48,827	0.35	1956	916	0.04	n.m.	n.m.	n.m.	n.m.
Namibia	AFR	1990	1,773	0.11	n.m.	n.m.	n.m.	1990	654	0.03	1990	284	0.15	1990
Nepal	SA	1961	1,218	0.08	1963	34,400	0.25	1966	1,072	0.04	1994	299	0.16	1969
Netherlands	n.a.	1945	35,753	2.21	1961	305,971	2.22	1956	56,381	2.35	1988	3,999	2.08	1966
New Zealand	n.a.	1961	7,486	0.46	1974	41,152	0.30	1961	3,833	0.16	n.m.	n.m.	n.m.	1980
Nicaragua	LAC	1946	858	0.05	1960	29,845	0.22	1956	965	0.04	1992	279	0.14	1995
Niger	AFR	1963	1,102	0.07	1963	19,302	0.14	1980	397	0.02	n.m.	n.m.	n.m.	1966
Nigeria	AFR	1961	12,905	0.80	1961	17,782	0.13	1961	21,893	0.91	1988	1,664	0.86	1966
Norway	n.a.	1945	10,232	0.63	1961	143,447	1.04	1956	17,849	0.74	1989	1,409	0.73	1967
Oman	MENA	1971	1,811	0.11	1960	26,927	0.20	1973	1,437	0.06	1989	343	0.18	1995
Pakistan	SA	1950	9,589	0.59	1960	116,830	0.85	1956	19,630	0.82	1988	1,340	0.70	1966
Palau	EAP	1997	266	0.02	1997	504	0.00	1997	274	0.01	1997	227	0.12	n.m.
Panama	LAC	1946	635	0.04	1961	10,185	0.07	1956	1,257	0.05	1997	408	0.21	1996

(continued)

Table D.1 Country Memberships and Voting Shares in Each Institution (continued)

Country	IBRD/IDA region	IBRD (founded 1945)			IDA (founded 1960)			IFC (founded 1956)			MIGA (founded 1988)			ICSID (founded 1966)
		Year joined	Votes	Percentage of total	Year joined	Votes	Percentage of total	Year joined	Votes	Percentage of total	Year joined	Votes	Percentage of total	Year joined
Papua New Guinea	EAP	1975	1,544	0.10	1975	15,750	0.11	1975	1,387	0.06	1991	273	0.14	1978
Paraguay	LAC	1945	1,479	0.09	1961	16,958	0.12	1956	686	0.03	1992	257	0.13	1983
Peru	LAC	1945	5,581	0.35	1961	20,428	0.15	1956	7,148	0.30	1991	834	0.43	1983
Philippines	EAP	1945	7,094	0.44	1960	16,583	0.12	1957	12,856	0.53	1994	661	0.34	1989
Poland	ECA	1946	11,158	0.69	1988	314,678	2.28	1987	7,486	0.31	1990	941	0.49	n.m.
Portugal	n.a.	1961	5,710	0.35	1992	36,684	0.27	1966	8,574	0.36	1988	850	0.44	1984
Qatar	MENA	1972	1,346	0.08	n.m.	n.m.	n.m.	n.m.	n.m.	n.m.	1996	418	0.22	n.m.
Romania	ECA	1972	4,261	0.26	n.m.	n.m.	n.m.	1990	2,911	0.12	1992	1,155	0.60	1975
Russian Federation	ECA	1992	45,045	2.79	1992	39,082	0.28	1993	81,592	3.39	1992	5,705	2.96	n.m.
Rwanda	AFR	1963	1,296	0.08	1963	20,312	0.15	1975	556	0.02	2002	309	0.16	1979
St. Kitts and Nevis	LAC	1984	525	0.03	1987	7,888	0.06	1996	888	0.04	1999	227	0.12	1995
St. Lucia	LAC	1980	802	0.05	1982	27,231	0.20	1982	324	0.01	1988	265	0.14	1984
St. Vincent	LAC	1982	528	0.03	1982	4,883	0.04	n.m.	n.m.	n.m.	1990	265	0.14	2003
Samoa	EAP	1974	781	0.05	1974	18,441	0.13	1974	285	0.01	1988	227	0.12	1978
San Marino	n.a.	2000	845	0.05	n.m.	n.m.	n.m.	n.m.	n.m.	n.m.	n.m.	n.m.	n.m.	n.m.
São Tomé and Principe	AFR	1977	745	0.05	1977	6,414	0.05	n.m.	n.m.	n.m.	n.m.	n.m.	n.m.	n.m.
Saudi Arabia	MENA	1957	45,045	2.79	1960	488,093	3.54	1962	30,312	1.26	1988	5,705	2.96	1980
Senegal	AFR	1962	2,322	0.14	1962	39,095	0.28	1962	2,549	0.11	1988	433	0.22	1967
Serbia and Montenegro	ECA	1993	1,847	0.11	1993	29,374	0.21	1993	2,053	0.09	1993	584	0.30	n.m.
Seychelles	AFR	1980	513	0.03	n.m.	n.m.	n.m.	1981	277	0.01	1992	227	0.12	1978
Sierra Leone	AFR	1962	968	0.06	1962	17,551	0.13	1962	473	0.02	1996	309	0.16	1966
Singapore	n.a.	1966	570	0.04	2002	4,134	0.03	1968	427	0.02	1998	449	0.23	1968
Slovak Rep.	ECA	1993	3,466	0.21	1993	41,870	0.30	1993	4,707	0.20	1993	568	0.29	1994
Slovenia	ECA	1993	1,511	0.09	1993	22,300	0.16	1993	1,835	0.08	1993	357	0.19	1994
Solomon Islands	EAP	1978	763	0.05	1980	518	0.00	1980	287	0.01	n.m.	n.m.	n.m.	1981
Somalia	AFR	1962	802	0.05	1962	10,506	0.08	1962	333	0.01	n.m.	n.m.	n.m.	1968
South Africa	AFR	1945	13,712	0.85	1960	39,579	0.29	1957	16,198	0.67	1994	1,839	0.95	n.m.

Country	Region	Year	Amount	%	Year	Amount	%	Year	Amount	%	Year	Amount	%	Year
Spain	n.a.	1958	28,247	1.75	1960	85,714	0.62	1960	37,276	1.55	1988	2,442	1.27	1994
Sri Lanka	SA	1950	4,067	0.25	1961	56,067	0.34	1956	7,385	0.31	1988	551	0.29	1967
Sudan	AFR	1957	1,100	0.07	1960	22,484	0.16	1960	361	0.02	1991	383	0.20	1973
Suriname	LAC	1978	662	0.04	n.m.	n.m.	n.m.	n.m.	n.m.	n.m.	2003	259	0.13	n.m.
Swaziland	AFR	1969	690	0.04	1969	15,630	0.11	1969	934	0.04	1990	235	0.12	1971
Sweden	n.a.	1951	15,224	0.94	1960	273,599	1.99	1956	27,126	1.13	1988	2,026	1.05	1967
Switzerland	n.a.	1992	26,856	1.66	1992	147,924	1.07	1992	41,893	1.74	1988	2,820	1.46	1968
Syrian Arab Rep.	MENA	1947	2,452	0.15	1962	10,351	0.08	1962	444	0.02	2002	345	0.18	n.m.
Tajikistan	ECA	1993	1,310	0.08	1993	20,568	0.15	1994	1,462	0.06	2002	251	0.13	n.m.
Tanzania	AFR	1962	1,545	0.10	1962	45,557	0.33	1962	1,253	0.05	1992	425	0.22	1992
Thailand	EAP	1949	6,599	0.41	1960	58,195	0.42	1956	11,191	0.47	2000	919	0.48	n.m.
Timor-Leste	EAP	2002	767	0.05	2002	558	0.00	n.m.	n.m.	n.m.	2002	227	0.12	2002
Togo	AFR	1962	1,355	0.08	1962	23,243	0.17	1962	1,058	0.04	1988	254	0.13	1967
Tonga	EAP	1985	744	0.05	1985	16,813	0.12	1985	284	0.01	n.m.	n.m.	n.m.	1990
Trinidad and Tobago	LAC	1963	2,914	0.18	1972	4,396	0.03	1971	4,362	0.18	1992	535	0.28	1967
Tunisia	MENA	1958	969	0.06	1960	2,793	0.02	1962	3,816	0.16	1988	333	0.17	1966
Turkey	ECA	1947	8,578	0.53	1960	94,605	0.69	1956	14,795	0.62	1988	991	0.51	1989
Turkmenistan	ECA	1992	776	0.05	n.m.	n.m.	n.m.	1997	1,060	0.04	1993	243	0.13	1992
Uganda	AFR	1963	867	0.05	1963	26,992	0.20	1963	985	0.04	1992	410	0.21	1966
Ukraine	ECA	1992	11,158	0.69	n.m.	n.m.	n.m.	1993	9,157	0.38	1994	941	0.49	2000
United Arab Emirates	MENA	1972	2,635	0.16	1981	1,367	0.01	1977	4,283	0.18	1993	549	0.28	1982
United Kingdom	n.a.	1945	69,647	4.31	1960	688,291	5.00	1956	121,265	5.04	1988	8,742	4.59	1967
United States	n.a.	1945	265,219	16.40	1960	1,913,640	13.89	1956	569,629	23.70	1988	31,481	16.34	1966
Uruguay	LAC	1946	3,062	0.19	n.m.	n.m.	n.m.	1968	3,819	0.16	1993	379	0.20	2000
Uzbekistan	ECA	1992	2,743	0.17	1992	746	0.01	1993	4,123	0.17	1993	352	0.18	1995
Vanuatu	EAP	1981	836	0.05	1981	13,821	0.10	1981	305	0.01	1988	227	0.12	n.m.
Venezuela, R. B. de	LAC	1946	20,611	1.27	n.m.	n.m.	n.m.	1956	27,838	1.16	1994	1,604	0.83	1995
Vietnam	EAP	1956	1,218	0.08	1960	15,454	0.11	1967	696	0.03	1994	565	0.29	n.m.
Yemen, Rep. of	MENA	1969	2,462	0.15	1970	40,727	0.30	1970	965	0.04	1996	332	0.17	n.m.
Zambia	AFR	1965	3,060	0.19	1965	33,199	0.24	1965	1,536	0.06	1988	495	0.26	1970
Zimbabwe	AFR	1980	3,575	0.22	1985	20,742	0.15	1980	2,370	0.10	1992	413	0.21	1994
TOTALS	184	1,617,412	100.00	164	13,773,312	100.00	175	2,403,931	100.00	161	192,678	100.00	139

Note: Columns may not total 100 because of rounding. Also, 0.00 signifies less than 0.005 percent.

n.a. = High-income countries that currently do not borrow or receive financing or advisory services from the World Bank or IFC. These countries are not necessarily classified as Part I relative to IDA. AFR = Africa; EAP = East Asia and the Pacific; ECA = Europe and Central Asia; LAC = Latin America and the Caribbean; MENA = Middle East and North Africa; SA = South Asia.

n.m. = Nonmember.

Source: World Bank Corporate Secretariat. Information is current as of July 15, 2003.

APPENDIX E

Constituencies of the Executive Directors

Under the Articles of Agreement of the International Bank for Reconstruction and Development (IBRD), the five member countries having the largest number of shares subscribed appoint five executive directors; the remaining member countries elect the other executive directors. At present, IBRD's board consists of 24 executive directors. Of these, five were appointed by the largest shareholders—the United States, Japan, Germany, France, and the United Kingdom (see figure E.1)—and 19 were elected by IBRD's governors to represent constituencies formed during the election process.

Under the Articles of Agreement of the International Development Association (IDA) and the International Finance Corporation (IFC), the executive directors of IBRD serve ex officio as executive directors of IDA and as members of the Board of Directors of IFC. The Multilateral Investment Guarantee Agency (MIGA) has its own separate Board of Directors, also consisting of 24 members. All members of the MIGA board are elected.

Regular elections of executive directors are held every two years, normally at the time of the annual meetings. Elections are coordinated by the Bank Group's Corporate Secretariat, which anticipates changes in constituency groupings resulting from new memberships or political events, as well as increases in members' capital subscriptions and the corresponding changes in voting power. The Corporate Secretariat also verifies the credentials of governors who are entitled to vote.

In the event that an executive director elected during the regular election terminates service before the next regular election, the constituency affected by the vacancy holds an interim election for a successor. The interim election is conducted either by mail vote or during an annual meeting that does not fall on a regular election year.

IBRD

Figure E.1 and table E.1 show the voting power of the largest shareholders of IBRD and the voting shares of directors of IBRD, respectively.

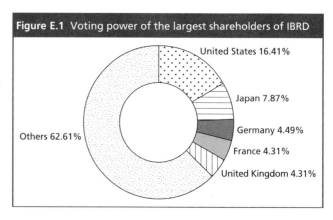

Figure E.1 Voting power of the largest shareholders of IBRD

United States 16.41%

Japan 7.87%

Germany 4.49%

France 4.31%

United Kingdom 4.31%

Others 62.61%

Table E.1 Voting Shares of Directors of IBRD

	Nationality of executive director	Constituency	Number of votes	Percentage of total votes
Appointed directors:				
1	United States	United States	265,219	16.41
2	Japan	Japan	127,250	7.87
3	Germany	Germany	72,649	4.49
4	France	France	69,647	4.31
5	United Kingdom	United Kingdom	69,647	4.31
Elected directors:				
6	Austria, casting the votes of	Austria, Belarus, Belgium, Czech Republic, Hungary, Kazakhstan, Luxembourg, Slovak Republic, Slovenia, Turkey	77,669	4.80
7	República Bolivariana de Venezuela, casting the votes of	Costa Rica, El Salvador, Guatemala, Honduras, Mexico, Nicaragua, Spain, República Bolivariana de Venezuela	72,786	4.50
8	Netherlands, casting the votes of	Armenia, Bosnia and Herzegovina, Bulgaria, Croatia, Cyprus, Georgia, Israel, former Yugoslav Republic of Macedonia, Moldova, Netherlands, Romania, Ukraine	72,208	4.47
9	Canada, casting the votes of	Antigua and Barbuda, The Bahamas, Barbados, Belize, Canada, Dominica, Grenada, Guyana, Ireland, Jamaica, St. Kitts and Nevis, St. Lucia, St. Vincent and the Grenadines	62,217	3.85
10	Brazil, casting the votes of	Brazil, Colombia, Dominican Republic, Ecuador, Haiti, Panama, Philippines, Suriname, Trinidad and Tobago	58,124	3.60
11	Italy, casting the votes of	Albania, Greece, Italy, Malta, Portugal, San Marino, Timor-Leste	56,705	3.51

	Nationality of executive director	Constituency	Number of votes	Percentage of total votes
12	Australia, casting the votes of	Australia, Cambodia, Kiribati, Republic of Korea, Marshall Islands, Federated States of Micronesia, Mongolia, New Zealand, Palau, Papua New Guinea, Samoa, Solomon Islands, Vanuatu	55,800	3.45
13	Uganda, casting the votes of	Angola, Botswana, Burundi, Eritrea, Ethiopia, The Gambia, Kenya, Lesotho, Liberia, Malawi, Mozambique, Namibia, Nigeria, Seychelles, Sierra Leone, South Africa, Sudan, Swaziland, Tanzania, Uganda, Zambia, Zimbabwe	55,190	3.41
14	India, casting the votes of	Bangladesh, Bhutan, India, Sri Lanka	54,945	3.40
15	Pakistan, casting the votes of	Afghanistan, Algeria, Ghana, Islamic Republic of Iran, Iraq, Morocco, Pakistan, Tunisia	55,602	3.34
16	Denmark, casting the votes of	Denmark, Estonia, Finland, Iceland, Latvia, Lithuania, Norway, Sweden	54,039	3.34
17	Switzerland, casting the votes of	Azerbaijan, Kyrgyz Republic, Poland, Serbia and Montenegro, Switzerland, Tajikistan, Turkmenistan, Uzbekistan	47,943	2.97
18	China, casting the votes of	China	45,049	2.79
19	Saudi Arabia, casting the votes of	Saudi Arabia	45,045	2.79
20	Russian Federation, casting the votes of	Russian Federation	45,045	2.79
21	Kuwait, casting the votes of	Bahrain, Arab Republic of Egypt, Jordan, Kuwait, Lebanon, Libya, Maldives, Oman, Qatar, Syrian Arab Republic, United Arab Emirates, Republic of Yemen	43,984	2.72
22	Thailand, casting the votes of	Brunei Darussalam, Fiji, Indonesia, Lao People's Democratic Republic, Malaysia, Myanmar, Nepal, Singapore, Thailand, Tonga, Vietnam	41,096	2.54
23	Argentina, casting the votes of	Argentina, Bolivia, Chile, Paraguay, Peru, Uruguay	37,499	2.32
24	Guinea-Bissau, casting the votes of	Benin, Burkina Faso, Cameroon, Cape Verde, Central African Republic, Chad, Comoros, Democratic Republic of Congo, Republic of Congo, Côte d'Ivoire, Djibouti, Equatorial Guinea, Gabon, Guinea, Guinea-Bissau, Madagascar, Mali, Mauritania, Mauritius, Niger, Rwanda, São Tomé and Principe, Senegal, Togo	32,252	2.00
			1,616,610	100.00

Note: Individual percentages may not total 100 because of rounding. Somalia did not participate in the 2002 regular election of executive directors. Information is current as of July 15, 2003.
Source: World Bank Group Corporate Secretariat.

IDA

Figure E.2 and table E.2 show the voting power of the largest shareholders of IDA and the voting shares of directors of IDA, respectively.

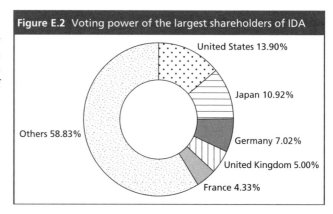

Figure E.2 Voting power of the largest shareholders of IDA

- United States 13.90%
- Japan 10.92%
- Germany 7.02%
- United Kingdom 5.00%
- France 4.33%
- Others 58.83%

Table E.2 Voting Shares of Directors of IDA

	Nationality of executive director	Constituency	Number of votes	Percentage of total votes
Appointed directors:				
1	United States	United States	1,913,640	13.90
2	Japan	Japan	1,502,886	10.92
3	Germany	Germany	966,302	7.02
4	United Kingdom	United Kingdom	688,291	5.00
5	France	France	596,483	4.33
Elected directors:				
6	Denmark, casting the votes of	Denmark, Finland, Iceland, Latvia, Norway, Sweden	683,380	4.97
7	Austria, casting the votes of	Austria, Belgium, Czech Republic, Hungary, Kazakhstan, Luxembourg, Slovak Republic, Slovenia, Turkey	611,808	4.45
8	India, casting the votes of	Bangladesh, Bhutan, India, Sri Lanka	596,440	4.33
9	Canada, casting the votes of	Barbados, Belize, Canada, Dominica, Grenada, Guyana, Ireland, St. Kitts and Nevis, St. Lucia, St. Vincent and the Grenadines	583,649	4.24
10	Uganda, casting the votes of	Angola, Botswana, Burundi, Eritrea, Ethiopia, The Gambia, Kenya, Lesotho, Liberia, Malawi, Mozambique, Nigeria, Sierra Leone, South Africa, Sudan, Swaziland, Tanzania, Uganda, Zambia, Zimbabwe	550,225	4.00
11	Switzerland, casting the votes of	Azerbaijan, Kyrgyz Republic, Poland, Serbia and Montenegro, Switzerland, Tajikistan, Uzbekistan	519,793	3.78
12	Italy, casting the votes of	Albania, Greece, Italy, Portugal, Timor-Leste	502,901	3.65
13	Netherlands, casting the votes of	Armenia, Bosnia and Herzegovina, Croatia, Cyprus, Georgia, Israel, former Yugoslav Republic of Macedonia, Moldova, Netherlands	500,327	3.64

	Nationality of executive director	Constituency	Number of votes	Percentage of total votes
14	Saudi Arabia, casting the votes of	Saudi Arabia	488,093	3.55
15	Australia, casting the votes of	Australia, Cambodia, Kiribati, Republic of Korea, Marshall Islands, Federated States of Micronesia, Mongolia, New Zealand, Palau, Papua New Guinea, Samoa, Solomon Islands, Vanuatu	420,963	3.06
16	Brazil, casting the votes of	Brazil, Colombia, Dominican Republic, Ecuador, Haiti, Panama, Philippines, Trinidad and Tobago	415,483	3.02
17	Guinea-Bissau, casting the votes of	Benin, Burkina Faso, Cameroon, Cape Verde, Central African Republic, Chad, Comoros, Democratic Republic of Congo, Republic of Congo, Côte d'Ivoire, Djibouti, Equatorial Guinea, Gabon, Guinea, Guinea-Bissau, Madagascar, Mali, Mauritania, Mauritius, Niger, Rwanda, São Tomé and Principe, Senegal, Togo	411,957	2.99
18	Thailand, casting the votes of	Fiji, Indonesia, Lao People's Democratic Republic, Malaysia, Myanmar, Nepal, Singapore, Thailand, Tonga, Vietnam	387,404	2.81
19	República Bolivariana de Venezuela, casting the votes of	Costa Rica, El Salvador, Guatemala, Honduras, Mexico, Nicaragua, Spain, República Bolivariana de Venezuela	297,725	2.16
20	Kuwait, casting the votes of	Arab Republic of Egypt, Jordan, Kuwait, Lebanon, Libya, Maldives, Oman, Syrian Arab Republic, United Arab Emirates, Republic of Yemen	296,822	2.16
21	China, casting the votes of	China	273,252	1.99
22	Pakistan, casting the votes of	Afghanistan, Algeria, Ghana, Islamic Republic of Iran, Iraq, Morocco, Pakistan, Tunisia	272,525	1.98
23	Argentina, casting the votes of	Argentina, Bolivia, Chile, Paraguay, Peru	243,375	1.77
24	Russian Federation, casting the votes of	Russian Federation	39,082	0.28
			13,762,806	100.00

Note: Individual percentages may not total 100 because of rounding. Somalia did not participate in the 2002 regular election of executive directors. Information is current as of July 15, 2003.
Source: World Bank Group Corporate Secretariat.

IFC

Figure E.3 and table E.3 show the voting power of the largest shareholders of IFC and the voting shares of directors of IFC, respectively.

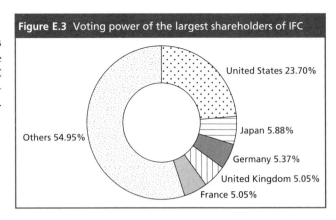

Figure E.3 Voting power of the largest shareholders of IFC

United States 23.70%

Japan 5.88%

Germany 5.37%

United Kingdom 5.05%

France 5.05%

Others 54.95%

Table E.3 Voting Shares of Directors of IFC

	Nationality of executive director	Constituency	Number of votes	Percentage of total votes
Appointed directors:				
1	United States	United States	569,629	23.70
2	Japan	Japan	141,424	5.88
3	Germany	Germany	129,158	5.37
4	France	France	121,265	5.05
5	United Kingdom	United Kingdom	121,265	5.05
Elected directors:				
6	Austria, casting the votes of	Austria, Belarus, Belgium, Czech Republic, Hungary, Kazakhstan, Luxembourg, Slovak Republic, Slovenia, Turkey	125,221	5.21
7	Italy, casting the votes of	Albania, Greece, Italy, Portugal	98,866	4.11
8	India, casting the votes of	Bangladesh, India, Sri Lanka	98,264	4.09
9	República Bolivariana de Venezuela, casting the votes of	Costa Rica, El Salvador, Guatemala, Honduras, Mexico, Nicaragua, Spain, República Bolivariana de Venezuela	97,478	4.06
10	Canada, casting the votes of	Antigua and Barbuda, The Bahamas, Barbados, Belize, Canada, Dominica, Grenada, Guyana, Ireland, Jamaica, St. Kitts and Nevis, St. Lucia	92,944	3.87
11	Denmark, casting the votes of	Denmark, Estonia, Finland, Iceland, Latvia, Lithuania, Norway, Sweden	86,693	3.61
12	Netherlands, casting the votes of	Armenia, Bosnia and Herzegovina, Bulgaria, Croatia, Cyprus, Georgia, Israel, former Yugoslav Republic of Macedonia, Moldova, Netherlands, Romania, Ukraine	86,515	3.60
13	Russian Federation, casting the votes of	Russian Federation	81,592	3.39
14	Brazil, casting the votes of	Brazil, Colombia, Dominican Republic, Ecuador, Haiti, Panama, Philippines, Trinidad and Tobago	75,980	3.16

	Nationality of executive director	Constituency	Number of votes	Percentage of total votes
15	Australia, casting the votes of	Australia, Cambodia, Kiribati, Republic of Korea, Marshall Islands, Federated States of Micronesia, Mongolia, New Zealand, Palau, Papua New Guinea, Samoa, Solomon Islands, Vanuatu	73,309	3.05
16	Argentina, casting the votes of	Argentina, Bolivia, Chile, Paraguay, Peru, Uruguay	64,144	2.67
17	Switzerland, casting the votes of	Azerbaijan, Kyrgyz Republic, Poland, Serbia and Montenegro, Switzerland, Tajikistan, Turkmenistan, Uzbekistan	62,601	2.60
18	Thailand, casting the votes of	Fiji, Indonesia, Lao People's Democratic Republic, Malaysia, Myanmar, Nepal, Singapore, Thailand, Tonga, Vietnam	59,912	2.49
19	Uganda, casting the votes of	Angola, Botswana, Burundi, Eritrea, Ethiopia, The Gambia, Kenya, Lesotho, Liberia, Malawi, Mozambique, Namibia, Nigeria, Seychelles, Sierra Leone, South Africa, Sudan, Swaziland, Tanzania, Uganda, Zambia, Zimbabwe	58,873	2.45
20	Pakistan, casting the votes of	Afghanistan, Algeria, Ghana, Islamic Republic of Iran, Iraq, Morocco, Pakistan, Tunisia	46,377	1.93
21	Kuwait, casting the votes of	Bahrain, Arab Republic of Egypt, Jordan, Kuwait, Lebanon, Libya, Maldives, Oman, Syrian Arab Republic, United Arab Emirates, Republic of Yemen	34,079	1.42
22	Saudi Arabia, casting the votes of	Saudi Arabia	30,312	1.26
23	China, casting the votes of	China	24,750	1.03
24	Guinea-Bissau, casting the votes of	Benin, Burkina Faso, Cameroon, Cape Verde, Central African Republic, Chad, Comoros, Democratic Republic of Congo, Republic of Congo, Côte d'Ivoire, Djibouti, Equatorial Guinea, Gabon, Guinea, Guinea-Bissau, Madagascar, Mali, Mauritania, Mauritius, Niger, Rwanda, Senegal, Togo	22,947	0.95
			2,403,598	100.00

Note: Individual percentages may not total 100 because of rounding. Somalia did not participate in the 2002 regular election of executive directors. Information is current as of July 15, 2003.
Source: World Bank Group Corporate Secretariat.

MIGA

Figure E.4 and table E.4 show the voting power of the largest shareholders of MIGA and the voting shares of directors of MIGA, respectively.

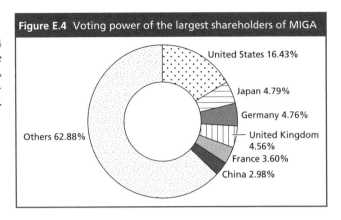

Figure E.4 Voting power of the largest shareholders of MIGA

United States 16.43%

Japan 4.79%

Germany 4.76%

United Kingdom 4.56%

France 3.60%

China 2.98%

Others 62.88%

Table E.4 Voting Shares of Directors of MIGA

	Nationality of director	Constituency	Number of votes	Percentage of total votes
Directors elected by 6 largest shareholders:				
1	United States	United States	31,481	16.43
2	Japan	Japan	9,156	4.79
3	Germany	Germany	9,113	4.76
4	United Kingdom	United Kingdom	8,742	4.56
5	France	France	6,889	3.60
6	China	China	5,707	2.98
Directors elected by other shareholders:				
7	Belgium, casting the votes of	Austria, Belarus, Belgium, Czech Republic, Hungary, Kazakhstan, Luxembourg, Slovak Republic, Slovenia, Turkey	10,681	5.57
8	Netherlands, casting the votes of	Armenia, Bosnia and Herzegovina, Bulgaria, Croatia, Cyprus, Georgia, Israel, former Yugoslav Republic of Macedonia, Moldova, Netherlands, Romania, Ukraine	10,134	5.29
9	Uganda, casting the votes of	Angola, Botswana, Burundi, Eritrea, Ethiopia, The Gambia, Kenya, Lesotho, Malawi, Mozambique, Namibia, Nigeria, Seychelles, Sierra Leone, South Africa, Sudan, Swaziland, Tanzania, Uganda, Zambia, Zimbabwe	9,663	5.04
10	Canada, casting the votes of	The Bahamas, Barbados, Belize, Canada, Dominica, Grenada, Guyana, Ireland, Jamaica, St. Kitts and Nevis, St. Lucia, St. Vincent and the Grenadines	8,974	4.68

	Nationality of director	Constituency	Number of votes	Percentage of total votes
11	Italy, casting the votes of	Albania, Greece, Italy, Malta, Portugal, Timor-Leste	7,482	3.91
12	Denmark, casting the votes of	Denmark, Estonia, Finland, Iceland, Latvia, Lithuania, Norway, Sweden	7,382	3.85
13	Kuwait, casting the votes of	Bahrain, Arab Republic of Egypt, Jordan, Kuwait, Lebanon, Libya, Oman, Qatar, Syrian Arab Republic, United Arab Emirates, Republic of Yemen	6,603	3.45
14	Brazil, casting the votes of	Brazil, Colombia, Dominican Republic, Ecuador, Haiti, Panama, Philippines, Trinidad and Tobago	6,408	3.34
15	Thailand, casting the votes of	Fiji, Indonesia, Lao People's Democratic Republic, Malaysia, Nepal, Singapore, Thailand, Vietnam	5,940	3.10
16	Australia, casting the votes of	Australia, Cambodia, Republic of Korea, Federated States of Micronesia, Mongolia, Palau, Papua New Guinea, Samoa, Vanuatu	5,921	3.09
17	Guinea-Bissau, casting the votes of	Benin, Burkina Faso, Cameroon, Cape Verde, Central African Republic, Chad, Democratic Republic of Congo, Republic of Congo, Côte d'Ivoire, Equatorial Guinea, Guinea, Madagascar, Mali, Mauritania, Mauritius, Rwanda, Senegal, Togo	5,842	3.05
18	Saudi Arabia, casting the votes of	Saudi Arabia	5,705	2.98
19	Russian Federation, casting the votes of	Russian Federation	5,705	2.98
20	República Bolivariana de Venezuela, casting the votes of	Costa Rica, El Salvador, Guatemala, Honduras, Nicaragua, Spain, República Bolivariana de Venezuela	5,679	2.97
21	Switzerland, casting the votes of	Azerbaijan, Kyrgyz Republic, Poland, Serbia and Montenegro, Switzerland, Turkmenistan, Uzbekistan	5,486	2.86
22	India, casting the votes of	Bangladesh, India, Sri Lanka	4,552	2.38
23	Pakistan, casting the votes of	Algeria, Ghana, Morocco, Pakistan, Tunisia	4,393	2.29
24	Argentina, casting the votes of	Argentina, Bolivia, Chile, Paraguay, Peru, Uruguay	3,960	2.07
			191,600	100.00

Note: Individual percentages may not total 100 because of rounding. Afghanistan, Gabon, Suriname, and Tajikistan joined MIGA after the 2002 regular election of directors. Information is current as of July 15, 2003.
Source: World Bank Group Corporate Secretariat.

World Bank Sectors

Sectors are high-level groupings of economic activities based on the types of goods or services produced. They are aligned with the United Nations classification of economic sectors used as a point of reference, are mutually exclusive, and are used to indicate which part of the economy is supported by a given Bank intervention. Codes for the various sectors are shown below.

Agriculture, fishing, and forestry
AB   Agricultural extension and research
AJ   Animal production
AH   Crops
AT   Forestry
AI   Irrigation and drainage
AZ   General agriculture, fishing, and forestry sector

Law and justice, and public administration
BC   Central government administration
BE   Compulsory pension and unemployment insurance
BG   Law and justice
GH   Subnational government administration

Information and communications
CA   Information technology
CB   Media
CD   Postal services
CT   Telecommunications
CZ   General information and communications sector

Education
EL   Adult literacy and nonformal education
EC   Preprimary education
EP   Primary education
ES   Secondary education

ET   Tertiary education
EV   Vocational training
EZ   General education sector

Finance
FA   Banking
FK   Capital markets
FB   Health insurance
FC   Housing finance and real estate markets
FD   Noncompulsory pensions, insurance, and contractual savings
FE   Microfinance and small and medium enterprise finance
FG   Payment systems, securities clearance, and settlement
FZ   General finance sector

Health and other social services
JA   Health
JB   Other social services

Industry and trade
YA   Agricultural marketing and trade
YB   Agro-industry
YC   Housing construction
YY   Other domestic and international trade
YW   Other industry
YD   Petrochemicals and fertilizers
YZ   General industry and trade sector

Energy and mining
LA   District heating and energy-efficiency services
LB   Mining and other extractive
LC   Oil and gas
LD   Power
LE   Renewable energy
LZ   General energy sector

Transportation
TV   Aviation
TP   Ports, waterways, and shipping
TW   Railways
TA   Roads and highways
TZ   General transportation sector

Water, sanitation, and flood protection
WD   Flood protection
WA   Sanitation
WS   Sewerage
WB   Solid waste management
WC   Water supply
WZ   General water, sanitation, and flood

Additional Country Resources

World Bank and International Finance Corporation (IFC) regional Web sites serve as portals to country-specific Web sites or pages (see box G.1). Those country-specific Web pages typically provide a brief summary of activities and issues in the country, with links to specific projects, economic data and statistics, publications, Web sites of the country's government, and related news.

Countries that have relevant resources are included in the country listing that follows. See chapter 4 ("World Bank Group Countries and Regions") for regional categorizations. See appendix D for information about membership status within the five Bank Group institutions.

Bank Group offices sometimes maintain their own Web sites in addition to the regional sites listed in box G.1. These Web site addresses are provided, along with other contact information, in the country listing.

The country listing is arranged alphabetically by country. The listing includes the following information:

- *Bank Group Offices.* World Bank, IFC, and Multilateral Investment Guarantee Agency (MIGA) offices in member countries are listed, including World Bank libraries and public information centers (PICs) where applicable. Many World Bank country offices house a PIC that disseminates information on the Bank Group's work. Most PICs have project documents specific to the country in which the office is located. PIC Europe in Paris and PIC Tokyo offer the complete range of Bank operational documents for all member countries and maintain libraries of recent World Bank publications. The symbol 📖 indicates that a PIC is attached to a country office.

- *World Bank Depository and Regional Libraries.* Each depository library is entitled to a free copy of each formal publication of the Bank Group. A depository library must make its collection of Bank Group publications available to the public. Each regional library has a similar arrangement but receives only formal publications that are related to its World Bank region.

- *Distributors of World Bank Group Publications.* The Bank Group encourages customers outside the United States to order through their local distributor, but it also sells direct to all member countries.

Regional Web Sites

Sub-Saharan Africa
World Bank vice presidency: http://www.worldbank.org/afr
IFC regional department: http://www.ifc.org/africa
Public information centers: http://www.worldbank.org/infoshop/afric.htm

East Asia and the Pacific
World Bank vice presidency: http://lnweb18.worldbank.org/eap/eap.nsf
IFC regional department: http://www.ifc.org/asia
Public information centers: http://www.worldbank.org/infoshop/eap.htm

South Asia
World Bank vice presidency: http://lnweb18.worldbank.org/sar/sa.nsf
IFC regional department: http://www.ifc.org/southasia
Public information centers: http://www.worldbank.org/infoshop/s_asia.htm

Europe and Central Asia
World Bank vice presidency: http://lnweb18.worldbank.org/eca/eca.nsf
IFC regional department: http://www.ifc.org/europe
Public information centers: http://www.worldbank.org/infoshop/eca.htm

Latin America and the Caribbean
World Bank vice presidency: http://wbln0018.worldbank.org/lac
IFC regional department: http://www.worldbank.org/lac
Public information centers: http://www.worldbank.org/infoshop/lac.htm

Middle East and North Africa
World Bank vice presidency: http://lnweb18.worldbank.org/mna/mena.nsf
IFC regional department: http://www.ifc.org/mena
Public information centers: http://www.worldbank.org/infoshop/mena.htm

North America and Western Europe
World Bank Europe vice presidency: http://www.worldbank.org/europe

- *Publication Discount.* Bank Group publications are sold at discounts of 35 percent or 75 percent off the list price to customers in many developing countries, depending on the country's income level. These discounts are assessed annually on the basis of new economic data. Discounts listed below were valid through May 2003. For full listings, including all nonsovereign territories, see <http://publications.worldbank.org/discounts>.
- *Selected Titles.* A list is provided of selected formal Bank Group publications related to individual countries or a small group of countries.

Country Listing

Afghanistan

Bank Group offices
World Bank
Street No. 15, House No. 19
Wazir Akbar Khan
Kabul, Afghanistan
Tel: (0092) 7207 9192

Publication discount: 75 percent

Albania

Bank Group offices
World Bank
Deshmoret e 4 Shkurtit 34
Tirana, Albania
Tel: (355-42) 405-87
Fax: (355-42) 405-90

International Finance Corporation
(Same address as World Bank)
Tel: (355-42) 300-17
Fax: (355-42) 405-90

Depository and regional libraries
Scientific Library of Polytechnic University
[depository]
Sheshi "Nene Tereza"
Tirana, Albania
Tel: (355-42) 264-87
Fax: (355-42) 264-87
Web: http://irclibrary.homestead.com/
index.html

Distribution of Bank Group publications
Adrion Books
Sami Frasheri Str.
P20/1 Shk.1 Ap.2
Tirana, Albania
Tel: (355-42) 400-18
Fax: (355-42) 352-42
E-mail: adrion@albaniaonline.net

Publication discount: 75 percent

Selected titles
- *Albania: Filling the Vulnerability Gap*
- *The Albanian Collateral Law System Handbook*
- *Financing Efficiency and Equity in Albanian Education*
- *Household Welfare, the Labor Market, and Public Programs in Albania*
- *Poverty in Albania: A Qualitative Assessment*
- *Social Assistance in Albania: Decentralization and Targeted Transfers*
- *Structural Adjustment in the Transition: Case Studies from Albania, Azerbaijan, Kyrgyz Republic, and Moldova*

Algeria

Depository and regional libraries
Institut Supérieur de Gestion et de
Planification [depository]
Centre d'Information Documentaire
ISGP B.P. 179
Rue Hadj Messaoud Nourredine-Baha
(Ex. Lido)
Bordj-El-Kiffan
Algiers, Algeria 16120
Tel: (213 2) 20 33 81
Fax: (213 2) 20 33 47 or 20 32 70

Publication discount: 75 percent

Angola

Bank Group offices
World Bank
Rua Alfredo Troni (Edificio BPC)
14 Andar, CP 1331
Luanda, Angola
Tel: (244-2) 394877, 394677, or 394727
Fax: (244-2) 394784
Web: http://www.worldbank.org/afr/ao

Publication discount: 75 percent

Argentina

Bank Group offices
Banco Mundial
Edificio Bouchard
Bouchard 547, 3er Piso
1106 Buenos Aires, Argentina
Tel: (54-11) 4316-9700 or 4316-9744
Fax: (54-11) 4313-1233

International Finance Corporation
Torre Fortabat
Bouchard 680, Piso 11
1106 Buenos Aires, Argentina
Tel: (54-11) 4114-7200
Fax: (54-11) 4312-7184

Depository and regional libraries
Ministerio de Economía y Obras y Servicios
Públicos [depository]
Centro de Documentación e Información
Hipólito Yrigoyen 250
Piso 2do, Oficina 200
1310 Buenos Aires, Argentina

Tel: (54-11) 4349-5559 or 4349-5554
Fax: (54-11) 4349-5540 or 4349-8593
Web: http://cdi.mecon.gov.ar

UNEP Liaison Committee in Argentina
[regional]
Information Centre
Av. Velez Sarsfield 2300
5000 Córdoba, Argentina
Tel: (54-351) 468-8696
Fax: (54-351) 422-6304
Web: http://www.ceapnuma.org.ar

Universidad Nacional del Litoral [depository]
Facultad de Ciencias Económicas Biblioteca
25 de Mayo 1783
3000 Santa Fe, Argentina
Tel: (54-342) 457-1179, 457-1180, or 457-1181
Fax: (54-342) 457-1179, 457-1180, or 457-1181
Web: http://www.unl.edu.ar

Distribution of Bank Group publications
World Publications SA
Av. Córdoba 1877
1120 Buenos Aires, Argentina
Tel: (54-11) 4815-8156
Fax: (54-11) 4815-8156
E-mail: wpbooks@wpbooks.com.ar
Web: http://www.wpbooks.com.ar

Publication discount: 35 percent

Selected titles
* Argentina: From Insolvency to Growth
* Black December: Banking Instability, the Mexican Crisis, and Its Effect on Argentina
* Competition Policy and MERCOSUR

Armenia

Bank Group offices
World Bank
Republic Square
9 Vazgen Sargsyan Street
Yerevan 375010, Armenia
Tel: (374-1) 52-48-84
Fax: (374-1) 52-17-87

International Finance Corporation
Republic Square
2 Khorhertarani Street
Yerevan 10, Armenia
Tel: (374-2) 54-52-41
Fax: (374-1) 54-52-45

Depository and regional libraries
National Library of Armenia [depository]
72 Terian Street
Yerevan 375009, Armenia
Tel: (374-2) 52-77-82
Fax: (374-2) 52-97-11
Web: http://www.iatp.am/sites/nla/index.html

Publication discount: 75 percent

Selected titles
* Armenia: Restructuring to Sustain Universal General Education
* Armenia: The Challenge of Reform in the Agricultural Sector
* Growth Challenges and Government Policies in Armenia
* Utility Pricing and the Poor: Lessons from Armenia

Australia

Bank Group offices
International Finance Corporation and FIAS
Asia Pacific Regional Office
Level 18, CML Building
14 Martin Place
Sydney, NSW 2000, Australia
Tel: (61-2) 9223-7155
Fax: (61-2) 9223-7152

IFC South Pacific Project Facility
(Same address as above)
Tel: (61-2) 9233-7773
Fax: (61-2) 9223-2533

Depository and regional libraries
National Library of Australia [depository]
Parkes Place
Canberra, ACT 2600, Australia
Tel: (61-2) 6262-1111
Fax: (61-2) 6273-4322
Web: http://www.nla.gov.au

Distribution of Bank Group publications
D.A. Information Services
648 Whitehorse Road
Mitcham, Victoria 3132, Australia
Tel: (61-3) 9210-7777
Fax: (61-3) 9210-7788
E-mail: service@dadirect.com.au
Web: http://www.dadirect.com.au
[Also distributes to Fiji, Papua New Guinea, the Solomon Islands, Samoa, and Vanuatu]

Austria

Depository and regional libraries
Institut für Höhere Studien [depository]
Bibliothek
Stumpergasse 56
1060 Vienna, Austria
Tel: (43 1) 59991 236
Fax: (43 1) 59991 555
Web: http://www.ihs.ac.at

Distribution of Bank Group publications
UNO-VERLAG
Am Hofgarten 10
D-53113 Bonn
Tel: (49 228) 949 020
Fax: (49 228) 949 0222
E-mail: fischer@uno-verlag.de
Web: http://www.uno-verlag.de

Azerbaijan

Bank Group offices
World Bank and International Finance
Corporation 📖
91-95 Mirza Mansur St., Icheri Sheher
370004 Baku, Azerbaijan
Tel: (994-12) 92-28-07 or 92-19-41
Fax: (994-12) 92-14-79

Depository and regional libraries
Khazar University [regional]
Mehsety Street 11
370133 Baku, Azerbaijan
Tel: (994-12) 21-79-16
Fax: (994-12) 98-93-79
Web: http://www.khazar.org

M. F. Akhundov State Library
[depository]
Foreign Literature Department
ul. Khagani 29
370601 Baku, Azerbaijan
Tel: (994-12) 93-40-03 or 93-64-03

Distribution of Bank Group publications
ASLAN
T.Mammedov St., 20, Apt.4, Baku,
Azerbaijan 370021
Tel: (994 12) 97-16-63
Fax: (994 12) 97-78-42
E-mail: aslan47@mail.ru

Publication discount: 75 percent

Selected titles
• *Structural Adjustment in the Transition: Case*

Studies from Albania, Azerbaijan, Kyrgyz Republic, and Moldova

Bahrain

Depository and regional libraries
University of Bahrain [depository]
University Library
P.O. Box 32038
Sakhir, Bahrain
Tel: (973) 449 257
Fax: (973) 449 838
Web: http://www.uob.bh/library/
index.htm

Publication discount: 35 percent

Bangladesh

Bank Group offices
World Bank 📖
3A Paribagh, Ground Floor, Room 105
G.P.O. Box 97
Dhaka 1000, Bangladesh
Tel: (880-2) 861-056 through
861-068 or 966-9301 through
966-9308, ext. 105
Fax: (880-2) 863-220

International Finance Corporation
(Same address as World Bank)
Tel: (880-2) 861-1056 or 966-9301
Fax: (880-2) 861-7521
E-mail: Bangladesh@ifc.org

Depository and regional libraries
Bangladesh Academy for Rural Development
[depository]
Akhter Hameed Khan Library
Kotbari
Comilla 3503, Bangladesh
Tel: (880-81) 642-8415

Bangladesh Institute of Development Studies
[regional]
Library and Documentation Centre
Sher-e-Bangla Nagar
Dhaka 1207, Bangladesh
G.P.O. Box 3854
Dhaka 1000, Bangladesh
Tel: (880-2) 912-5004 or 911-8999
Fax: (880-2) 813-023
Web: http://www.bids-bd.org

Bangladesh Public Administration Training
Centre Library [depository]

Library and Training Aids
Savar
Dhaka 1343, Bangladesh
Tel: (880-2) 831-715 through 831-720
Fax: (880-2) 933-2016

Centre on Integrated Rural Development for
Asia and the Pacific [depository]
Documentation and Information Division
Chameli House
17 Topkhana Road
G.P.O. Box 2883
Dhaka 1000, Bangladesh
Tel: (880-2) 956-3384, 956-4776,
or 956-4772
Fax: (880-2) 956-2035

Micro Industfs Development Assistance and
Services Library [depository]
Recife
Dhanmondi R/Area
Dhaka 1209, Bangladesh
G.P.O. Box 800
Dhaka 1000, Bangladesh
Tel: (880-2) 816-0945, 816-1867, or 911-1920
Fax: (880-2) 811-1188 or 811-2680

Distribution of Bank Group publications
Micro Industries Development Assistance
and Services
House 5, Road 16
Dhanmondi R/Area
Dhaka 1209, Bangladesh
Tel: (880-2) 326-427
Fax: (880-2) 811-1188
E-mail: midas@aitlbd.net

Publication discount: 75 percent

Selected titles
* *Bangladesh: The Experience and Perceptions of Public Officials*
* *Bangladesh: Financial Accountability for Good Governance*
* *Bangladesh: From Counting the Poor to Making the Poor Count*
* *Bangladesh: Progress through Partnership*
* *The Bangladesh Rural Advancement Committee's Credit Programs: Performance and Sustainability*
* *Developing the Nonfarm Sector in Bangladesh: Lessons from Other Asian Countries*
* *Education Achievements and School Efficiency in Rural Bangladesh*
* *Grameen Bank: Performance and Sustainability*
* *Household and Intrahousehold Impact of the Grameen Bank and Similar Targeted Credit Programs in Bangladesh*

* *Leveling the Playing Field: Giving Girls an Equal Chance for Basic Education—Three Countries' Efforts*
* *The Role of Family Planning and Targeted Credit Programs in Demographic Change in Bangladesh*
* *Targeted Credit Programs and Rural Poverty in Bangladesh*

Barbados

Depository and regional libraries
University of the West Indies [depository]
Main Library
Cave Hill
Bridgetown, Barbados
Tel: (246) 417 4449
Fax: (246) 417 4460

Publication discount: 35 percent

Belarus

Bank Group offices
World Bank 📖
2A Gertsena Str.
Minsk 220030, Belarus
Tel: (375-172) 26-52-84
Fax: (375-172) 11-03-14
Web: http://www.worldbank.org.by

International Finance Corporation
6A Partizansky Prospekt
Minsk 220033, Belarus
Tel: (3725-172) 13-25-24
Fax: (3725-172) 22-74-40

Depository and regional libraries
Presidential Library [depository]
House of Government
Minsk 220010, Belarus
Tel: (375-172) 22-66-27
Fax: (375-172) 20-12-09

Publication discount: 75 percent

Selected titles
* *Belarus: Prices, Markets, and Enterprise Reform*
* *Farm Sector Restructuring in Belarus: Progress and Constraints*

Belgium

Bank Group offices
World Bank, European Union Liaison
Rue Montoyer 10, Bte 16
1000 Brussels, Belgium
Tel: (32 2) 552 00 52
Fax: (32 2) 552 00 25
Web: http://wbln0018.worldbank.org/EURVP/

web.nsf/Pages/Brussels%20HOME%20PAGE

Depository and regional libraries
University of Antwerp [depository]
UFSIA Central Library
Prinsstraat 9
2000 Antwerpen, Belgium
Tel: (32 3) 220 40 19
Fax: (32 3) 220 44 37
Web: http://lib.ua.ac.be

Distribution of Bank Group publications
Jean de Lannoy
Av. du Roi 202
1060 Brussels, Belgium
Tel: (32 2) 538 51 69
Fax: (32 2) 538 08 41
Web: http://www.jean-de-lannoy.be
E-mail: jean.de.lannoy@euronet.be

Benin

Bank Group offices
World Bank 📖
Zone Residentielle de la Radio
P.O. Box 03-2112
Cotonou, Benin
Tel: (229) 31-21-24, 31-23-08, or 31-52-69
Fax: (229) 31-27-51 or 31-58-39

Depository and regional libraries
Benin University Library [regional]
04 B.P. 789
Campus d'Abomey, Calavi
Cadjehoun, Cotonou, Benin
Tel: (229) 36-01-01
Fax: (229) 36-01-01

Publication discount: 75 percent

Bolivia

Bank Group offices
World Bank and International Finance
Corporation
Calle Fernando Guachalla #342
Edificio Victor, Piso 9
La Paz, Bolivia
Tel: (591-2) 244-3133
Fax: (591-2) 212-5065

Depository and regional libraries
Academia Nacional de Ciencias [depository]
Biblioteca
P.O. Box 5829
Av. 16 de Julio 1732
La Paz, Bolivia

Tel: (591-2) 319-748
Fax: (591-2) 379-681

Unidad de Análisis de Políticas Sociales y
Económicas Library [regional]
Centro de Documentación
P.O. Box 12087
Av. Mariscal Santa Cruz
Edificio Palacio de las Comunicaciones,
Piso 18
La Paz, Bolivia
Tel: (591-2) 379-493, 375-512, 374-628, or
369-905
Fax: (591-2) 372-333

Universidad Andina Simón Bolívar [regional]
Centro de Información, Biblioteca
P.O. Box 545
Sucre, Bolivia
Tel: (591-64) 602-65 or 620-21
Fax: (591-64) 608-33
Web: http://www.uasb.edu.bo

Distribution of Bank Group publications
Martínez Acchini Libros
Av. Arce 2132 Edificio
Illampu P.B.
5349 La Paz, Bolivia
Tel: (591-2) 278-3239
Fax: (591-2) 278-4209
E-mail: gerencia@martinezacchini.com

Publication discount: 75 percent

Selected titles
* *Agricultural Trade Policies in the Andean Group: Issues and Options*
* *The Demand for Medical Care: Evidence from Urban Areas in Bolivia*
* *An Environmental Study of Artisanal, Small and Medium Mining in Bolivia, Chile, and Peru*
* *Poverty and Nutrition in Bolivia*
* *Setting Priorities for Environmental Management: An Application to the Mining Sector in Bolivia*

Bosnia and Herzegovina

Bank Group offices
World Bank
Hamdije Kresevljakovica 19
71000 Sarajevo, Bosnia and Herzegovina
Tel: (387-33) 251-500 or 251-509
Fax: (387-71) 440-108
Web: http://www.worldbank.org.ba

International Finance Corporation and World
Bank Business Development/PIC 📖
(Same address as World Bank)
Tel: (387-33) 440-293
Fax: (387-33) 440-108

International Finance Corporation
Vase Palagica 12
51000 Banja Luka, Bosnia and Herzegovina
Tel: (387-33) 319-680
Fax: (387-33) 319-683

Depository and regional libraries
National and University Library of Bosnia and
Herzegovina [depository]
Zmaja od Bosne 8B
71000 Sarajevo, Bosnia and Herzegovina
Tel: (387-71) 275-312
Fax: (387-71) 533-204
Web: http://www.nub.ba

Publication discount: 75 percent

Selected titles
* *Bosnia and Herzegovina: From Recovery to
  Sustainable Growth*
* *Bosnia and Herzegovina: Post-Conflict
  Reconstruction*
* *Bosnia and Herzegovina: Toward Economic
  Recovery*

Botswana

Depository and regional libraries
Institute of Development Management
[regional]
Library
P.O. Box 1357
Mobutu and Tlokweng Rd. Circle
BNPC/IDM Building Complex
Gaborone, Botswana
Tel: (267) 312 371
Fax: (267) 313 296

Botswana National Library Service [regional]
329 Independence Avenue
Gaborone, Botswana
Tel: (267) 352 397
Fax: (267) 301 149

University of Botswana [depository]
Library
Private Bag
Maputo Drive
Gaborone 00390, Botswana
Tel: (267) 355 2300
Fax: (267) 357 291

Distribution of Bank Group publications
See South Africa

Publication discount: 35 percent

Brazil

Bank Group offices
Banco Mundial 📖
Setor Comercial Norte, Quadra 2, Lote A
Ed. Corporate Financial Center, Cj. 303/304
Brasília DF 70712-900, Brazil
Tel: (55-61) 329-1000
Fax: (55-61) 329-1010
Web: http://www.bancomundial.org.br

Banco Mundial
Edifício SUDENE
Cidade Universitária, Sala 108
Recife PE 50670-900, Brazil
Tel: (55-81) 3453-1644
Fax: (55-81) 3453-4624

Banco Mundial
Rua Oswaldo Cruz, 1
Ed. Beira Mar Trade Center, Sala 1710,
Meireles
Fortaleza CE 60125-150, Brazil
Tel: (55-85) 242-7200
Fax: (55-85) 242-7177

International Finance Corporation
Rua Redentor, 14
Ipanema
Rio de Janeiro CEP 22421-030, Brazil
Tel: (55-21) 2525-5850
Fax: (55-21) 2525-5879

International Finance Corporation
Av. Roque Petroni Jr. 999
8th Floor, Rooms 81 and 82
São Paulo SP CEP 04707-910, Brazil
Tel: (55-11) 5185-6888
Fax: (55-11) 5181-6890

Depository and regional libraries
Instituto de Pesquisa Economica Aplicada
[regional]
Coordenação de Documentação e Biblioteca
Caixa Postal 03784
Ed. BNDES, 2 andar
SBS
Brasília DF 70076-900, Brazil
Tel: (55-61) 315-5318
Fax: (55-61) 315-5148
Web: http://www.ipea.gov.br

Faculdade Federal de Odontologia de
Diamantina [depository]
Rua de Gloria 187, Centro
Diamantina MG 39100-00, Brazil
Tel: (55-38) 3531-1030

Universidade Federal de Pernambuco
[depository]
Biblioteca Setorial Reitor Edinaldo, CCSA
Av. Dos Economistas, S/N
Cidade Universitária
Recife PE 50732-970, Brazil
Tel: (55-81) 271-885, 271-8881
Fax: (55-81) 271-8364

Universidade Santa Ursula [depository]
Instituto de Ciencias Economicas e Gestao
Caixa Postal 16.086
Rua Fernando Ferrari 75
Predio VI, Sala 1102, Botafogo
Rio de Janeiro RJ 22231-040, Brazil
Tel: (55-21) 551-8648
Fax: (55-21) 551-1992
Web: http://www.usu.br

Fernand Braudel Institute of World Economics
[depository]
Library
Rua Ceara 2
Higienopolis
São Paulo SP 01243-010, Brazil
Tel: (55-11) 3824-9633
Fax: (55-11) 825-2637
Web: http://www.braudel.org.br

Distribution of Bank Group publications
Editora UNESP
Praça da Sé, 108
São Paulo, SP
CEP 01001-900
Tel: (11) 3242-7171
Fax: (011) 3242-7172
e-mail: feu@editora.unesp.br

Publicações Tecnicas Internacionais Ltda.
Rua Peixoto Gomide, 209
Bela Vista
São Paulo SP 01409-901, Brazil
Tel: (55-11) 259-6644
Fax: (55-11) 258-6990
E-mail: info@pti.com.br
Web: http://www.pti.com.br

Publication discount: 35 percent

Selected titles
- *Brazil: Critical Issues in Social Security*
- *Brazil: Forests in the Balance: Challenges of Conservation with Development*
- *Competition Policy and MERCOSUR*
- *Educação Secundaria no Brasil: Chegou a Hora (in Portuguese)*
- *Higher Education in Brazil: Challenges and Options*
- *Institutional and Entrepreneurial Leadership in the Brazilian Science and Technology Sector: Setting a New Agenda*
- *Macroeconomic Crises, Policies, and Growth in Brazil, 1964–90*

Bulgaria

Bank Group offices
World Bank 📖
World Trade Center, INTERPRED
36 Dragan Tsankov Blvd.
1057 Sofia, Bulgaria
Tel: (359-2) 969-7229
Fax: (359-2) 971-2045
Web: http://www.worldbank.bg

International Finance Corporation
(Same address as World Bank)
Tel: (359-2) 9181-4225
Fax: (359-2) 971-2045

Depository and regional libraries
American University in Bulgaria [depository]
University Library
1 Georgi Izmerliev Sq.
2700 Blagoevgrad, Bulgaria
Tel: (359-73) 738-8330
Fax: (359-73) 738-8377
Web: http://www.aubg.bg

Ivan Vazov National Library [regional]
17 Avk. Veleshki Str.
4000 Plovdiv, Bulgaria
Tel: (359-32) 625-046
Fax: (359-32) 267-623

Ljuben Karavelov Rousse Regional Library
[regional]
1 Dondukov-Korsakov Str.
7000 Rousse, Bulgaria
Tel: (359-82) 224-554
Fax: (359-82) 272-131

Bulgarian Academy of Sciences [depository]
Central Library
15 Noemvri Str. 1

1040 Sofia, Bulgaria
Tel: (359-2) 987-8966
Fax: (359-2) 986-2500
Web: http://www.cl.bas.bg

Center for the Study of Democracy
[depository]
Library
5 Alexander Zhendov
1113 Sofia, Bulgaria
Tel: (359-2) 971-3000, ext. 351
Fax: (359-2) 971-2233
Web: http://www.csd.bg

University of Economics [depository]
Library
Bul. "Kniaz Boris I" No. 77
9002 Varna, Bulgaria
Tel: (359-52) 225-031
Fax: (359-52) 225-031

Publication discount: 75 percent

Selected titles
* *Bulgaria: The Dual Challenge of Transition and Accession*
* *Bulgaria: Public Expenditure Issues and Directions for Reform*
* *The Current Regulatory Framework Governing Business in Bulgaria*
* *Financing Government in the Transition— Bulgaria: The Political Economy of Tax Policies, Tax Bases, and Tax Evasion*
* *Food and Agriculture in Bulgaria: The Challenge of Preparing for EU Accession*
* *From Transition to Accession: Developing Stable and Competitive Financial Markets in Bulgaria*
* *From Transition to EU Accession: The Bulgarian Labor Market During the 1990s*

Burkina Faso

Bank Group offices
World Bank 📖
Immeuble BICIA-B siège, 3e et 4e étage
B.P. 622
Ouagadougou 01, Burkina Faso
Tel: (226) 30 62 37 or 30 72 57
Fax: (226) 30 86 49

Depository and regional libraries
Centre Régional pour l'Eau Potable et
l'Assainissement [regional]
Codin
03 B.P. 7112

Ouagadougou 03, Burkina Faso
Tel: (226) 36 62 10 or 36 62 11
Fax: (226) 36 62 08
Web: http://www.oieau.fr/crepa

Publication discount: 75 percent

Selected titles
* *The Dynamics of Education Policymaking: Case Studies of Burkina Faso, Jordan, Peru, and Thailand*

Burundi

Bank Group offices
World Bank 📖
Avenue du 18 Septembre
P.O. Box 2637
Bujumbura, Burundi
Tel: (257) 22 24 43 or 22 32 69
Fax: (257) 22 60 05

Publication discount: 75 percent

Cambodia

Bank Group offices
World Bank Liaison Office 📖
164 Pasteur Street
Phnom Penh, Cambodia
Tel: (855-23) 211-751
Fax: (855-23) 721-752
Web: http://www.worldbank.org/kh

PIC 📖
113 Norodom Blvd.
Phnom Penh, Cambodia
Tel: (855-23) 213-538 or 213-639
Fax: (855-23) 210-504 or 213-373

International Finance Corporation and IFC
Mekong Project Development Facility
113 Norodom Blvd.
Sangkat Chaktomuk
Phnom Penh, Cambodia
Tel: (855-23) 210-922
Fax: (855-23) 215-157

Depository and regional libraries
Ministry of Economic and Finance Institute
[depository]
Street 92, Sangkat Wat Phnom
Khan Daun Penh
Phnom Penh, Cambodia
Tel: (855-23) 430-556
Fax: (855-23) 430-168

Cambodia Development Resource Institute
[regional]
56 Street 315
Tuol Kork
Phnom Penh, Cambodia
Tel: (855-23) 880-734
Fax: (855-23) 366-094
E-mail: cdri@camnet.com.kh
Web: http://www.cdri.org.kh

Publication discount: 75 percent

Selected titles
•   *A Poverty Profile of Cambodia*
•   *Private Solutions for Infrastructure in Cambodia*

Cameroon

Bank Group offices
World Bank 📖
1792 rue Bastos Ekoudou
P.O. Box 1128
Yaoundé, Cameroon
Tel: (237) 220 3815 or 216 876
Fax: (237) 221 0722
Web: http://www.worldbank.org/infoshop/
piccameroon.htm

International Finance Corporation
Immeuble Flatters
96 Flatters Street, Suite 305
B.P. 4616
Douala, Cameroon
Tel: (237) 428 033 or (237) 429 451
Fax: (237) 428 014

Depository and regional libraries
Buea University Library [depository]
P.O. Box 63
Fak Division SWP
Buea, Cameroon
Tel: (237) 322 134
Fax: (237) 432 272

University of Dschang [regional]
Central Library
B.P. 255
Dschang, Cameroon
Tel: (237) 451 351
Fax: (237) 451 381

University of Ngaoundere [regional]
Library
P.O. Box 454
Ngaoundere, Cameroon
Tel: (237) 225 2767 or 764 4872
Fax: (237) 225 2599

Catholic University of Central Africa
[depository]
Main Library
B.P. 11628
Yaoundé, Cameroon
Tel: (237) 237 400 or 237 401
Fax: (237) 237 402

Distribution of Bank Group publications
NK Découverte (Tiger Bookshop)
B.P. 12784
Yaoundé, Cameroon
Tel: (237) 220 6166
Fax: (237) 223 2745

Publication discount: 75 percent

Selected titles
•   *Cameroon: Forest Sector Development in a
    Difficult Political Economy*

Canada
Web: http://www.worldbank.org/canada

Depository and regional libraries
University of Ottawa Network [depository]
Reference, Morisset Library
65 University Private
Ottawa, Ontario K1N 9A5
Tel: (613) 562-5800, ext. 3655
Fax: (613) 562-5133
Web: http://www.uottawa.ca/library

Distribution of Bank Group publications
Renouf Publishing Co. Ltd.
5369 Canotek Road
Ottawa, Ontario K1J 9J3
Tel: (613) 745-2665
Fax: (613) 745-7660
E-mail: order.dept@renoufbooks.com
Web: http://www.renoufbooks.com

Selected titles
•   *Large Mines and the Community: Socioeconomic
    and Environmental Effects in Latin America,
    Canada, and Spain*

Central African Republic

Bank Group offices
World Bank
Rue des Missions
B.P. 819
Bangui, Central African Republic
Tel: (236) 616138 or 616577
Fax: (236) 616087

Publication discount: 75 percent

Chad

Bank Group offices

World Bank
Quartier Curvette St. Martin
B.P. 146
N'Djamena, Chad
Tel: (235-52) 3247 or 3360
Fax: (235-52) 4484

Publication discount: 75 percent

Chile

Depository and regional libraries

Dirección de Presupuestos [depository]
Centro de Documentación, Biblioteca
Teatinos No. 120, Piso 12, Of. 24-25
Santiago, Centro, Chile
Tel: (56 2) 6717113, ext. 228, 229, 230, 231,
or 354
Fax: (56 2) 6711577
Web: http://www.dipres.cl

Publication discount: 35 percent

Selected titles

* *Chile: Enhancing Agricultural Competitiveness and Alleviating Rural Poverty*
* *Chile: Recent Policy Lessons and Emerging Challenges*
* *Chile: The Adult Health Policy Challenge*
* *Chile Health Insurance Issues: Old Age and Catastrophic Health Costs*
* *Chile's High Growth Economy: Poverty and Income Distribution 1987–1998*
* *Closing the Gap in Access to Rural Communication: Chile 1995–2002*
* *La Construcción de un Mercado de Capitales: El Caso de Chile (in Spanish)*
* *An Environmental Study of Artisanal, Small, and Medium Mining in Bolivia, Chile, and Peru*
* *The Market for Water Rights in Chile: Major Issues*
* *Water Allocation and Water Markets: An Analysis of Gains from Trade in Chile*

China

Bank Group offices

World Bank Resident Mission 📖
Building A, Fuhua Mansion, Floors 8–9
No. 8, Chaoyangmen Beidajie
Dongcheng District
Beijing 100027, China
Tel: (86-10) 6554-3361, ext. 2030
Fax: (86-10) 6554-1686
Web: http://www.worldbank.org.cn/English

International Finance Corporation
Tower B, Fuhua Mansion, 9th Floor
No. 8, Chaoyangmen Beidajie
Beijing 100027, China
Tel: (86-10) 6554-4191
Fax: (86-10) 6554-4192

International Finance Corporation
Suite 1107, Asia Pacific Finance Tower
Citibank Plaza, 3 Garden Road
Central, Hong Kong, China
Tel: (852) 2509-8100
Fax: (852) 2509-9363

Depository and regional libraries

Institute of World Economics and Politics
[depository]
Library
Chinese Academy of Social Sciences
5 Jianguomennei Dajie
Beijing 100732, China
Tel: (86-1) 6513-7744
Fax: (86-1) 6512-6105

National Library of China [depository]
Section of International Organizations and
Foreign Governments Publications
39 Bai-Shi-Qiao Road, Hai Dian District
Beijing 100081, China
Tel: (86-10) 6841-5566, ext. 5674 or 5274
Fax: (86-1) 6841-9271
Web: http://www.nlc.gov.cn

Tsinghua University Library [depository]
Tsinghua University
Beijing 100084, China
Tel: (86-10) 6278-4591
Fax: (86-10) 6259-1758
E-mail: lgl-lib@mail.tsinghua.edu.cn or
tsg@mail.tsinghua.edu.cn
Web: http://www.lib.tsinghua.edu.cn

Jilin University [depository]
Library
Exchange and Gift Section
Jie Fang Da Lu 77
Changchun 130023, China
Tel: (86) 23189, ext. 313

Sichuan Provincial Library [depository]
15 Liansheng Xiang
Chengdu, Sichuan 610016, China
Tel: (86-28) 665-9219
Fax: (86-28) 666-6223

Chongqing Institute of Technology [regional]

Library
No. 4, Xingsheng Rd.
Yangjiapin
Chongqing 400050, China
Tel: (86-23) 6866-7556 or 6866-7449
Fax: (86-23) 6866-7294

Hong Kong Central Library [depository]
66 Causeway Road, Causeway Bay
Hong Kong, China
Tel: (852) 2921-0233
Fax: (852) 2881-5251

Wuhan University [depository]
Library of School of Business
Wuchang
Hubei 430072, China
Tel: (86-27) 8768-2120
Fax: (86-27) 8787-4150
Web: http://www.whu.edu.cn

Fudan University [depository]
School of Economics, Library
220 Handan Road
Shanghai 200433, China
Tel: (86-21) 6564-2668
Fax: (86-21) 6564-6456

Shanghai Academy of Social Sciences Library
[regional]
Acquisition
1575 Van Hang Tu Road
Shanghai 200042, China
Tel: (86-21) 6486-2266, ext. 1304
Fax: (86-21) 6427-6018

Shanghai University of Finance and Economics
[depository]
Library
777 Guoding Road
Shanghai 200433, China
Tel: (86-21) 6511-1000
Fax: (86-21) 6511-5680
Web: http://www.lib.shufe.edu.cn

Library of Nankai University [depository]
International Exchange
No. 94, Weijin Road
Tianjin 300071, China
Tel: (86-22) 2350-2410 or 2350-8763
Fax: (86-22) 2350-5633

University of Macao [depository]
Documentation Center of International

Library
P.O. Box 3001
Taipa, Macao, China
Tel: (853) 397-8186
Fax: (853) 397-8144
Web: http://www.umac.mo/dc

Distribution of Bank Group publications
China Book Import Center
35 Chegongzhuang Xilu
P.O. BOX 2825
Beijing 100044, China
Tel: (8610) 6843 7146
Fax: (8610) 6841 6126
E-mail: cbic5@mail.cibtc.com.cn

China Financial and Economic Publishing
House
Room No. 916, Xinzhi Massion
No. Jia 28, Fucheng Road, Haidan District
Beijing 100038, China
Tel: (86-10) 8819-0915
Fax: (86-10) 8819-0916
E-mail: shijingbook@yahoo.com

Chinese Corporation for Promotion
and Humanities
Building No. 7, 1-502
No. 81, Wu Ke Son Lu
Haidian District
Beijing 100039, China
Tel: (86-10) 6821-5048
Fax: (86-10) 6821-5048
E-mail: ccphibcd@yahoo.com

Publication discount: 75 percent

Selected titles
- *Accelerating China's Rural Transformation*
- *Assessing Markets for Renewable Energy for Rural Areas of Northwestern China*
- *At China's Table: Food Security Options*
- *China: A Strategy for International Assistance to Accelerate Renewable Energy Development*
- *China: Air, Land, and Water*
- *China: From Afforestation to Poverty Alleviation and Natural Forest Management*
- *China: Higher Education Reform*
- *China: Internal Market Development and Regulation*
- *China: Issues and Options in Greenhouse Gas Emissions Control*
- *China: Overcoming Rural Poverty*
- *China: Power Sector Regulation in a Socialist Market Economy*

- *China: The Achievement and Challenge of Price Reform*
- *China: Urban Land Management in an Emerging Market Economy*
- *China and the Knowledge Economy: Seizing the 21st Century*
- *China Engaged: Integration with the Global Economy*
- *China 2020: Development Challenges in the New Century*
- *China's Emerging Private Enterprises: Prospects for the New Century China's Management of Enterprise Assets: The State as Shareholder*
- *China's Non-Bank Financial Institutions: Trust and Investment Companies*
- *The Chinese Economy: Fighting Inflation, Deepening Reforms*
- *Clear Water, Blue Skies: China's Environment in the New Century*
- *Corporate Governance and Enterprise Reform in China: Building the Institutions of Modern Markets*
- *The Dynamics of Urban Growth in Three Chinese Cities*
- *Energy Demand in Five Major Asian Developing Countries: Structure and Prospects*
- *Enterprise Reform in China: Ownership, Transition, and Performance*
- *Financing Health Care: Issues and Options for China*
- *Fostering Competition in China's Power Markets*
- *Liquefied Natural Gas in China: Options for Markets, Institutions, and Finance*
- *Macroeconomic Reform in China: Laying the Foundation for a Socialist Economy*
- *Mobilizing Domestic Capital Markets for Infrastructure Financing: International Experience and Lessons for China*
- *Multipurpose River Basin Development in China*
- *Old Age Security: Pension Reform in China*
- *Policy Options for Reform of Chinese State-Owned Enterprises*
- *Sharing Rising Incomes: Disparities in China*

Colombia

Bank Group offices
International Finance Corporation
Carrera 7, No. 71-21, Torre A
Piso 16, Edificio Fiduagraria
Santafé de Bogotá, Colombia
Tel: (57 1) 326-3600
Fax: (57 1) 317-4380

Depository and regional libraries
Universidad de Antioquia [regional]
Centro de Documentación

Calle 67, No. 53-108
Medellin, Colombia
Tel: (57 4) 210-5841 or 210-5844
Fax: (57 4) 210-5843

Banco de la Republica [depository]
Biblioteca Luis Angel Arango
Calle 11, No. 4-14
Santafé de Bogotá, Colombia
Tel: (57 1) 342-1111 or 282-7516
Fax: (57 1) 286-3881

Universidad Externado de Colombia [regional]
Biblioteca
Calle 12, No. 1-17 Este
Apartado Aéreo 034141
Santafé de Bogotá, Colombia
Tel: (57 1) 341-8196
Fax: (57 1) 341-8196

Distribution of Bank Group publications
Alfaomega Grupo Editor, S.A.
Calle 106ª No. 22-56
Bogotá, D.C.
Colombia
Tel: 619 7677
E-mail: scliente@alfaomega.com.co
Web: http://www.alfaomega.com.co

Infoenlace Ltda.
Av. Chile No. 13-23, Piso 3
Edificio Nueva Granada
Santafé de Bogotá, Colombia
Tel: (57 1) 600-9480 or 600-9482
Fax: (57 1) 248-0808 or 217-6435
E-mail: servicliente@infoenlace.com.co
Web: http://www.infoenlace.com.co

Publication discount: 75 percent

Selected titles
- *Agricultural Trade Policies in the Andean Group: Issues and Options*
- *Cali, Colombia: Toward a City Development Strategy*
- *Colombia: The Economic Foundation of Peace*
- *Colombia: Essays on Conflict, Peace, and Development*
- *Colombia: Paving the Way for a Results-Oriented Public Sector*
- *Colombia's Pension Reform: Fiscal and Macroeconomic Effects*
- *Courting Turmoil and Deferring Prosperity: Colombia between 1960 and 1990*
- *Review of Colombia's Agriculture and Rural Development Strategy*

- *Urban Poor Perceptions of Violence and Exclusion in Colombia*
- *Violence in Colombia: Building Sustainable Peace and Social Capital*

Republic of Congo

Bank Group offices
World Bank
Immeuble Arc
Avenue Amilcar Cabral, 5ème étage
B.P. 14536
Brazzaville, Republic of Congo
Tel: (242) 83-55-01
Fax: (242) 83-55-02

Publication discount: 75 percent

Demoftic Republic of Congo

Depository and regional libraries
Centre d'Etudes Pour l'Action Sociale [regional]
Library
B.P. 5717
9, Avenue Père Boka
Kinshasa, Gombe, Democratic Republic of Congo
Tel and Fax: (243 12) 884 685

Publication discount: 75 percent

Costa Rica

Depository and regional libraries
INCAE Library [depository]
Apartado 960
Alajuela 4050, Costa Rica
Tel: (506) 437 2276
Fax: (506) 433 9101
Web: http://www.incae.ac.cr

University of Costa Rica [depository]
Instituto de Investigaciones en Ciencias Economica
Library
San Pedro de Montes de Oca
San José, Costa Rica
Tel: (506) 207 5290
Fax: (506) 224 3682

Publication discount: 75 percent

Selected titles
- *Attracting High Technology Investment: Intel's Costa Rican Plant*
- *Costa Rica: A Pension Reform Strategy*

- *Costa Rica: Forest Strategy and the Evolution of Land Use*

Côte d'Ivoire

Bank Group offices
World Bank and International Finance Corporation 📖
Corner of Booker Washington and Jacques Aka Streets
B.P. 1850
Cocody, Abidjan, Côte d'Ivoire
Tel: (225) 44-22-27
Fax: (225) 44-16-87
Web: http://www.banquemondialeci.org/centre.html

IFC Africa Project Development Facility Office
Immeuble CCIA, 17th Floor
Abidjan-01, Côte d'Ivoire
Tel: (225) 21-96-97 or 21-23-03
Fax: (225) 21-61-51

MIGA
E-mail: Contact William Dadzie,
kdadzie@worldbank.org

Depository and regional libraries
African Development Bank [depository]
Library
01 B.P. 1387
Abidjan-01, Côte d'Ivoire
Tel: (225) 20-20-49-74 or 20-20-48-71
Fax: (225) 20-20-49-48

Institut Africain pour le Développement Economique et Social [regional]
Documentation
15, Avenue Jean Mermoz Cocody
08 B.P. 2088
Abidjan-08, Côte d'Ivoire
Tel: (225) 44-15-94 or 44-15-95
Fax: (225) 44-84-38

Distribution of Bank Group publications
Centre d'Edition et de Diffusion Africaines
04 B.P. 541
Abidjan-04, Côte d'Ivoire
Tel: (225) 24-65-10
Fax: (225) 25-05-67
E-mail: info@ceda-ci.com
Web: http://www.ceda-ci.com

Publication discount: 75 percent

Selected titles
- *Côte d'Ivoire: Country Assistance Review (in French)*

- *Determinants of Fertility and Child Mortality in Côte d'Ivoire and Ghana*
- *Unconditional Demand for Health Care in Côte d'Ivoire: Does Selection on Health Status Matter?*

Croatia

Bank Group offices
World Bank and International Finance Corporation 📖
Trg. J. F. Kennedya 6b, III Floor
10000 Zagreb, Croatia
Tel: (385-1) 23-87-222
Fax: (385-1) 23-87-200
Web: http://www.worldbank.hr

Depository and regional libraries
University Library Rijeka [regional]
Dolac 1
51000 Rijeka, Croatia
Tel: (385-51) 33-69-11
Fax: (385-51) 33-20-06

University of Split [depository]
Faculty of Economics
Radovanova 13
21000 Split, Croatia
Tel: (385-21) 36-60-33
Fax: (385-21) 36-60-26

National and University Library [depository]
Official Publications Collections
Hrvatske bratske zajednice bb
10000 Zagreb, Croatia
Tel: (385-1) 61-64-001
Fax: (385-1) 61-64-185
Web: http://www.nsk.hr

Distribution of Bank Group publications
Tamaris
Petrinjska 11
10000 Zagreb, Croatia
Tel: (385-1) 48-82-680
Fax: (385-1) 48-82-681

Publication discount: 35 percent

Selected titles
- *Regaining Fiscal Sustainability and Enhancing Effectiveness in Croatia: A Public Expenditure and Institutional Review*

Cyprus

Depository and regional libraries
Cyprus College [depository]
Library

6, Diogenes Street, Engomi
P.O. Box 2006
1516 Nicosia, Cyprus
Tel: (357 2) 713 000
Fax: (357 2) 662 051
Web: http://www.cycollege.ac.cy

Czech Republic

Bank Group offices
International Finance Corporation
Husova 5
1100 00 Prague, Czech Republic
Tel: (420-2) 24 401 402
Fax: (420-2) 24 401 41

Depository and regional libraries
Ekonomicko-správní Fakulta
Masarykovy Univerzity v Brne [regional]
Stredisko vedeckˇch informací
ESF MU, SVI
Lipova 41 A
659 79 Brno, Czech Republic
Tel: (420-5) 4352 3202
Fax: (420-5) 4352 3222
Web: http://www.econ.muni.cz/svi

State Scientific Library [depository]
Smetanovy sady 2
305 48 Plzen, Czech Republic
Tel: (420-19) 722 4249 or 722 6482
Fax: (420-19) 224 776

Charles University in Prague [depository]
CERGE-EI Library
P.O. Box 882
Politickych veznu 7
111 21 Prague 1, Czech Republic
Tel: (420-2) 24 005 180 or 24 005 145
Fax: (420-2) 24 211 374 or 24 227 143
Web: http://library.cerge.cuni.cz

National Library in Prague [depository]
Central Library of Economic Sciences
Klementinum 190
Prague 1, Czech Republic
Tel: (420-2) 21 663 260
Fax: (420-2) 21 663 261
Web: http://www.nkp.cz

Distribution of Bank Group publications
Dovoz Tisku Praha
Suweco CZ, CR 01/1751
Ceskomoravska 21 180 21
Prague 9, Czech Republic
Tel: (420-2) 66 035 364

Web: http://import@suweco.cz

Publication discount: 35 percent

Selected titles
- *Czech Republic: Capital Market Review*
- *Czech Republic: Completing the Transformation of Banks and Enterprises*
- *Czech Republic: Enhancing the Prospects for Growth with Fiscal Stability*
- *Czech Republic: Intergovernmental Fiscal Relations in the Transition*
- *Czech Republic: Toward EU Accession*
- *Food and Agriculture in the Czech Republic: From a "Velvet" Transition to the Challenges of EU Accession*
- *Overcoming Obstacles to Liberalization of the Telecom Sector in Estonia, Poland, the Czech Republic, Slovenia, and Hungary: An Overview of Key Policy Concerns and Potential Initiatives to Facilitate the Transition Process*
- *Private Sector Development during Transition: The Visegrad Countries*
- *Trade and Cost Competitiveness in the Czech Republic, Hungary, Poland, and Slovenia*

Denmark

Depository and regional libraries
Copenhagen Business School Library [depository]
Handelshogskolens Bibliotek
Solbjerg Plads 3
2000 Frederiksberg, Denmark
Tel: (45 38) 153666
Fax: (45 38) 153663
E-mail: hbk.lib@cbs.dk
Web: http://www.cbs.dk/library

Distribution of Bank Group publications
Samfundslitteratur
Solbjerg Plads 3
2000 Frederiksberg, Denmark
Tel: (45 38) 153870
Fax: (45 38) 153856
E-mail: ck@sl.cbs.dk
Web: http://www.sl.cbs.dk

Dominican Republic

Bank Group offices
International Finance Corporation
Calle Virgilio Díaz Ordoñez #36
Edificio Mezzo Tempo, Suite 401
Santo Domingo, Dominican Republic
Tel: (809) 566-6815
Fax: (809) 566-7746

Depository and regional libraries
Pontificia Universidad Católica Madre y Maestra [depository]
Sistema de Bibliotecas
Apartado 2748
Av. Abraham Lincoln Esq. Romulo Betancourt
Santo Domingo, Dominican Republic
Tel: (809) 534-0111, ext. 234 or 235
Fax: (809) 534-7060

Publication discount: 75 percent

Selected titles
- *The Demand for Health Care in Latin America: Lessons from the Dominican Republic and El Salvador*
- *Surveillance of Agricultural Prices and Trade: A Handbook for the Dominican Republic*

Ecuador

Bank Group offices
Banco Mundial
Calle 12 de Octubre y Cordero
World Trade Center
Torre B, Piso 13
Quito, Ecuador
Tel: (593-2) 220-204
Fax: (593-2) 220-205

Depository and regional libraries
Universidad San Francisco de Quito [depository]
Library
P.O. Box 17-12-841
Via Interoceánica y Jardines del Este Cumbayá
Quito, Ecuador
Tel: (593-2) 895-723, ext. 373
Fax: (593-2) 890-070

Distribution of Bank Group publications
Libri Mundi, Librería Internacional
Juan Leon Mera 851
P.O. Box 17-01-3029
Quito, Ecuador
Tel: (593-2) 521-606
Fax: (593-2) 504-209
E-mail: librimu1@librimundi.com.ec

Publication discount: 75 percent

Selected titles
- *Agricultural Trade Policies in the Andean Group: Issues and Options*
- *Constructing an Indicator of Consumption for the Analysis of Poverty: Principles and Illustrations*

with Reference to Ecuador
* *Crisis and Dollarization in Ecuador: Stability, Growth, and Social Equity*
* *Ecuador Gender Review: Issues and Recommendations*
* *Ecuador Poverty Report*

Arab Republic of Egypt

Bank Group offices
World Bank 📖
1191 Corniche El Nil Street
World Trade Center, 15th Floor
Cairo, Egypt
Tel: (20-2) 574-1670
Fax: (20-2) 574-1676

International Finance Corporation
World Trade Center
1191 Corniche El Nil Street
Boulac
Cairo, Egypt
Tel: (20-2) 579-9900 or 579-6565
Fax: (20-2) 579-2211

Depository and regional libraries
General Organization of the Alexandria Library [depository]
63 Soter Street
Shatby
Alexandria, Egypt
Tel: (20-3) 422-5002 or 422-3010
Fax: (20-3) 422-5002

Institute of National Planning [depository]
Documentation and Publishing Center
P.O. Box 11765
Salah Salem Street
Nasr City
Cairo, Egypt
Tel: (20-2) 263-6047
Fax: (20-2) 262-1151

Cairo University [regional]
Center for Agricultural Economic Studies Library
Faculty of Agriculture
Giza, Egypt
Tel: (20-2) 570-0995
Fax: (20-2) 570-0995

Distribution of Bank Group publications
MERIC (Middle East Readers Information Center)
2 Bahrat Aly Street

Building D, 1st Floor, Apt. 24
Cairo, Egypt
Tel: (20-2) 341-3824
Fax: (20-2) 341-9355
E-mail: order@meric-co.com
Web: http://www.meobserver.com.eg

Middle East Observer
41 Sherif Street
11111 Cairo, Egypt
Tel: (20-2) 392-6919
Fax: (20-2) 393-9732
E-mail: inquiry@meobserver.com
Web: http://www.meobserver.com
[For publications in French only]

Publication discount: 75 percent

Selected titles
* *Egypt in the Global Economy: Strategic Choices for Savings, Investment, and Long-Term Growth*
* *School Quality, Achievement Bias, and Dropout Behavior in Egypt*

El Salvador

Depository and regional libraries
Fundación Salvadoreña para el Desarrollo Económico y Social [depository]
Economic and Social Studies Department
Boulevard y Urbanización Santa Elena
Edificio Fusades
Antiguo Cuscatlan
La Libertad, El Salvador
Tel: (503) 278 3366
Fax: (503) 278 3371
Web: http://www.fusades.com.sv

Distribution of Bank Group publications
Editoriales La Ceiba S.A de C.V.
Plaza del Sol Local 1, Calle del Mediterráneo
Col. La Sultana
San Salvador, El Salvador
Tel: (503) 243 0931
E-mail: laceiba@navegante.com.sv

Publication discount: 75 percent

Selected titles
* *The Demand for Health Care in Latin America: Lessons from the Dominican Republic and El Salvador*
* *El Salvador: Meeting the Challenge of Globalization*
* *El Salvador: Post-Conflict Reconstruction*
* *El Salvador: Rural Development Study*

Estonia

Depository and regional libraries
National Library of Estonia [depository]
Tonismagi 2
Tallinn 15189, Estonia
Tel: (37 2) 630 7105
Fax: (37 2) 631 1417
Web: http://www.nlib.ee

Distribution of Bank Group publications
Krisostomus
Kuutri 16
Tartu 50002, Estonia
Tel: (37 27) 441 627
Fax: (37 27) 423 345
E-mail: Kriso@Kriso.Ee

Publication discount: 35 percent

Selected titles
* *Cost Benefit Analysis of Private Sector Environmental Investments: A Case Study of the Kunda Cement Factory*
* *Estonia: Implementing the EU Accession Agenda*
* *Estonia: The Transition to a Market Economy*
* *Overcoming Obstacles to Liberalization of the Telecom Sector in Estonia, Poland, the Czech Republic, Slovenia, and Hungary: An Overview of Key Policy Concerns and Potential Initiatives to Facilitate the Transition Process*

Ethiopia

Bank Group offices
World Bank and International Finance Corporation 📖
Worbek House, Ground Floor, Building Entrance
P.O. Box 5515, Bole Road
Addis Ababa, Ethiopia
Tel: (251-1) 627 700, ext. 207 or 208
Fax: (251-1) 627 717
Web: http://www.worldbank.org/afr/et

Depository and regional libraries
Addis Ababa University [depository]
Faculty of Business and Economics Library
P.O. Box 1176
Addis Ababa, Ethiopia
Tel: (251-1) 124 928 or 553 900 ext. 241 or 242
Fax: (251-1) 550 655

National Archives and Library of Ethiopia [depository]
P.O. Box 717
Addis Ababa, Ethiopia

Tel: (251-1) 530 058 or 512 241
Fax: (251-1) 512 889

United Nations Economic Commission for Africa [regional]
DISD/Library
P.O. Box 3001
Addis Ababa, Ethiopia
Tel: (251-1) 510 280
Fax: (251-1) 510 2180

Mekelle University [regional]
Faculty of Business and Econ Library
P.O. Box 451
Mekelle, Tigray, Ethiopia
Tel: (251-3) 400 144
Fax: (251-3) 402 044

Distribution of Bank Group publications
T.G.B. Roman Trading Enterprise
P.O. BOX 2076 code 1110
Addis Ababa
Ethiopia
Tel: 251-1-635973
E-mail: tesfayeg@telecom.net.et

Publication discount: 75 percent

Selected titles
* *Case Studies in War-to-Peace Transition: The Demobilization and Reintegration of Ex-Combatants in Ethiopia, Namibia, and Uganda*
* *Ethiopia: Social Sector Report*
* *The Impact of Economic Reforms on Rural Households in Ethiopia: A Study from 1989–1995*
* *Implementing the Ethiopian National Policy for Women: Institutional and Regulatory Issues*

Fiji

Depository and regional libraries
University of the South Pacific [depository]
Library
P.O. Box 1168
Suva, Fiji
Tel: (679) 313 900
Fax: (679) 300 830

Publication discount: 75 percent

Finland

Depository and regional libraries
Helsinki School of Economics [depository]
Library
Leppäsuonkatu 9 E

P.O. Box 149
00101 Helsinki, Finland
Tel: (358 9) 4313 8431
Fax: (358 9) 4313 8539
Web: http://helecon.hkkk.fi/library

Distribution of Bank Group publications
Akateeminen Kirjakauppa
PL 128 (Keskuskatu 1)
00101 Helsinki, Finland
Tel: (358 9) 121 4385
Fax: (358 9) 121 4450
E-mail: sps@akateeminen.com
Web: http://www.akateeminen.com

France

Bank Group offices
World Bank and World Bank Institute 📖
66, avenue d'Iéna
75116 Paris, France
Tel: (33-1) 40 69 30 10
Fax: (33-1) 40 69 30 64
Web: http://wbln0018.worldbank.org/eurvp/
web.nsf/Pages/EURVP+Home+Page

International Finance Corporation
(Same address as World Bank)
Tel: (33-1) 40 69 30 60
Fax: (33-1) 47 20 77 71

MIGA
(Same address as World Bank)
Tel: (33-1) 40 69 32 75
Fax: (33-1) 47 23 74 36

Depository and regional libraries
Documentation Française [depository]
Bibliothèque
29, quai Voltaire
75344 Paris Cedex 07, France
Tel: (33-1) 40 15 72 05
Fax: (33-1) 40 15 72 30

Distribution of Bank Group publications
Editions Eska
DJB/Offilib
12, rue du Quatre-Septembre
75002 Paris, France
Tel: (33-1) 42 86 55 66
Fax: (33-1) 42 60 45 35
E-mail: eska@club-internet.fr
Web: http://www.offilib.fr

The Gambia

Depository and regional libraries
Department of State for Trade Industry and
Employment [regional]
Documentation Center
Independence Dr.
Banjul, The Gambia
Tel: (220) 228 868
Fax: (220) 227 757

Management Development Institute
[depository]
Library and Documentation Centre
P.O. Box 2553
Serrekunda, The Gambia
Tel: (220) 392 873, 394 906, 392 871,
or 392 872
Fax: (220) 394 905

Publication discount: 75 percent

Georgia

Bank Group offices
World Bank and International Finance
Corporation
5A 1st Drive, Chavchavadze Ave.
Tbilisi 380079, Georgia
Tel: (995 32) 91-30-96 or 91-26-89
Fax: (995 32) 91-34-78 or (995 32) 91-23-71
Web: http://www.worldbank.org.ge

Depository and regional libraries
The National Parliamentary Library of Georgia
[depository]
7 Lado Gudiashvili Str.
Tbilisi 380005, Georgia
Tel: (995 32) 99-92-86
Fax: (995 32) 99-80-95
Web: http://www.nplg.gov.ge

Distribution of Bank Group publications
Prospero's Books
34 Rustaveli Ave.
Tbilisi 380008, Georgia
Tel and Fax: (995 32) 92-35-92
E-mail: prospero@access.sanet.ge

Publication discount: 75 percent

Germany

Bank Group offices
International Finance Corporation
Bockenheimer Landst 109

60325 Frankfurt, Germany
Tel: (49-69) 7434-8230
Fax: (49-69) 7434-8239

Depository and regional libraries
Staatsbibliothek zu Berlin, Preussischer
Kulturbesitz [depository]
Abteilung Amtsdruckschriften und
Internationaler
Amtlicher Schriftentausch
Potsdamer Strasse 33
10785 Berlin, Germany
Tel: (49-30) 266-2471
Fax: (49-30) 266-2341
Web: http://www.sbb.spk-berlin.de

Distribution of Bank Group publications
UNO-Verlag
Am Hofgarten 10
53113 Bonn, Germany
Tel: (49-228) 949 020
Fax: (49-228) 949 0222
E-mail: info@uno-verlag.de
Web: http://www.uno-verlag.de

Data Service and Information
Tel: (49-2843) 3220
E-mail: dsi@dsidata.com
Web: http://www.dsidata.com
[For electronic products only]

Selected titles
• *Intellectual Property Protection, Direct Investment,
   and Technology Transfer: Germany, Japan, and the
   United States*

Ghana

Bank Group offices
World Bank 📖
69 Dr. Isert Road
North Ridge Residential Area
P.O. Box M.27
Accra, Ghana
Tel: (233-21) 229-681 or 220-837
Fax: (233-21) 227-887

International Finance Corporation and Africa
Project Development Facility
150 A, Roman House
Roman Ridge
Accra, Ghana
Tel: (233-21) 778-109 or 779-805
Fax: (233-21) 776-245 or 774-961

Depository and regional libraries
University of Ghana [depository]
Balme Library
P.O. Box 24, Legon
Accra, Ghana
Tel: (233-21) 767-303
Fax: (233-21) 502-701

Ghana Institute of Management and Public
Administration [depository]
Library and Documentation Centre
Gimpa Greenhill
P.O. Box 50
Achimota, Ghana
Tel: (233-21) 401-683
Fax: (233-21) 405-805

University of Cape Coast [depository]
University Library
University Post Office
Cape Coast, Ghana
Tel: (233-42) 33482

Distribution of Bank Group publications
Epp Books Services
P.O. Box 44
TUC
Accra, Ghana
Tel: (233-21) 778-843
Fax: (233-21) 779-099
E-mail: epp@africaonline.com.gh

Publication discount: 75 percent

Selected titles
• *Contraceptive Use in Ghana: The Role of Service
   Availability, Quality, and Price*
• *Delayed Primary School Enrollment and Child
   Malnutrition in Ghana: An Economic Analysis*
• *Determinants of Fertility and Child Mortality in
   Côte d'Ivoire and Ghana*
• *Ghana Country Assistance Review: A Study in
   Development Effectiveness*
• *The Impact of the Quality of Health Care on
   Children's Nutrition and Survival in Ghana*
• *Investment in Human Capital: Schooling Supply
   Restraints in Rural Ghana*
• *Small Enterprises Adjusting to Liberalization in
   Five African Countries*
• *Supply and Demand for Finance of Small
   Enterprises in Ghana*

Greece

Depository and regional libraries
Centre of Planning and Economic Research
[depository]

Library
22, Hippokratous Str.
10680 Athens, Greece
Tel: (30 1) 362 8911
Fax: (30 1) 363 0122 or 361 1136
Web: http://www.kepe.gr

Distribution of Bank Group publications
Papasotiriou S.A.
35, Stournara Str.
10682 Athens, Greece
Tel: (30 1) 364 1826
Fax: (30 1) 364 8254
E-mail: pap4@ioa.forthnet.gr
Web: http://www.papasotiriou.gr

Guatemala

Bank Group offices
Banco Mundial
13 Calle 3-40, Zona 10
Edificio Atlantis, Nivel 14
Guatemala City, Guatemala
Tel: (502) 366-2044
Fax: (502) 366-1936 or 366-2033

International Finance Corporation
(Same address as Banco Mundial)
Tel: (502) 367-2275
Fax: (502) 366-9851

Depository and regional libraries
Banco de Guatemala [depository]
Biblioteca
7 Avenida 22-01, Zona 1
Guatemala City, Guatemala
Tel: (502) 230-6222
Fax: (502) 238-909
Web: http://www.banguat.gob.gt

Distribution of Bank Group publications
Librería Artemis Edinter, S.A.
12 Calle 10-55, Zona 1
Guatemala City, Guatemala
Tel: (502) 220-3645
Fax: (502) 232-9004
E-mail: artemisedint@gold.guate.net

Publication discount: 75 percent

Guinea

Bank Group offices
World Bank
Immeuble de l'Archevêché
Face Baie des Anges
B.P. 1420

Conakry, Guinea
Tel: (224) 41-27-70, 41-13-91, or 41-50-61
Fax: (224) 41-50-94

Distribution of Bank Group publications
Les Editions Ganndal
B.P. 542, Conakry - Rep. de Guinee
Tel/Fax: +224 46 35 07
E-mail: ganndal@afribone.net.gn

Publication discount: 75 percent

Selected titles
* *Measuring the Burden of Disease and the Cost-Effectiveness of Health Interventions: A Case Study in Guinea*

Guyana

Depository and regional libraries
Bank of Guyana [depository]
Library Division, Research Department
P.O. Box 1003
1 Ave. of the Republic
Georgetown, Guyana
Tel: (592 2) 632 50 through 632 59 or 632 61 through 632 65
Fax: (592 2) 729 65
Web: http://www.bankofguyana.org.gy

Publication discount: 75 percent

Selected titles
* *Institutional Environment and Public Officials' Performance in Guyana*

Haiti

Distribution of Bank Group publications
Culture Diffusion
76, Ave. John Brown (Lalue)
Port-au-Prince, Haiti
Tel: (509) 511 8090
Fax: (509) 223 4858

Publication discount: 75 percent

Honduras

Bank Group offices
Banco Mundial
Centro Financiero BANEXPO
Blvd. San José Bosco
4to. Piso, Colonial Payaqui
Apartado 3591
Tegucigalpa, Honduras
Tel: (504) 239-4551, 239-4552, 239-4553,

239-4554, or 239-4560
Fax: (504) 239-4555

Depository and regional libraries
Unidad de Apoyo Técnico [depository]
Library
Apartado Postal 4822
Edificio Ejecutivo Las Lomas, 4 Piso
Tegucigalpa, Honduras
Tel: (504) 239-2024, 239-2025, 239-4058, or
239-4059

SECPLAN [depository]
Coord y Presupuesto
P.O. Box 1327
Tegucigalpa, Honduras

Publication discount: 75 percent

Selected titles
· *Honduras: Toward Better Health Care for All*
· *The Participation of Nongovernmental Organizations in Poverty Alleviation: A Case Study of the Honduras Social Investment Fund Project*

Hungary

Bank Group offices
World Bank 📖
Bajcsy-Zsilinszky ut 42-46, 5th Floor
1054 Budapest, Hungary
Tel: (36-1) 374-9500
Fax: (36-1) 374-9510
Web: http://www.worldbank.hu

Depository and regional libraries
National Bank of Hungary [regional]
Research Library
Szabadság tér 8-9
1850 Budapest, Hungary
Tel: (36 1) 332-2722
Fax: (36 1) 331-9379
Web: http://www.mnb.hu

Janus Pannonius University Library
[depository]
Pf. 227
7601 Pécs, Hungary
Tel: (36 72) 325-466
Fax: (36 72) 324-780

Distribution of Bank Group publications
Euro Info Service
Szt. Istvan krt. 12. III emelet 1/A

1137 Budapest, Hungary
Tel: (36 1) 329-2487 or 329-2170
Fax: (36 1) 349-2053
E-mail: euroinfo@euroinfo.hu
Web: http://www.euroinfo.hu

Publication discount: 35 percent

Selected titles
· *Household Responses to Poverty and Vulnerability, Volume 2: Confronting Crisis in Angyalfold, Budapest, Hungary*
· *Hungary: A Regulatory and Structural Review of Selected Infrastructure Sectors*
· *Hungary: Foreign Trade Issues in the Context of Accession to the EU*
· *Hungary: Modernizing the Subnational Government System*
· *Hungary: Structural Reforms for Sustainable Growth*
· *Overcoming Obstacles to Liberalization of the Telecom Sector in Estonia, Poland, the Czech Republic, Slovenia, and Hungary: An Overview of Key Policy Concerns and Potential Initiatives to Facilitate the Transition Process*
· *The Pharmaceutical Industry in India and Hungary: Policies, Institutions, and Technological Development*
· *Private Sector Development during Transition: The Visegrad Countries*
· *Privatization of the Power and Natural Gas Industries in Hungary and Kazakhstan*
· *Trade and Cost Competitiveness in the Czech Republic, Hungary, Poland, and Slovenia*

India

Bank Group offices
World Bank 📖
70 Lodi Estate
New Delhi 110 003, India
Tel: (91-11) 461-7241 through 461-7244 or
461-9491 through 491-9493
Fax: (91-11) 461-9393

International Finance Corporation
No. 1, Panchseel Marg, Chanakyapuri
New Delhi 110 021, India
Tel: (91-11) 611-1306
Fax: (91-11) 611-1281
E-mail: SouthAsia@ifc.org

International Finance Corporation
Godrej Bhavan, 3rd Floor
Murzban Road
Fort, Mumbai 200 001, India
Tel: (91-22) 231-1235
Fax: (91-22) 231-1236

Depository and regional libraries

Indian Institute of Management, Ahmedabad
[depository]
Vikram Sarabhai Library
Vastrapur
Ahmedabad, Gujarat 380 015, India
Tel: (91-79) 640-7241 or 640-7263
Fax: (91-79) 642-7896

Guru Nanak Dev University [depository]
Punjab School of Economics Library
Amritsar, Punjab 143 005, India
Tel: (91-183) 258-841
Fax: (91-183) 258-819 or 258-820

Annamalai University [depository]
Sir C. P. Ramasamy Iyyer Library
Tamil Nadu, Annamalai Nagar 608 002, India
Tel: (91-44) 381-55
Fax: (91-44) 381-45 or 380-80

Institute for Social and Economic Change
[depository]
Library
Nagarabhavi P.O.
ISEC Campus
Bangalore, Karnataka 560 072, India
Tel: (91-80) 321-5468, 321-5592, or 321-5519
Fax: (91-80) 321-7008
Web: http://www.isec.ac.in

University of Mumbai [depository]
Jawaharlal Nehru Library
Vidyanagari
Santacruz (East)
Mumbai 400 098, India
Tel: (91-22) 652-6091, ext. 471, 472, or 380

Centre for Studies in Social Sciences, Calcutta
[depository]
Library
R-1 Baishnabghata-Patuli Township
Calcutta 700 094, India
Tel: (91-33) 462-7252 or 462-5794
Fax: (91-33) 462-6183

Institute of Economic Growth [depository]
University Enclave
Malkangang Road
Delhi 110 007, India
Tel: (91-11) 725-7365, 725-7288, or 725-7425
Fax: (91-11) 725-7410
Web: http://www.ieg.nic.in

Prof. S. S. Basavanal Library [depository]
Karnataka University

Pavate Nagar
Dharwad, Karnataka 580 003, India
Tel: (91-836) 742-291
Fax: (91-836) 747-884

Center for Economic and Social Studies
[regional]
Library
Nizamia Observatory Campus
Begumpet
Hyderabad, Andhra Pradesh 500 016, India
Tel: (91-40) 331-2789 or 332-6780
Fax: (91-40) 332-6808

Institute of Development Studies [depository]
Library
8-B Jhalana Institutional Area
Jaipur 302 002, India
Tel: (91-141) 270-5726
Fax: (91-141) 270-5348
Web: http://www.ids.org

Giri Institute of Development Studies
[depository]
Sector "O"
Aliganj Housing Scheme
Lucknow, Uttar Pradesh 226 020, India
Tel: (91-522) 373-640, 324-294, or 325-021
Fax: (91-522) 373-640

Uttar Pradesh Academy of Administration
[depository]
Library and Documentation Center
Mallital
Nainital, India
Tel: (91-5942) 361-49, 350-11, or 360-68
Fax: (91-5942) 352-03

Indian Institute of Public Administration
[depository]
Library
Indraprastha Estate
Ring Road
New Delhi 110 002, India
Tel: (91-11) 341-5383
Fax: (91-11) 331-9956

Institute for Financial Management and
Research [depository]
H. T. Parekh Library
30 Kothari Road
Nungambakkam, Chennai 600 034, India
Tel: (91-44) 827-3801
Fax: (91-44) 827-9208
Web: http://www.ifmr.com

Punjabi University [depository]
Department of Economics, Library
Patiala, Punjab 147 002, India
Tel: (91-175) 282-461 through 282-465,
ext. 6103
Fax: (91-175) 282-881

Gokhale Institute of Politics and Economics
[depository]
Library
Pune, Maharashtra 411 004, India
Tel: (91-212) 565-0287
Fax: (91-212) 565-2579 or 567-5600

Pt. Ravishankar Shukla University [depository]
Pt. Sundar Lal Sharma Library
Raipur, Madhya Pradesh 492 010, India
Tel: (91-771) 534-356 or 224-649
Fax: (91-771) 234-283

Kerala University Library [depository]
Palayam
Trivandrum, Kerala 695 034, India
Tel: (91-471) 247-7844
Fax: (91-471) 244-7158
Web: http://www.keralauniversity.edu

British Library (Ahmedabad) [regional]
Bhaikaka Bhavan
Law Garden
Ellisbridge
Ahmedabad 380 006, India

British Library (Hyderabad) [regional]
Sarovar Centre, 5-9-22
Hyderabad 500 063, India

British Library (Bangalore) [regional]
39 St. Mark's Road
Bangalore 560 001, India

Distribution of Bank Group publications
Allied Publishers Ltd.
751 Mount Road
Madras 600 002, India
Tel: (91-44) 852-3938
Fax: (91-44) 852-0649
E-mail: aplchn@vsnl.net

Bookwell Head Office
2/72, Nirankari Colony
Delhi, 110 009
Tel: (91-11) 725-1283
Sales Office: 24/4800, Ansari Road
Darya Ganj

New Delhi 110 002, India
Tel: (91-11) 326-8786 or 325-7264
Fax: (91-11) 328-1315
E-mail: bkwell@nde.vsnl.net.in

Anand Associates
1219 Stock Exchange Tower
12th Floor
Dalal Street
Mumbai 400 023, India
Tel: (91-22) 272-3065 or 272-3066
Fax: (91-22) 272-3067
E-mail: thrupti@vsnl.com
Web: http://www.myown.org

Team Spirit (India) Pvt. Ltd.
B-1, Hirak Centre
Sardar Patel Chowk
Nehru Park
Vastrapur
Ahmedabad 380 015, India
Tel: (91-79) 676-4489
E-mail: business@teamspiritindia.net

Publication discount: 75 percent

Selected titles
- *Better Health Systems for India's Poor: Findings, Analysis, and Options*
- *Energy Demand in Five Major Asian Developing Countries: Structure and Prospects*
- *Incentives for Joint Forest Management in India: Analytical Methods and Case Studies*
- *India: Achievements and Challenges in Reducing Poverty*
- *India: Alleviating Poverty through Forest Development*
- *India: Five Years of Stabilization and Reform and the Challenges Ahead*
- *India: Macroeconomics and Political Economy, 1964–1991*
- *India: Sustaining Rapid Economic Growth*
- *India: The Challenges of Development*
- *India: The Dairy Revolution*
- *India's Family Welfare Program: Moving to a Reproductive and Child Health Approach*
- *India's Public Distribution System: A National and International Perspective*
- *Leapfrogging? India's Information Technology Industry and the Internet*
- *Measuring the Impact of Climate Change on Indian Agriculture*
- *Participation in Project Preparation: Lessons from World Bank-Assisted Projects in India*
- *The Pharmaceutical Industry in India and Hungary: Policies, Institutions, and Technological Development*

- *Satisfying Urban Thirst: Water Supply Augmentation and Pricing Policy in Hyderabad City, India*
- *Transferring Irrigation Management to Farmers in Andhra Pradesh, India*

Indonesia

Bank Group offices
World Bank and International Finance Corporation 📖
Jakarta Stock Exchange Building, Tower 2
Floor 12
Sudirman Central Business District
Jl. Jenderal, Sudirman Kav. 52-53
Jakarta 12190, Indonesia
Tel: (62 21) 5299 3000 or 5299 3001 (main);
(62 21) 5299 3146 or 5299 3140 (direct)
Fax: (62 21) 5299 3002 or 5299 3111
Web: http://www.worldbank.or.id

Depository and regional libraries
Universitas Udayana [regional]
Departemen Pendidikan Nasional
UPT Perpustakaan
Kampus Bukit-Jimbaran
Bali 80364, Indonesia
Tel: (62 361) 702 772
Fax: (62 361) 702 765

Bandung Institute of Technology Library
[regional]
Central Library
Jalan Ganesya 10a
Bandung 40132, Indonesia
Tel: (62 22) 250 0089
Fax: (62 22) 250 0089

Bogor Agricultural University Library
[depository]
P.O. Box 199
Kampus IPB Darmaga
Bogor 16001, Indonesia
Tel: (62 251) 621 073
Fax: (62 251) 623 166
Web: http://www.ipb.ac.id

Catholic University of Indonesia [regional]
Centre for Societal Development Studies
Library
Jalan Jenderal, Sudirman 51
Jakarta 12930, Indonesia
Tel: (62 21) 570 3306
Fax: (62 21) 573 4355
Web: http://www.atmajaya.ac.id

National Library of Indonesia [depository]
Deputy of Collection Dev. and Inf. Svc.
Jl. Salemba Raya 28A
Jakarta, Pusat 10002, Indonesia
Tel: (62 21) 315 4864
Fax: (62 21) 310 3554

Sekretariat General of DPR RI [depository]
Library
KA Unit Perpustakaan
Jalan Gatot Subroto
Jakarta, Pusat 10270, Indonesia
Tel: (62 21) 575 6079
Fax: (62 21) 575 6068

University of Mataram [regional]
Library
Jl. Majapahit 62
Lombok NTB, Indonesia
Tel: (62 370) 632 470
Fax: (62 370) 636 041

Universitas Sam Ratulangi [regional]
Departemen Pendidikan Nasional
UPT Perpustakaan
Jalan Kampus
Manado 95115, Indonesia
Tel: (62 431) 863 386
Fax: (62 431) 863 386
E-mail: upt-perp-unsrat@yahoo.com

University of North Sumatra [regional]
University Library
Jalan Perpustakaan 1
Kampus USU
Medan 20155, Indonesia
Tel: (62 61) 821 3526
Fax: (62 61) 821 3108

Riau University [regional]
Central Library
Kampus Bina Widya, Km 12.5
Simpang Baru
Pekanbaru 28293, Indonesia
Tel: (62 761) 63276
Fax: (62 761) 63276

Mulawarman University [regional]
UPT Perpustakaan
Kotak Pos 1068
Jl. Kuaro Kampus Gunung Kelua
Samarinda, Indonesia
Tel: (62 541) 739 892
Fax: (62 541) 739 892
E-mail: perpus@yahoo.com
Web: http://www.unmul.ac.id

Sepuluh Nopember Institute of Technology
(ITS) Library [depository]
UPT Perpustakaan ITS
Kampus ITS, Sukolilo
Surabaya 60111, Indonesia
Tel: (62 31) 593 774
Fax: (62 31) 593 7774

Universitas Diponegoro [regional]
UPT Perpustakaan
Jl. Prof. Sudarto, SH
Gedung Widya Puraya
Tembalang-Semarang, Indonesia
Tel: (62 24) 746 0042
Fax: (62 24) 746 0036

Hasanuddin University Library [depository]
Tamalanrea, Km 10
Ujung Pandang 90245, Indonesia
Tel and Fax: (62 411) 587 027
Web: http://www.unhas.ac.id

Distribution of Bank Group publications
Ada Utama
JL Melawai Raya 22, Room #5,
Kebayoran Baru,
Jakarta,
Tel: +62 21 727 93614,
E-mail: Adautama@Cbn.Net.Id

Publication discount: 75 percent

Selected titles
- *Energy Demand in Five Major Asian Developing Countries: Structure and Prospects*
- *Indonesia: Environment and Development*
- *Indonesia: The Challenges of World Bank Involvement in Forests*
- *Macroeconomic Policies, Crises, and Long-Term Growth in Indonesia, 1965–90*
- *The Microfinance Revolution: Lessons from Indonesia*

Islamic Republic of Iran

Depository and regional libraries
Iran Banking Institute [depository]
Library
205 Pasdaran Ave.
P.O. Box 19395
Tehran, Iran
Tel: (98 21) 284 8000
Fax: (98 21) 284 2618

Distribution of Bank Group publications
Ketab Sara Co. Publishers
P.O. Box 15745-733

Tehran 15117, Iran
Tel: (98 21) 871 6104
Fax: (98 21) 871 2479
E-mail: ketab-sara@neda.net.ir

Kowkab Publishers
P.O. Box 19575-511
Tehran, Iran
Tel: (98 21) 258 3723
Fax: (98 21) 258 3723
E-mail: info@kowkabpublishers.com

Publication discount: 75 percent

Ireland

Depository and regional libraries
University of Dublin [depository]
Trinity College Library
College Street
Dublin 2, Ireland
Tel: (353 1) 608 2342
Fax: (353 1) 671 9003
Web: http://www.tcd.ie/library/opub.htm

Israel

Depository and regional libraries
Development Study Center [depository]
Library
P.O. Box 2355
Rehovot 76122, Israel
Tel: (972 8) 947 4111
Fax: (972 8) 947 5884

Distribution of Bank Group publications
Yozmot Literature Ltd.
P.O. Box 56055
3 Yohanan Hasandlar St.
Tel Aviv 61560, Israel
Tel: (972 3) 5285 397
Fax: (972 3) 5285 397

Italy

Bank Group offices
World Bank
Via Labicana, 110
00184 Rome, Italy
Tel: (39 06) 77 7101
Fax: (39 06) 70 96046

Depository and regional libraries
University of Rome, La Sapienza [depository]
Contabilita Naz. e Analisi dei Processi Sociali
Library
Piazzale A. Moro, 5

00185 Rome, Italy
Tel: (39 06) 445 3828
Fax: (39 06) 499 10720

Distribution of Bank Group publications
Licosa Libreria Commissionaria
Sansoni S.P.A.
Via Duca di Calabria 1/1
50125 Firenze, Italy
Tel: (39 55) 648 31
Fax: (39 55) 641 257
E-mail: licosa@licosa.com
Web: http://www.licosa.com

Jamaica

Bank Group offices
World Bank
Caribbean PIC 📖
University of the West Indies
Mona, Kingston 7, Jamaica
Tel: (876) 977-4366
Fax: (876) 927-1926
E-mail: cpic@uwimona.edu.jm

Depository and regional libraries
Planning Institute of Jamaica [depository]
Documentation and Data Center
8 Ocean Boulevard
Kingston Mall, Jamaica
Tel: (876) 967-3690, 967-3691, or 967-3692
Fax: (876) 967-3688 or 967-4900

Distribution of Bank Group publications
Ian Randle Publishers Ltd.
11 Cunningham Avenue
Kingston 6, Jamaica
Tel: (876) 978-0739 or 978-0745
Fax: (876) 978-1156
E-mail: sales@ianrandlepublishers.com
Web: http://www.ianrandlepublishers.com

Publication discount: 75 percent

Selected titles
*   *Chronic Illness and Retirement in Jamaica*
*   *Health Care in Jamaica: Quality, Outcomes, and Labor Supply*
*   *Urban Poverty and Violence in Jamaica*

Japan

Bank Group offices
World Bank 📖
10th Floor, Fukoku Seimei Building
2-2-2 Uchidaiwai-cho, Chiyoda-ku

Tokyo 100-0011, Japan
Tel: (81-3) 3597-6665
Fax: (81-3) 3597-6695
Web: http://www.worldbank.or.jp

International Finance Corporation
(Same address as World Bank)
Tel: (81-3) 3597-6657
Fax: (81-3) 3597-6698

MIGA
(Same address as World Bank)
Tel: (81-3) 3597-9100
Fax: (81-3) 3597-9101
E-mail: mkogiso@worldbank.org

Depository and regional libraries
National Diet Library [depository]
Special Materials Department
Official Publications Division
1-10-1 Nagata-cho, Chiyoda-ku
Tokyo 100-8924, Japan
Tel: (81-3) 3581-2331
Fax: (81-3) 3581-2290

Distribution of Bank Group publications
Eastern Book Service
3-13 Hongo 3-chome, Bunkyo-ku
Tokyo 113, Japan
Tel: (81-3) 3818-0861
Fax: (81-3) 3818-0864
E-mail: orders@svt-ebs.co.jp
Web: http://www.svt-ebs.co.jp

Selected titles
*   *Catching Up to Leadership: The Role of Technology-Support Institutions in Japan's Casting Sector*
*   *Intellectual Property Protection, Direct Investment, and Technology Transfer: Germany, Japan, and the United States*
*   *Policy-Based Finance: The Experience of Postwar Japan*

Jordan

Depository and regional libraries
University of Jordan [depository]
Library
Queen Rania Al-Abdullah
Amman, Jordan
Tel: (962 6) 5355 000 or 5355 099, ext. 3135
Fax: (962 6) 5355 570
Web: http://www.ju.edu.jo

Distribution of Bank Group publications
Global Development Forum
P.O. Box 941488

Amman 11194, Jordan
Tel: (962 6) 4656 124
Fax: (962 6) 4656 123
E-mail: gdf@index.com.jo or
gdf@ngoglobalforum.org

Publication discount: 75 percent

Selected titles
- *The Dynamics of Education Policymaking: Case Studies of Burkina Faso, Jordan, Peru, and Thailand*
- *Hashemite Kingdom of Jordan: Health Sector Study*
- *Poverty Alleviation in Jordan in the 1990s: Lessons for the Future*

Kazakhstan

Bank Group offices
World Bank and International Finance Corporation 📖
41 Kazibeck bi Street, 4th Floor
480100 Almaty, Kazakhstan
Tel: (7-3272) 980 580
Fax: (7-3272) 980 581
Web: http://www.worldbank.org.kz

World Bank
Samal-12
473000 Astana, Kazakhstan
Tel: (7-3172) 580 555
Fax: (7-3272) 580 342

Depository and regional libraries
National Library of Kazakhstan [depository]
Abai av. 14
Almaty, Kazakhstan
Tel: (7-3272) 627 956
Fax: (7-3272) 696 586
Web: http://www.nlrk.kz

Publication discount: 75 percent

Selected titles
- *Kazakhstan: A Review of Farm Restructuring*
- *Privatization of the Power and Natural Gas Industries in Hungary and Kazakhstan*

Kenya

Bank Group offices
World Bank 📖
Hill Park Building, Upper Hill Road
P.O. Box 30577
Nairobi, Kenya
Tel: (254-2) 260-400 or 260 484
Fax: (254-2) 260-380 or 260-381
Web: http://www.worldbank.org/afr/ke

International Finance Corporation
(Same address as World Bank)
Tel: (254-2) 260-341 or 720-467
Fax: (254-2) 260-383 or 717-390

IFC Africa Project Development Facility
International House, 6th Floor
P.O. Box 46534
Nairobi, Kenya
Tel: (254-2) 217-368, 217-369, or 217-370
Fax: (254-2) 339-121 or 330-436

Depository and regional libraries
Moi University [depository]
Library
P.O. Box 3900
Eldoret, Kenya
Tel: (254-321) 433-09, 437-20, or 436-20
Fax: (254-321) 432-75

University of Eastern Africa, Baraton
[depository]
Library
P.O. Box 2500
Eldoret, Kenya
Tel: (254) 326-2625
Fax: (254) 326-2263

Kenya National Library Services
[depository]
National Reference and Bibliography Dept.
NR and BD
P.O. Box 30573
Ngong Road
Nairobi, Kenya
Tel: (254-2) 725-550 or 725-551
Fax: (254-2) 721-749

Kenyatta University [depository]
Moi Library
P.O. Box 43844
Thika Road
Nairobi, Kenya
Tel: (254-2) 810-187
Fax: (254-2) 810-759
Web: http://www.knls.or.ke

Egerton University [depository]
Library
P.O. Box 536
Njoro, Kenya
Tel: (254-37) 612-65
Fax: (254-37) 613-89

Distribution of Bank Group publications
Legacy Books
Loita House
P.O. Box 68077
Nairobi, Kenya
Tel: (254-2) 330-853
Fax: (254-2) 330-854
E-mail: info@legacybookshop.com

Publication discount: 75 percent

Selected titles
*   *Agricultural Pricing Policy in Eastern Africa:
    A Macroeconomic Simulation for Kenya, Malawi,
    Tanzania, and Zambia*
*   *Land Resource Management in Machakos District,
    Kenya 1930–1990*

Republic of Korea

Bank Group offices
International Finance Corporation
Youngpoong Building, 11th Floor
Chongro-ku
Seoul 110-110, Korea
Tel: (82-2) 399-0905 or 399-0906
Fax: (82-2) 399-0915

Depository and regional libraries
Chonnam National University [regional]
Library
300 Yongbong-dong Puk-gu
Kwangju 500-757, Korea
Tel: (82-62) 530-3531
Fax: (82-62) 530-3529

Korea Development Institute Library
[depository]
Library
207-41 Chungnyangri-dong
Dongdaemun-ku
Seoul 130-012, Korea
Tel: (82-2) 958-4262
Fax: (82-2) 958-4261
Web: http://www.kdi.re.kr

Seoul National University Library
[depository]
International Documents Room
San 56-1 Shillim-dong, Gwanag-gu
Seoul 151-736, Korea
Tel: (82-2) 880-8070
Fax: (82-2) 878-2730

Distribution of Bank Group publications
Eulyoo Publishing Co. Ltd.

46-1 Susong-dong
Jongro-gu
Seoul, Korea
Tel: (82-2) 734-3515
Fax: (82-2) 732-9154
E-mail: eulyoo@chollian.net

Dayang Intelligence Co.
954-22 Banghae-dong, Socho-ku
Seoul, Korea
Tel: (82-2) 582-3588
Fax: (82-2) 521-8827
E-mail: dybook@kornet.net
Web: http://www.dayang.co.kr

Sejong Books Inc.
81-4 Neung-dong
Kwangjin-ku
Seoul 143-180, Korea
Tel: (82-2) 498-0300
Fax: (82-2) 3409-0321
Web: http://www.sejongbooks.com

Publication discount: 35 percent

Selected titles
*   *Credit Policies and the Industrialization of Korea*
*   *The Distribution of Income and Wealth in Korea*
*   *Energy Demand in Five Major Asian Developing
    Countries: Structure and Prospects*
*   *Korea: A Case of Government-Led Development*
*   *Korea and the Knowledge-based Economy: Making
    the Transition*
*   *Regulated Deregulation of the Financial System in
    Korea*

Kosovo (Serbia and Montenegro)

Bank Group offices
World Bank 📖
35 Tirana Street
38000 Priština, Kosovo
Tel: (381-38) 249-459
Fax: (381-38) 249-780

Distribution of Bank Group publications
See Albania

Publication discount: 75 percent

Selected titles
*   *Building Peace in South East Europe:
    Macroeconomic Policies and Structural Reforms
    Since the Kosovo Conflict*
*   *Kosovo: Economic and Social Reforms for Peace
    and Reconciliation*

Kuwait

Depository and regional libraries
Arab Planning Institute [depository]
P.O. Box 5834
Safat 13059, Kuwait
Tel: (965) 484 7540 or 484 3130,
ext. 311
Fax: (965) 484 2935 or 464 1868
Web: http://www.arab-api.org

Kyrgyz Republic

Bank Group offices
World Bank
214 Moskovskaya Street
Bishkek 720010, Kyrgyz Republic
Tel: (996-312) 21-74-63
Fax: (996-312) 61-03-56
Web: http://worldbank.org.kg

International Finance Corporation
(Same address as World Bank)
Tel: (996-312) 61-06-50
Fax: (996-312) 61-03-56

Publication discount: 75 percent

Selected titles
* *Kyrgyz Republic: Fiscal Sustainability Study*
* *Kyrgyz Republic: Strategy for Rural Growth and Poverty Alleviation*
* *Structural Adjustment in the Transition: Case Studies from Albania, Azerbaijan, Kyrgyz Republic, and Moldova*

Lao People's Democratic Republic

Bank Group offices
World Bank 📖
Patou Xay, Nehru Road
Vientiane, Lao PDR
Tel: (856-21) 414-209, ext. 266
Fax: (856-21) 414-210

International Finance Corporation and IFC
Mekong Project Development Facility
Pathou Xay, Nehru Road
P.O. Box 9690
Vientiane, Lao PDR
Tel: (856-21) 450-017
Fax: (856-21) 450-020

Latvia

Bank Group offices
World Bank and International Finance
Corporation 📖

Smilsu Street 8
5th Floor
1162 Riga, Latvia
Tel: (371-7) 22-07-44
Fax: (371-7) 82-80-58
E-mail: LatviaOffice@worldbank.org
Web: http://www.worldbank.org.lv

Depository and regional libraries
Liepajas Central Scientific Library [regional]
Zivju Street 7
3401 Liepaja, Latvia
Tel: (371-3) 42-45-70
Web: http://www.czb.anet.lv

National Library of Latvia [depository]
K. Barona Str. 14
1423 Riga, Latvia
Tel: (371-7) 28-08-51 or 28-76-11
Fax: (371-7) 28-08-51
Web: http://www.lnb.lv

Distribution of Bank Group publications
Janis Roze
15/3 Miera Street
1001 Riga, Latvia
Tel: (371-7) 50-15-62
Fax: (371-7) 37-09-22

Publication discount: 75 percent

Selected titles
* *Latvia: The Transition to a Market Economy*

Lebanon

Bank Group offices
World Bank 📖
UN House, 6th Floor
Riad El-Sohl Square
P.O. Box 11-8577
Beirut, Lebanon
Tel: (961-1) 987 800
Fax: (961-1) 986 600

Publication discount: 35 percent

Lesotho

Depository and regional libraries
Lesotho National Library Services
[depository]
P.O. Box 52
Maseru 100, Lesotho
Tel: (266) 313 034
Fax: (266) 310 194

National University of Lesotho [regional]
Thomas Mofolo Library
P.O. Roma 180
Lesotho

Publication discount: 75 percent

Selected titles
- *Lesotho: Development in a Challenging Environment: A Joint World Bank–African Development Bank Evaluation*

Libya

Depository and regional libraries
Economics Research Center [depository]
Documentation and Information,
Library
P.O. Box 1300
132 Nasser Street
Benghazi, Libya
Tel: (218 61) 909 8198
Fax: (218 61) 909 0753

Publication discount: 35 percent

Lithuania

Bank Group offices
World Bank
Jogailos g. 4
2001 Vilnius, Lithuania
Tel: (370-5) 210-76-80
Fax: (370-5) 210-76-81
E-mail: office@worldbank.lt
Web: http://www.worldbank.lt

Library 📖
Litimpeks Bank Building
IBRD/IFC Office, 12th Floor (entrance from Benediktiniu Str.)
Vilniaus Str. 28
2600 Vilnius, Lithuania
Tel: (370-2) 618-262
Fax: (370-2) 226-829

Depository and regional libraries
Kaunas County Public Library [regional]
Radastu 2
3000 Kaunas, Lithuania
Tel: (370-7) 324-248
Fax: (370-7) 324-250
Web: http://www.kvb.lt

P. Visinskis Siauliai County Public Library [regional]
Ausros Aleja 62

5419 Siauliai, Lithuania
Tel: (370-41) 523-748
Fax: (370-41) 523-750
Web: http://www.savb.lt

Martynas Mazvydas National Library of Lithuania [depository]
Gedimino pr. 51
2600 Vilnius, Lithuania
Tel: (370-2) 629-023 or 628-112
Fax: (370-2) 629-023 or 627-129
Web: http://www.lnb.lt

Distribution of Bank Group publications
Humanitas
Zemaiciu Str. 31
3000 Kaunas, Lithuania
Tel: (370-7) 423-664 or 220-333
Fax: (370-7) 423-653

Publication discount: 75 percent

Selected titles
- *Lithuania: An Opportunity for Economic Success (Volume I: Main Report)*
- *Lithuania: An Opportunity for Success (Volume II: Analytical Background)*

Macedonia, Former Yugoslav Republic of

Bank Group offices
World Bank and International Finance Corporation
34 Leninova Street
91000 Skopje, Macedonia
Tel: (389-2) 11-71-59
Fax: (389-2) 11-76-27
Web: http://www.worldbank.org.mk

Depository and regional libraries
University "Ss. Cyril and Methodius" [depository]
Faculty of Economics, Library
P.O. Box 550
Bul. Krste Misrkov BB
91000 Skopje, Macedonia
Tel: (389-91) 11-64-66 or 22-32-45
Fax: (389-91) 11-87-01
Web: http://www.eccf.ukim.edu.mk

Publication discount: 75 percent

Madagascar

Bank Group offices
World Bank 📖

Anosy (près Ministère des Affaires Etrangères)
1, Rue Andriamifidy L. Razafimanantsoa
B.P. 4140
Antananarivo, Madagascar
Tel: (261-20) 22-560-22
Fax: (261-20) 22-333-38
Web: http://www.worldbank.org/infoshop/
madag.htm

Publication discount: 75 percent

Selected titles
*   *Education and Training in Madagascar: Toward a Policy Agenda for Economic Growth and Poverty Reduction*
*   *Madagascar: An Agenda for Growth and Poverty Reduction (in French)*
*   *Population Growth, Shifting Cultivation, and Unsustainable Agricultural Development: A Case Study in Madagascar*

Malaysia

Depository and regional libraries
Yayasan Sabah [depository]
Borneo Research Library
Locked Bag 190
88745 Kota Kinabalu, Sabah, Malaysia
Tel: (60 88) 426 484
Fax: (60 88) 427 077

Asian and Pacific Development Center [regional]
Library
Pesiaran Duta
P.O. Box 12224
50770 Kuala Lumpur, Malaysia
Tel: (60 3) 651 1088
Fax: (60 3) 651 0316

South East Asian Central Banks [regional]
Research and Training Centre, Library
Lorong Universiti A
59100 Kuala Lumpur, Malaysia
Tel: (60 3) 758 5600
Fax: (60 3) 757 4616

Pustaka Negeri Sarawak [regional] (Sarawak State Library)
Jalan Pustaka off Jalan Stadium
Petra Jaya
93502 Kuching, Sarawak, Malaysia
Tel: (60 82) 442 000
Fax: (60 82) 449 944
E-mail: librarian@sarawaknet.gov.my
Web: http://www.pustaka-sarawak.com

Distribution of Bank Group publications
University of Malaya Cooperative Bookshop, Ltd.
P.O. Box 1127, Jalan Pantai Baru
59700 Kuala Lumpur, Malaysia
Tel: (60 3) 756 5000
Fax: (60 3) 755 4424
E-mail: umkoop@tm.net.my

MDC Publishers Printers Sdn. Bhd.
MDC Building
2718, Jalan Permata Empat
Taman Permata, Ulu Kelang
53300 Kuala Lumpur, Malaysia
Tel: (60 3) 4108 6600
Fax: (60 3) 4108 1506
E-mail: mdcpp@mdcpp.com.my
Web: http://www.mdcpp.com.my

Publication discount: 35 percent

Selected titles
*   *Investing in Maternal Health in Malaysia and Sri Lanka*
*   *Malaysia: Enterprise Training, Technology, and Productivity*
*   *Malaysia: Growth, Equity, and Structural Transformation*

Malawi

Bank Group offices
World Bank 📖
2nd Floor, Development House
P.O. Box 30557
Capital City
Lilongwe 3, Malawi
Tel: (265) 780 611
Fax: (265) 781 158

Depository and regional libraries
Chitedze Agricultural Research Station [depository]
Agricultural Research and Technical Services
P.O. Box 158
Lilongwe, Malawi
Tel: (265) 767 222
Fax: (265) 784 184

National Library Service [depository]
Technical Services Department
P.O. Box 30314
Capital City
Lilongwe 3, Malawi
Tel: (265) 783 700
Fax: (265) 781 616

University of Malawi [depository]
Chancellor College Library
P.O. Box 280
Zomba, Malawi
Tel: (265) 522 222
Fax: (265) 523 225

Distribution of Bank Group publications
Book Sales and Distribution Company Ltd.
P.O. Box 32008
Chichiri
Blantyre 3, Malawi
Tel and Fax: (265) 1620 073 or (265) 1636 049
E-mail: bsad@africa-online.net

Publication discount: 75 percent

Selected titles
• *Agricultural Pricing Policy in Eastern Africa: A
  Macroeconomic Simulation for Kenya, Malawi,
  Tanzania, and Zambia*
• *Leveling the Playing Field: Giving Girls an Equal
  Chance for Basic Education—Three Countries'
  Efforts*
• *Small Enterprises Adjusting to Liberalization in
  Five African Countries*
• *Who Benefits from Public Education Spending in
  Malawi?: Results from the Recent Education
  Reform*

Malta

Depository and regional libraries
Central Bank of Malta [depository]
Information Services
Castille Place
Valletta CMR 01, Malta
Tel: (356) 247 480
Fax: (356) 247 489
Web: http://www.centralbankmalta.com

Mali

Bank Group offices
World Bank
Immeuble SOGEFIH
Quartier du Fleuve
Centre Commercial rue 321
B.P. 1864
Bamako, Mali
Tel: (223) 22-22-83, 22-32-01, 22-88-67, or
22-88-69
Fax: (223) 22-66-82

PIC 📖
Centre Djoliba (Centre Ville)
B.P. 1864

Bamako, Mali
Tel: (223) 22-22-83 or 22-32-01
Fax: (223) 22-66-82 or 22-88-67

Depository and regional libraries
Centre Djoliba [depository]
Documentation et Debats Publics
B.P. 298
Avenue Modibo KEITA
Rue Raymond Poincare Porte 8
Bamako, Mali
Tel: (223) 22-83-32
Fax: (223) 22-46-50
Web: http://www.malinet.ml/pratique/
centredjo

Publication discount: 75 percent

Selected titles
• *Small Enterprises Adjusting to Liberalization in
  Five African Countries*

Mauritania

Bank Group offices
World Bank 📖
Socogim Tevragh Zeina, Villa No. 30, Lot A
Quartier Socogim
B.P. 667
Nouakchott, Mauritania
Tel: (222) 25-10-17 or 25-13-59
Fax: (222) 25-13-34

Publication discount: 75 percent

Mauritius

Depository and regional libraries
National Library of the Republic of Mauritius
[depository]
2nd Floor
Fon Sing Building
Edith Cavell Street
Port-Louis, Mauritania
Tel: (230) 211-9891
Fax: (230) 210-7173
E-mail: natlib@itnet.mu

Publication discount: 35 percent

Mexico

Bank Group offices
World Bank
Torre Mural
Insurgentes Sur 1605, Piso 24
San José Insurgentes
Mexico D.F. 03900, Mexico

Tel: (52 5) 480-4200
Fax: (52 5) 480-4271

International Finance Corporation
Prado Sur 240, Piso 4
Suite 402
Lomas de Chapultepec
Mexico D.F. 11000, Mexico
Tel: (52 5) 5520-6191
Fax: (52 5) 5520-5659

Depository and regional libraries
Banco de México [depository]
Biblioteca
Apartado Postal No. 98 Bis
Marconi No. 2, Col. Centro
Delegación Cuauhtemoc
Mexico D.F. 06059, Mexico
Tel: (52 5) 237-2376
Fax: (52 5) 237-2380

Instituto Tecnológico y de Estudios Superiores
de Monterrey (ITESM) [regional]
Biblioteca, Centro de Información
Campus Monterrey
Avenida Eugenio Garza Sada, No. 2501
Sucursal de Correos "J" Monterrey
Nuevo Leon 64849, Mexico
Tel: (52 8) 358-2000, ext. 4020
Fax: (52 8) 358-6850

Distribution of Bank Group publications
Alfaomega Grupo Editor
Pitágoras 1139
Col. Del Valle
México D.F.
México
Tel: (52) 5575 5022
Fax: (52) 5575 2420
E-mail: universitaria@alfaomega.com.mx

Publication discount: 35 percent

Selected titles
- *Beyond Privatization: The Second Wave of Telecommunications Reforms in Mexico*
- *Black December: Banking Instability, the Mexican Crisis, and Its Effect on Argentina*
- *The Economics of Gender in Mexico: Work, Family, State, and Market*
- *Irrigation Management Transfer in Mexico: Process and Progress*
- *Latin America after Mexico: Quickening the Pace*
- *Managing Disaster Risk in Mexico: Market Incentives for Mitigation Investment*
- *Mexico: A Comprehensive Development Agenda*

for the New Era
- *Private Solutions for Infrastructure in Mexico*

Mongolia
Bank Group offices
World Bank
11-A Peace Avenue
Ulaanbaatar 210648, Mongolia
Tel: (976-1) 312-647
Fax: (976-1) 312-645
Web: http://www.worldbank.org.mn

International Finance Corporation
(Same address as World Bank)
Tel: (976-1) 312-694
Fax: (976-1) 312-696

Depository and regional libraries
Women for Social Progress Movement
[depository]
"Parliament" Internet library
Building of National History Museum
Northern Entrance, Room 2
POB-20A
Ulaanbaatar 11, Mongolia
Tel: (976-1) 328-291
Fax: (976-1) 322-340
E-mail: wsp@magicnet.mn

Publication discount: 75 percent

Moldova
Bank Group offices
World Bank
76/6 Sciusev Street
2012 Chisinau, Moldova
Tel: (373-2) 237-065
Fax: (373-2) 237-053

International Finance Corporation
(Same address as World Bank)
Tel: (373-2) 233-565 or 232-737
Fax: (373-2) 233-908

Depository and regional libraries
Academy of Economic Studies [depository]
Library
59 Banulescu-Bodoni Str.
2005 Chisinau, Moldova
Tel: (373-2) 242-663
Fax: (373-2) 221-968
Web: http://www.lib.ase.md

Publication discount: 75 percent

Selected titles

- *Land Reform and Farm Restructuring in Moldova: Progress and Prospects*
- *Moldova: Moving to a Market Economy*
- *Moldova: Poverty Assessment*
- *Structural Adjustment in the Transition: Case Studies from Albania, Azerbaijan, Kyrgyz Republic, and Moldova*

Morocco

Bank Group offices
World Bank and International Finance Corporation 📖
7, rue Larbi Ben Abdellah
Souissi, Ravat, Morocco
Tel: (212-7) 63 60 50
Fax: (212-7) 63 60 51

Depository and regional libraries
Centre National de Documentation [depository]
Avenua Al Haj Cherkaoui
Quartier des Ministeres
Haut Agdal 10100, Morocco
B.P. 826
10004 Rabat, Morocco
Tel: (212 37) 77 30 13
Fax: (212 37) 77 31 34
E-mail: cnd@cnd.mpep.gov.ma
Web: http://www.cndportal.net.ma

Selected titles
- *Changing Patterns of Illiteracy in Morocco: Assessment Methods Compared*
- *How Does Schooling of Mothers Improve Child Health?: Evidence from Morocco*
- *Royaume du Maroc: Participation du secteur prive dans les infrastructures (in French)*

Mozambique

Bank Group offices
World Bank and International Finance Corporation
Avenue Kenneth Kaunda, 1224
Caixa Postal 4053
Maputo, Mozambique
Tel: (258-1) 492-841, 492-851, 492-861, or 492-871
Fax: (258-1) 492-893

Depository and regional libraries
National Library of Mozambique [depository]
25 de Setembro Av #1348

CP 141 Maputo, Mozambique
Tel: (258-1) 425-676

Universidade Eduardo Mondlane [depository]
Directorate of the Documentation Services
P.O. Box 1169
Avenida Julius Nyerere
Campus Universitario
Maputo, Mozambique
Tel: (258-1) 492-875
Fax: (258-1) 493-174
E-mail: bibweb@nambu.uem.mz

Publication discount: 75 percent

Selected titles
- *Rebuilding the Mozambique Economy: Assessment of a Development Partnership*

Namibia

Depository and regional libraries
National Library of Namibia [depository]
Library and Archives Services
Private Bag 13349
Chr. Mugabe/Korner Street
Windhoek, Namibia
Tel: (264 61) 293 5300
Fax: (264 61) 293 5321

Publication discount: 75 percent

Selected titles
- *Case Studies in War-to-Peace Transition: The Demobilization and Reintegration of Ex-Combatants in Ethiopia, Namibia, and Uganda*

Nepal

Bank Group offices
World Bank 📖
Yak and Yeti Hotel Complex
Lal Durbar, Durbar Marg
G.P.O. Box 798
Kathmandu, Nepal
Tel: (977-1) 226 792 or 226 793, ext. 102
Fax: (977-1) 225 112
Web: http://www.bishwabank.org.np

International Finance Corporation
(Same address as World Bank)
Tel: (977-1) 268 123 or 439 571
Fax: (977-1) 223 443
E-mail: SouthAsia@ifc.org

Depository and regional libraries
Tribhuvan University [depository]

Central Library
Kirtipur, Kathmandu, Nepal
Tel: (977-1) 330 834
Fax: (977-1) 331 964
Web: http://www.nepalnet.org.np/tucl/
home.htm

Distribution of Bank Group publications
Everest Media International Services (P.) Ltd.
G.P.O. Box 5443
Kathmandu, Nepal
Tel: (977-1) 416 026
Fax: (977-1) 250 176
E-mail: emispltd@wlink.com.np

Bazaar International
228 Sanchaya Kosh Building
G.P.O. Box 2480, Tridevi Marg
Kathmandu, Nepal
Tel: (977-1) 255 125
Fax: (977-1) 229 437
E-mail: bazaar@mos.com.np

Publication discount: 75 percent

Selected titles
*   *Forest Management in Nepal: Economics and Ecology*
*   *Urban Air Quality Management Strategy in Asia: Kathmandu Valley Report*

Netherlands

Depository and regional libraries
Royal Tropical Institute (KIT) [depository]
Information, Library and Documentation (IBD)
U.N. Collection
P.O. Box 95001
1090 HA Amsterdam, Netherlands
Tel: (31 20) 568 8316
Fax: (31 20) 665 4423
Web: http://www.kit.nl

Distribution of Bank Group publications
De Lindeboom/Internationale Publicaties b.v.
M.A. de Ruyterstraat 20A
7482 BZ Haaksbergen, Netherlands
Tel: (31 53) 574 0004
Fax: (31 53) 572 9296
E-mail: books@delindeboom.com
Web: http://www.delindeboom.com

New Zealand

Depository and regional libraries
Parliamentary Library [depository]

International Documents Section
Parliament House
Wellington 1, New Zealand
Tel: (64 4) 471 9611
Fax: (64 4) 471 2551
Web: http://www.ps.parliament.govt.nz/
library.htm

Nicaragua

Bank Group offices
Banco Mundial
De los Semaforos de la Centroamérica
400 mts. abajos
Segundo Piso Edificio SYSCOM
Managua, Nicaragua
Tel: (505-2) 70-000
Fax: (505-2) 70-0077

Depository and regional libraries
Instituto Centroamericano de Administración
de Empresas [depository]
Library
P.O. Box 2485
Km. 15-1/2 Carretera Sur
Managua 2, Nicaragua
Tel: (505-2) 658-141
Fax: (505-2) 658-617

Distribution of Bank Group publications
Hispamer
Costado Este UCA
Managua, Nicaragua
Tel: (505-2) 78-1210
Fax: (505-2) 78-0825
E-mail: hispamer@cablenet.com.ni
Web: http://www.hispamer.com.ni

Publication discount: 75 percent

Niger

Bank Group offices
World Bank 📖
42 rue des Dallols
B.P. 12402
Niamey, Niger
Tel: (227) 73 59 29 or 73 49 66
Fax: (227) 73 55 06

Publication discount: 75 percent

Selected titles
*   *The Niger Household Energy Project: Promoting Rural Fuelwood Markets and Village Management of Natural Woodlands*

Nigeria

Bank Group offices
World Bank 📖
Plot 433 Yakubu Gowon Crescent, Opp.
ECOWAS Secretariat
Asokoro District
P.O. Box 2826
Garki Abuja, Nigeria
Tel: (234-9) 3145269 or 3145275
Fax: (234-9) 3145267

International Finance Corporation and Africa
Project Development Facility
Maersk House
Plot 121 Louis Solomon Close
Off Ahmadu Bello Way
Victoria Island
Lagos, Nigeria
Tel: (234-1) 2626455 through 2626464
Fax: (234-1) 2626465 or 2626466

Depository and regional libraries
Nnamdi Azikiwe University [depository]
University Library
P.M.B. 5025
Awka
Anambra State, Nigeria
Tel: (234-90) 503265

University of Calabar Library [depository]
P.M.B. 1115
Calabar
Cross River State, Nigeria
Tel: (234-87) 221697
Fax: (234-87) 221766

Nigerian Institute of Social and Economic
Research [depository]
Library
P.M.B. 5
U.I. Post Office
Ojoo
Ibadan, Nigeria
Tel: (234-2) 8102904, ext. 243
Fax: (234-2) 8101194

Nigerian Industrial Development Bank Ltd.
[regional]
Library
P.O. Box 2357
63/71, Broad Str.
Lagos, Nigeria
Tel: (234-1) 2662259, 2663470, or 2663495,
ext. 18
Fax: (234-1) 2665286 or 2666733

Nigerian Institute of International Affairs
[regional]
13/15 Kofo Abayomi Road
Victoria Island
G.P.O. Box 1727
Lagos, Nigeria
Tel: (234-1) 22615606
Fax: (234-1) 22611360

University of Nigeria [depository]
Nnamdi Azikiwe Library
Anambra UL
Nsukka, Enugu State, Nigeria
Tel: (234-42) 771444
Fax: (234-42) 770644

Distribution of Bank Group publications
University Press Plc
Three Crowns Building Jericho
P.M.B. 5095
Ibadan, Nigeria
Tel: (234-22) 411356
Fax: (234-22) 412056
E-mail: unipress@skannet.com

Publication discount: 75 percent

Selected titles
* *Contraceptive Use and the Quality, Price, and
  Availability of Family Planning in Nigeria*
* *State, Community, and Local Development in
  Nigeria*

Norway

Depository and regional libraries
Chr. Michelsen Institute [depository]
Library
Fantoftvegen 38
5892 Bergen, Norway
Tel: (47 5) 557 4191
Fax: (47 5) 557 4166
Web: http://www.cmi.no/library/library.htm

Oman

Depository and regional libraries
Oman Ministry of National Economy
[depository]
Information and Documentation Center
Box 881 PC 113
Muscat, Oman
Tel: (968) 604 852
Fax: (968) 698 467
Web: http://www.moneoman.gov.om

Publication discount: 35 percent

Pakistan

Bank Group offices
World Bank 📖
20-A, Shahrah-e-Jamhuriat
Ramna 5 (G-5/1)
Islamabad, Pakistan
Tel: (92-51) 279-641
Fax: (92-51) 279-648
Web: http://www.worldbank.org.pk

International Finance Corporation
(Same address as World Bank)
Tel: (92-51) 2279-631, 2279-632, or 2279-633
Fax: (92-51) 2824-335

Depository and regional libraries
University of Agriculture [depository]
Department of Library
Faisalabad, Pakistan
Tel: (92-411) 625-583
Fax: (92-411) 647-846

Pakistan Institute of Development Economics
[depository]
Library and Documentation Division
P.O. Box 1091
Islamabad 44000, Pakistan
Tel: (92-51) 921-4041 or 920-6610
Fax: (92-51) 921-0886

Applied Economics Research Centre
[depository]
Library
University of Karachi
P.O. Box 8403
University Road
Karachi 75270, Pakistan
Tel: (92-21) 496-4284, 474-749, or 474-384
Fax: (92-21) 496-9229

Lahore University of Management Sciences
[regional]
Library
Opposite Sector U
L.C.C.H.S, Lahore-Cantt.
Lahore 54792, Pakistan
Tel: (92-42) 572-2670 through 572-2679
Fax: (92-42) 572-2591
E-mail: library.lums.edu.pk

Punjab Economic Research Institute
[depository]
Planning and Development Department
Government of Punjab

184-M, Gulberg-III
Lahore 54660, Pakistan
Tel: (92-42) 588-4947
Fax: (92-42) 588-4948

Pakistan Academy for Rural Development
[depository]
Library
P.O. University Town
Peshawar, Pakistan
Tel: (92-521) 921-6200 through 921-6202
Fax: (92-91) 921-6278

University of Baluchistan [depository]
Central Library
Sariab Road
Quetta, Pakistan
Tel: (92-81) 921-1247
Fax: (92-81) 921-1288, 921-1277

Distribution of Bank Group publications
Mirza Book Agency
65 Shahrah-e-Quaid-e-Azam
Lahore 54000, Pakistan
Tel: (92-42) 735-3601
Fax: (92-42) 576-3714
E-mail: merchant@brain.net.pk

Oxford University Press
5 Bangalore Town, Sharae Faisal
P.O. Box 13033
Karachi 75350, Pakistan
Tel: (92-21) 446-307, 449-032, or 440-532
Fax: (92-21) 454-7640 or 449-032
Web: http://www.oup.com.pk

Pak Book Corporation
Aziz Chambers 21
Queen's Road
Lahore, Pakistan
Tel: (92-42) 636-3222 or 636-0885
Fax: (92-42) 636-2328
E-mail: pbc@brain.net.pk

Publication discount: 75 percent

Selected titles
*   *Improving Women's Health in Pakistan*
*   *Leveling the Playing Field: Giving Girls an Equal Chance for Basic Education—Three Countries' Efforts*
*   *The Next Ascent: An Evaluation of the Aga Khan Rural Support Program, Pakistan*
*   *Strategic Reforms for Agricultural Growth in Pakistan*

Panama

Depository and regional libraries
Universidad de Panamá [depository]
Sistema de Bibliotecas de la Universidad de
Panamá
Biblioteca Interamericana Simón Bolivar
Campus Universitario
Estafeta Universitaria
Panama City, Panama
Tel: (507) 223 8786
Fax: (507) 223 3734

Publication discount: 35 percent

Selected titles
* *Panama Poverty Assessment: Priorities and
  Strategies for Poverty Reduction*

Papua New Guinea

Depository and regional libraries
University of Papua New Guinea [depository]
Michael Somare Library
P.O. Box 319
University Post Office
National Capital District
Tel: (675) 326 7280 or 326 7480
Fax: (675) 326 7187
Web: http://www.ps.parliament.govt.nz/
library.htm

Publication discount: 75 percent

Selected titles
* *Gender Analysis in Papua New Guinea*

Paraguay

Depository and regional libraries
Universidad Nacional de Asunción
[depository]
Facultad de Ciencias Agrarias
Biblioteca
Casilla de Correos No. 1618
Asunción, Paraguay
Tel: (595 21) 585 606, 585 609, or 585 613
Fax: (595 21) 585 612

Ministry of Finance (CIDDI) [depository]
Information, Documentation, and
Dissemination Center
Chile 252 c/Palma, 1st Floor
P.O. Box 473
Asunción, Paraguay
Tel: (595 21) 440 010 or 440 017, ext. 271
Fax: (595 21) 448 283

Distribution of Bank Group publications
Ediciones Técnicas Paraguayas
Blas Garay 106 (es 4°) e/ Ind.
Nacional Asunción, Paraguay
Tel: (595 21) 496 778
E-mail: etp@cmm.com.py

Publication discount: 75 percent

Selected titles
* *Competition Policy and MERCOSUR*
* *Surveillance of Agricultural Price and Trade
  Policies: A Handbook for Paraguay*

Peru

Bank Group offices
Banco Mundial
Avenida Alvarez Calderón 185
Piso 7, San Isidro
Lima, Peru
Tel: (51-1) 615-0660
Fax: (51-5) 421-7241

Depository and regional libraries
Banco Central de Reserva del Perú
[depository]
Centro de Inform y Documentación
Jiron Lampa No. 474
Apartado Postal No. 1958
Lima 100, Peru
Tel: (51-1) 427-6250
Fax: (51-1) 427-5880
Web: http://www.bcrp.gob.pe

Distribution of Bank Group publications
Fundación del Libro Universitario - LIBUN
Av. Arequipa N° 3845, Lima 18, Perú
Telefax: (511) 421-0160 / 421-0190 / 440-6587
E-mail: libun@libun.edu.pe
Web: http://www.libun.edu.pe

Publication discount: 75 percent

Selected titles
* *Agricultural Trade Policies in the Andean Group:
  Issues and Options*
* *The Dynamics of Education Policymaking: Case
  Studies of Burkina Faso, Jordan, Peru, and
  Thailand*
* *An Environmental Study of Artisanal, Small, and
  Medium Mining in Bolivia, Chile, and Peru*
* *Peru: Improving Health Care for the Poor*
* *Peruvian Education at a Crossroads: Challenges
  and Opportunities for the 21st Century*
* *Poverty and Social Developments in Peru,
  1994–1997*

Philippines

Bank Group offices

World Bank Resident Mission and Knowledge
for Development Center
Taipan Place Building, 23rd and Ground
Floors
Emerald Avenue, Ortigas Center
Pasig City, Philippines
Tel: (63-2) 637-5855, ext. 3003; (63-2)
917-3034 or 637-5855
Fax: (63-2) 917-3050 or 637-5870
Web: http://www.worldbank.org.ph

International Finance Corporation
11th Floor, Tower One
Ayala Triangle, Ayala Avenue
Makati City 1200, Philippines
Tel: (63-2) 848-7333 or 848-7338
Fax: (63-2) 848-7339

Depository and regional libraries

Saint Mary's University [depository]
University Library
Bayombong, Nueva Vizcaya
Region 02, Philippines
Tel: (63-78) 321-3650
Fax: (63-78) 321-2117

Panay State Polytechnic College [depository]
Department of Library Services
PSPC Mambusao
Capiz 5807, Philippines
Tel: (63-36) 647-0212 or 647-0101

University of San Carlos [depository]
Library System
P. del Rosario Street
Cebu City 6000, Philippines
Tel: (63-32) 254-0432
Fax: (63-32) 254-0432
Web: http://www.econ.upd.edu.ph/aboutupse/
library.htm

Notre Dame University [depository]
Data Resource Centre
Notre Dame Avenue
Cotabato City 9600, Philippines
Tel: (63-64) 421-2698
Fax: (63-64) 421-4312
E-mail: ndu@ndu.fapenet.org

University of Southeastern Philippines
[depository]
Library

Bo. Obrero
Davao City 8000, Philippines
Tel: (63-82) 221-7741
Fax: (63-82) 221-7737

University of the Philippines Los Banos
[depository]
University Library
UP Los Banos
4031 College
Laguna, Philippines
Tel: (63-49) 536-2326 or 536-2235
Fax: (63-49) 536-5081
Web: http://www.uplb.edu.ph/admin/ovcre/lib

Asian Institute of Management [depository]
Eugenio Lopez Foundation Building
Joseph R. McMicking Campus
123 Paseo de Rosas
Makati City 1260, Philippines
Tel: (63-2) 817-2663
Fax: (63-2) 893-3338 or 867-2114
E-mail: wbpublications@dataserve.aim.edu.ph
Web: http://www.aim.edu.ph

National Economic and Development
Authority [depository]
Library
St. Josemaria Escriva Drive
Pasig City 1600, Philippines
Tel: (63-2) 631-3757 or 631-0945 through
631-0956, ext. 113
Fax: (63-2) 631-3282 or 631-3731
Web: http://www.neda.gov.ph

University of the Philippines [depository]
School of Economics
Library
Diliman
Quezon City 1101, Philippines
Tel: (63-2) 927-2044
Fax: (63-2) 921-3359
Web: http://www.econ.upd.edu.ph/aboutupse/
library.htm

Western Mindanao State University
[depository]
Library, College of Public Administration and
Development Studies
San José Road, Baliwasan
Zamboanga City 7000, Philippines
Tel: (63-62) 993-0944 or 992-2837
Fax: (63-62) 991-1231
E-mail: library@wmsu.edu.ph
Web: http://www.wmsu.edu.ph

Distribution of Bank Group publications
F & J de Jesus, Inc.
7636 Guijo cor. Sacred Heart Sts.,
San Antonio Village 1200 Makati City,
Philippines
Tel: +632 8902213/8902208/8995997
Fax: +632 8969095
E-mail: fnjph@yahoo.com

International Booksource Center Inc.
1127-A Antipolo St.
Barangay, Venezuela
Makati City, Philippines
Tel: (63-2) 896-6501
Fax: (63-2) 896-6497

Asian Institute of Management
(Same as under Depository and Regional
Libraries)

Publication discount: 75 percent

Selected titles
*   *Household Responses to Poverty and Vulnerability,*
    Volume 3: Confronting Crisis in Commonwealth,
    Metro Manila, Philippines
*   *The Manila Water Concession: A Key Government*
    Official's Diary of the World's Largest Water
    Privatization
*   *Philippines: From Crisis to Opportunity*

Poland

Bank Group offices
World Bank
Warsaw Financial Center, 9th Floor
53 Emilii Plater St.
00-113 Warsaw, Poland
Tel: (48-22) 520-8000
Fax: (48-22) 520-8001
Web: http://www.worldbank.org.pl

International Finance Corporation
(Same address as World Bank)
Tel: (48-22) 520-6100
Fax: (48-22) 520-6101

Depository and regional libraries
Gdánsk Institute for Market Economics
[regional]
Library
Do Studzienki 63
80-227 Gdánsk, Poland
Tel: (48-58) 341-1535
Fax: (48-58) 341-0620

Krakow University of Economics [depository]

Main Library
ul. Rakowicka 27
31-510 Krakow, Poland
Tel: (48-12) 421-0336 or 616-7739
Fax: (48-12) 421-0706

Narodowy Bank Polski [depository]
Research Department
Central Library
ul. Swietokrzyska 11/21
00-919 Warsaw, Poland
Tel: (48-22) 653-1773 or 826-7786
Fax: (48-22) 653-1593
Web: http://www.nbp.pl

Distribution of Bank Group publications
International Publishing Service
Ul. Piekna 31/37
00-677 Warsaw, Poland
Tel: (48-2) 628-6089
Fax: (48-2) 621-7255
E-mail: books@ips.com.pl
Web: http://www.ips.com.pl

A.B.E. Marketing
Ul. Grzybowska 37A
00-855 Warsaw, Poland
Tel: (48-22) 654-0675
Fax: (48-22) 682-2233 or 682-17 24
E-mail: info@abe.com.pl

Ars Polona
7 Krakowskie Przedmiescie
00-950 Warsaw, Poland
Tel: (42-22) 826-4758
E-mail: Books119@Arspolona.Com.Pl

Publication discount: 35 percent

Selected titles
*   *Competitiveness and Employment: A Framework*
    for Rural Development in Poland
*   *Overcoming Obstacles to Liberalization of the*
    Telecom Sector in Estonia, Poland, the Czech
    Republic, Slovenia, and Hungary: An Overview of
    Key Policy Concerns and Potential Initiatives to
    Facilitate the Transition Process
*   *Poland: Complying with EU Environmental*
    Legislation
*   *Poland: Income Support and the Social Safety Net*
    during the Transition
*   *Poland: Policies for Growth with Equity*
*   *Poland Country Assistance Review: Partnership*
    in a Transition Economy
*   *Poland's Labor Market: The Challenge of Job*
    Creation
*   *Private Sector Development during Transition:*

The Visegrad Countries
- *The Role of Foreign Direct Investment and Trade Policies in Poland's Accession to the European Union*
- *Trade and Cost Competitiveness in the Czech Republic, Hungary, Poland, and Slovenia*
- *Welfare and the Labor Market in Poland: Social Policy during Economic Transition*

Portugal

Depository and regional libraries
Universidade do Minho [depository]
Servicos de Documentação
Largo do Paço
4709 Braga codex, Portugal
Tel: (351 53) 604 150 or 604 151
Fax: (351 53) 678 590

Universidade da Beira Interior [depository]
Servicos de Documentacio
Rua-R. Marquês d'Ávila e Bolama
6200 Covilha, Portugal
Tel: (351 75) 319 826
Fax: (351 75) 319 744

Instituto Superior de Economia e Gestão [depository]
Biblioteca CID/ISEG
Rua Miguel Lupi, 20
1200 Lisboa, Portugal
Tel: (351 1) 392 2888
Fax: (351 1) 397 2684

Romania

Bank Group offices
World Bank
Boulevard Dacia 83, Sector 2
Bucharest, Romania
Tel: (40-1) 210-1804
Fax: (40-1) 210-2021
Web: http://www.worldbank.org.ro

International Finance Corporation
(Same address as World Bank)
Tel: (40-1) 211-2866
Fax: (40-1) 211-3141

Depository and regional libraries
Institute for World Economy [depository]
Library
Calea 13 Septembrie, Nr. 13
Sector 5 C.P. 42-13
Bucharest 76117, Romania
Tel: (40-1) 410-5596
Fax: (40-1) 410-5020

Biblioteca Centrala Universitara "Lucian Blaga" [depository]
Economics Reading Room
Str. Clinicilor Nr. 2
3400 Cluj-Napoca
Tel: (40-64) 197-092
Fax: (40-64) 197-633

Publication discount: 75 percent

Selected titles
- *Financial Markets, Credit Constraints, and Investment in Rural Romania*

Russian Federation

Bank Group offices
World Bank
Bolshaya Molchanovka, 36, Building 1
121069 Moscow, Russia
Tel: (7-095) 745-7000
Fax: (7-095) 967-1209
Web: http://www.worldbank.org.ru/eng

International Finance Corporation
7/5 Bolshaya Dmitrovka, Building 2
103009 Moscow, Russia
Tel: (7-095) 755-8818
Fax: (7-095) 755-8296

Depository and regional libraries
Kuban State University [depository]
149 Stavropolskaya ul.
350040 Krasnodar, Russia
Tel: (7-8612) 699-552
Fax: (7-8612) 339-887

Institute of International Economic and Political Studies [depository]
Library
Novocheryomushkinskaya, 46
117418 Moscow, Russia
Tel: (7-095) 128-8843
Fax: (7-095) 310-7061

Russian Economic Academy (named after G. V. Plekhanov) [regional]
Library
Stremjanny per., d. 36, korp. 3
113054 Moscow, Russia
Tel: (7-095) 236-8645
Fax: (7-095) 237-9232

Russian State Library [depository]
Foreign Acquisition and International Stock Exchange
3 Vozdvizhenka

101000 Moscow, Russia
Tel: (7-095) 202-8317
Fax: (7-095) 202-8317

St. Petersburg Economics and Finance
University [regional]
Library
30/32 Ekaterininskii Canal
191023 St. Petersburg, Russia
Tel: (7-812) 110-5711
Fax: (7-812) 110-5717
Web: http://www.lib.finec.ru

Voronezh State University [regional]
Scientific Library
Pr. Revolyutsii 24
394000 Voronezh, Russia
Tel: (7-732) 553-559
Fax: (7-732) 502-200

Distribution of Bank Group publications
Izdatelstvo "Ves Mir"
9 a, Kolpachnly pereulok
101831 Moscow, Russia
Tel: (7-95) 923-6839 or 923-8568
Fax: (7-95) 925-4269
E-mail: vesmirorder@vesmirbooks.ru
Web: http://www.vesmirbooks.ru

Publication discount: 35 percent

Selected titles
- *Agricultural Reform in Russia: A View from the Farm Level*
- *Assisting Russia's Transition: An Unprecedented Challenge*
- *Building Trust: Developing the Russian Financial Sector*
- *Case-by-Case Privatization in the Russian Federation: Lessons from International Experience*
- *Dismantling Russia's Nonpayments System: Creating Conditions for Growth*
- *Enterprise Restructuring, Pollution, and Economic Policy in Russia*
- *Fiscal Management in Russia*
- *Food and Agricultural Policy in Russia: Progress to Date and the Road Forward*
- *Improving Women's Health Services in the Russian Federation: Results of a Pilot Project*
- *Investment Policy in Russia*
- *Reforming Education in the Regions of Russia*
- *The Role of Women in Rebuilding the Russian Economy*
- *Russia: Creating Private Enterprises and Efficient Markets*

- *Russia: Forest Policy during Transition*
- *Reforming Education in the Regions of Russia Subnational Budgeting in Russia: Preempting a Potential Crisis*
- *Russia: The Banking System during Transition*
- *Russian Federation: Toward Medium-Term Viability*
- *Russian Trade Policy Reform for WTO Accession*
- *Russian Views of the Transition in the Rural Sector: Structures, Policy Outcomes, and Adaptive Responses*
- *Russia's Transition to a New Federalism*
- *Social Assessments for Better Development: Case Studies in Russia and Central Asia*
- *The TB and HIV/AIDS Epidemics in the Russian Federation*
- *Unemployment, Restructuring, and the Labor Market in Eastern Europe and Russia*

Rwanda

Bank Group offices
World Bank 📖
SORAS Building
Boulevard de la Revolution
B.P. 609
Kigali, Rwanda
Tel: (250) 72-204 or 77-746
Fax: (250) 76-385

Distribution of Bank Group publications
Bookshop Ikirezi
Avenue de la Paix
P.O. Box 443, Kigali
Tel: + 250 571314 / 570298
Fax: + 250 571314
E-mail: Ikirezi@Rwanda1.Com

Publication discount: 75 percent

Samoa

Depository and regional libraries
National University of Samoa [depository]
P.O. Box 5768
Apia, Samoa
Tel: (685) 20072
Fax: (685) 20938

Publication discount: 75 percent

Saudi Arabia

Bank Group offices
World Bank
UNDP Building
King Faisal Street

Riyadh, Saudi Arabia
Tel: (966-1) 483 4956
Fax: (966-1) 488 5311

Depository and regional libraries
Ministry of Planning [depository]
Library and Documentation Department
P.O. Box 358
University Street
Riyadh 11182, Saudi Arabia
Tel: (966-1) 401 0417
Fax: (966-1) 405 2051
Web: http://www.planning.gov.sa

Publication discount: 35 percent

Senegal
Bank Group offices
World Bank 📖
3, place de l'Independence
Immeuble SDIH
5ème Étage
B.P. 3296
Dakar, Senegal
Tel: (22-1) 823-3630, ext. 132
Fax: (22-1) 823-7993

International Finance Corporation
3, place de l'Independence
Immeuble SDIH, 7th Floor
B.P. 3296
Dakar, Senegal
Tel: (22-1) 822-9561 or 822-6470
Fax: (22-1) 823-7993

Depository and regional libraries
U.N. African Institute for Economic
Development and Planning [regional]
Library
Rue du 18 juin
B.P. 3186
Dakar, Senegal
Tel: (22-1) 823-1020
Fax: (22-1) 822-2964

Université Cheikh Anta Diop de Dakar
[depository]
Bibliothèque
B.P. 2006
Dakar, Senegal
Tel: (22-1) 824-6981 or 823-0279
Fax: (22-1) 824-2379
Web: http://www.ucad.sn

Publication discount: 75 percent

Selected titles
*   *Small Enterprises Adjusting to Liberalization in Five African Countries*

Serbia and Montenegro
Bank Group offices
World Bank
Bulevar Kralja Aleksandra 86-90
Belgrade, Serbia
Tel: (381-11) 3023 723
Fax: (381-11) 3023 732
Web: http://www.worldbank.org.yu

PIC/Library 📖
Kneginje Zorke 96-98
11000 Belgrade, Serbia
Tel: (381-11) 3023 750
Fax: (381-11) 3023 740

Depository and regional libraries
Institute of Economic Sciences
[depository]
Library
Zmaj Jovina 12
11000 Belgrade, Serbia
Tel: (381-11) 622 357
Fax: (381-11) 181 471
E-mail: ien@ien.bg.ac.yu
Web: http://www.ien.bg.ac.yu

Library/Research Center [regional]
National Bank of Yugoslavia
Bulevar Kralja Aleksandra 15
11000 Belgrade, Serbia
Tel: (381-11) 3240 992
Fax: (381-11) 3240 992
E-mail: biblio@nbj.sv.gov.yu
Web: http://www.nbj.yu

University of Podgorica [regional]
Library
Cetinjski put bb
81000 Podgorica, Montenegro
Tel: (381-81) 265 013
Fax: (381-81) 265 013

Publication discount: 75 percent

Selected titles
*   *Building Peace in South East Europe: Macroeconomic Policies and Structural Reforms Since the Kosovo Conflict*
*   *Kosovo: Economic and Social Reforms for Peace and Reconciliation*

Sierra Leone

Bank Group offices
World Bank Liaison Office
14 Wilberforce Street
Freetown, Sierra Leone
Tel: (232-22) 227-488 or 227-555
Fax: (232-22) 228-555

Publication discount: 75 percent

Selected titles
• *Health Reform in Africa: Lessons from Sierra Leone*

Singapore

Bank Group offices
World Bank
10 Shenton Way, #15-08
MAS Building
Singapore 079117
Phone: (65) 6324 4612
Fax: (65) 6324 4615
Web: http://www.worldbank.org/sg

Multilateral Investment Guarantee Agency
(Same address as World Bank)
Tel: (65) 6324 4612
Fax: (65) 6324 4615

Depository and regional libraries
National Library Board [depository]
91 Stamford Road
Singapore 178896
Tel: (65) 337 7355
Fax: (65) 332 3248
Web: http://www.nlb.gov.sg

Distribution of Bank Group publications
Taylor and Francis
240 Macpherson Road, #08-01
Pines Industrial Building
Singapore 348574
Tel: (65) 741 5166
Fax: (65) 742 9356
E-mail: info@hemisphere.com.sg
[Also distributes to Brunei, China, Myanmar, and Taiwan (China)]

Selected titles
• *Judiciary-Led Reforms in Singapore: Framework, Strategies, and Lessons*

Slovak Republic

Bank Group offices
World Bank
Grosslingova 35

811 09 Bratislava, Slovak Republic
Tel: (421) 2-59 337 317
Fax : (421) 2-59 337 450
Web: http://www.worldbank.sk

Depository and regional libraries
Slovak Academy of Sciences [depository]
Central Library
Klemensova 19
814 67 Bratislava 1, Slovak Republic
Tel: (421) 2-52 926 321
Fax: (421) 2-52 921 733
Web: http://www.uk.sav.sk

Distribution of Bank Group publications
Slovart G.T.G. Ltd.
Krupinská 4
P.O. Box 152
852 99 Bratislava 5, Slovak Republic
Tel: (427) 2-63 839 471, 2-63 839 472, or 2-63 839 473
Fax: (427) 2-63 839 485
E-mail: gtg@internet.sk

Publication discount: 35 percent

Selected titles
• *Private Sector Development during Transition: The Visegrad Countries*
• *Slovak Republic: A Strategy for Growth and European Integration*
• *Slovak Republic: Living Standards, Employment, and Labor Market Study*
• *Slovakia: Restructuring for Recovery*

Slovenia

Depository and regional libraries
Centre for International Cooperation and Development [regional]
Library
Kardeljeva ploscad
1000 Ljubljana, Slovenia
Tel: (386 61) 168 1372
Fax: (386 61) 168 1585

Institute for Economic Research [depository]
Library
Kardeljeva ploscad 17
1000 Ljubljana, Slovenia
Tel: (386 61) 345 787
Fax: (386 61) 342 760
Web: http://www.ier.si

Distribution of Bank Group publications
Gospodarski vestnik Publishing Group
Dunajska cesta 5

1000 Ljubljana, Slovenia
Tel: (386 61) 133 8347
Fax: (386 61) 133 8030

Selected titles
- *Communal Infrastructure in Slovenia: Survey of Investment Needs and Policies Aimed at Encouraging Private Sector Participation*
- *Overcoming Obstacles to Liberalization of the Telecom Sector in Estonia, Poland, the Czech Republic, Slovenia, and Hungary: An Overview of Key Policy Concerns and Potential Initiatives to Facilitate the Transition Process*
- *Slovenia: Economic Transformation and EU Accession, Volume 1: Summary Report*
- *Slovenia: Economic Transformation and EU Accession, Volume 2, Main Report*
- *Trade and Cost Competitiveness in the Czech Republic, Hungary, Poland, and Slovenia*

South Africa

Bank Group offices
World Bank
1st Floor, Equity Court
1250 Pretoria Street
P.O. Box 12629
Hatfield 0028
Pretoria, South Africa
Tel: (27-12) 342-3111
Fax: (27-12) 342-5511 or 342-5151

International Finance Corporation
1st Floor Oxford Gate
Hyde Park Lane
Johannesburg 2196, South Africa
Tel: (27-11) 341-9000
Fax: (27-11) 325-0582 or 325-1901

IFC Africa Project Development Facility
Ground Floor, Victoria Gate West
Hyde Park Lane, Hyde Park
Johannesburg 2196, South Africa
Tel: (27-11) 325-0720
Fax: (27-11) 325-0729 or 325-0393

International Finance Corporation
1 Thibault Square, 13th Floor
Capetown 8001, South Africa
Tel: (27-21) 418-7180
Fax: (27-21) 418-7183

MIGA
Tel: (27-11) 341-9000
E-mail: kkwaku@worldbank.org

Depository and regional libraries
University of Fort Hare [depository]
Library
Private Bag X1322
Alice 5700, South Africa
Tel: (27-40) 602-2612 or 602-2042
Fax: (27-40) 653-1423

National Library of South Africa [depository]
Cape Town Division
P.O. Box 496
Cape Town 8000, South Africa
Tel: (27-21) 424-6320
Fax: (27-21) 423-3359 or 424-4848

National Library of South Africa [depository]
Pretoria Division
Foreign Official Publication Section
P.O. Box 397
239 Vermeulen Street
Pretoria 0001, South Africa
Tel: (27-12) 321-8931
Fax: (27-12) 325-5984
Web: http://www.nlsa.ac.za

Distribution of Bank Group publications
Oxford University Press Southern Africa
P.O. Box 12119
N1 City 7463
Cape Town, South Africa
Tel: (27-21) 595-4400
Fax: (27-21) 595-4430
E-mail: oxford@oup.co.za

Anglia Book and Freight
Consolidators (Pty) Ltd
P.O. Box 140
Sedgefield 6573, South Africa
Tel: (27-44) 343-3068
Fax: (27-44) 343-3066

Publication discount: 75 percent

Selected titles
- *Economic Integration and Trade Liberalization in Southern Africa: Is There a Role for South Africa?*

Spain

Depository and regional libraries
ESADE [depository]
Library
Avenida de Pedralbes 60-62
08034 Barcelona, Spain
Tel: (34 93) 280 6162
Fax: (34 93) 204 8105

Distribution of Bank Group publications
Mundi-Prensa Libros, S.A.
Castello 37
28001 Madrid, Spain
Tel: (34 91) 436 3700
Fax: (34 91) 575 3998
E-mail: libreria@mundiprensa.es
Web: http://www.mundiprensa.es

Mundi-Prensa Barcelona
Tel: (34 3) 488 3492
E-mail: barcelona@mundiprensa.es

Selected titles
- *Large Mines and the Community: Socioeconomic and Environmental Effects in Latin America, Canada, and Spain*

Sri Lanka

Bank Group offices
World Bank
73/5 Galle Road
Colombo 3, Sri Lanka
Tel: (94-1) 448-070
Fax: (94-1) 440-357

International Finance Corporation
(Same address as World Bank)
Tel: (94-1) 448-070, ext. 325
Fax: (94-1) 471-536
E-mail: SriLanka@ifc.org

Depository and regional libraries
Central Bank of Sri Lanka [regional]
Library and Information Center
Level 9
30 Janadhipathi Mawatha
P.O. Box 590
Colombo 1, Sri Lanka
Tel: (94-1) 873-247
Fax: (94-1) 867-383

Marga Institute [depository]
Information Services Division
93/10 Dutugemenu Street
Kirulapone
Colombo 6, Sri Lanka
Tel: (94-1) 828-544
Fax: (94-1) 828-597
Web: http://www.lanka.net/marga

Distribution of Bank Group publications
Vijitha Yapa Bookshop
Unity Plaza
2 Galle Road, Colombo 4

Sri Lanka
Tel: +94-11 259-6960
E-mail: Vijiyapa@Sri.Lanka.Net
Web: http://www.vijithayapabookshop.com

Publication discount: 75 percent

Selected titles
- *Investing in Maternal Health in Malaysia and Sri Lanka*
- *Sri Lanka's Rubber Industry: Succeeding in the Global Market*
- *Sri Lanka's Tea Industry: Succeeding in the Global Market*

Sudan

Depository and regional libraries
Arab Organization for Agricultural Development [depository]
Arab Center for Agricultural Documentation
P.O. Box 474
St. No. 7, Al-Amarat
Khartoum, Sudan
Tel: (249 11) 472 176 or 472 183
Fax: (249 11) 471 402

Swaziland

Depository and regional libraries
University of Swaziland [depository]
Library
Private Bag No. 4
Kwaluseni, Swaziland
Tel: (268) 518 4011 or 518 5108
Fax: (268) 518 276

Publication discount: 75 percent

Sweden

Depository and regional libraries
Library for Economic Sciences [depository]
Uppsala University
Box 513
751 20 Uppsala, Sweden
Tel: (46 18) 471 1461
Fax: (46 18) 510 149
E-mail: ekonomikum@ub.uu.se
Web: http://www.ub.uu.se/sam/ekon

Distribution of Bank Group publications
Akademibokhandeln
Master Samuelsgatan 32
103 94 Stockholm, Sweden
Tel: (46 8) 613 6100
Fax: (46 8) 222 543
Web: http://www.akademibokhandeln.se

Switzerland

Bank Group offices
3, chemin Louis-Dunant
Case Postale 66
1211 Geneva 20, Switzerland
Tel: (41-22) 748-1000
Fax: (41-22) 748-1030

Depository and regional libraries
Mandat International
Documentation Centre
31, chemin William Rappard
1293 Bellevue, Switzerland
Tel: (41-22) 959-8855
Fax: (41-22) 959-8851
Web: http://www.mandint.org

Distribution of Bank Group publications
ADECO Van Diermen Editions Techniques
Ch. de Lacuez 41
1807 Blonay, Switzerland
Tel: (41-21) 943-2673
Fax: (41-21) 943-3605

Librarie Payot S.A.
Cotes-de-Montbenon 30
1002 Lausanne, Switzerland
Tel: (41-21) 341-3229
Fax: (41-21) 341-3235
E-mail: institutionnel@payot-librairie.ch

Taiwan, China

Distribution of Bank Group publications
Tycoon Information Inc.
Attn: Ms. Eileen Chen
5 Floor, No. 500
Chang-Chun Road
Taipei 105, Taiwan, China
Tel: (866 2) 8712 8886
Fax: (886 2) 8712 4747 or 8712 4777
E-mail: tycoon00@ms36.hinet.net

Tajikistan

Bank Group offices
World Bank and International Finance
Corporation 📖
Rudaki Avenue 105
Dushanbe 743001, Tajikistan
Tel: (992) 372 21-03-81 or 372 21-07-56
Fax: (992) 372 51-00-42

Publication discount: 75 percent

Selected titles
* *Tajikistan: The Transition to a Market Economy*

Tanzania

Bank Group offices
World Bank
Samora Avenue
P.O. Box 2054
Dar-es-Salaam, Tanzania
Tel: (255-51) 36410 or 38355
Fax: (255-51) 113039
Web: http://www.worldbank.org/afr/tz

PIC 📖
50 Mirambo Street
Dar-es-Salaam 4th Floor
P.O. Box 2054
Dar-es-Salaam, Tanzania
Tel: (255-51) 114575, 114577, or 116199
Fax: (255-51) 3039

Depository and regional libraries
Eastern and Southern African Management
Institute [depository]
Library and Documentation Center
P.O. Box 3030
Njiro Hill
Arusha, Tanzania
Tel: (255-27) 2508384
Fax: (255-27) 2508285

Institute of Finance Management [depository]
Library and Information
P.O. Box 3918
Shabaan Robert Street
Dar-es-Salaam, Tanzania
Tel: (255-51) 123666 or 112931 through
112934
Fax: (255-51) 112935

Publication discount: 75 percent

Selected titles
* *Agricultural Pricing Policy in Eastern Africa: A Macroeconomic Simulation for Kenya, Malawi, Tanzania, and Zambia*
* *Agriculture in Tanzania Since 1986: Follower or Leader of Growth?*
* *Land Degradation in Tanzania: Perception from the Village*
* *The Quality and Availability of Family Planning Services and Contraceptive Use in Tanzania*
* *Small Enterprises Adjusting to Liberalization in Five African Countries*
* *Tanzania: Social Sector Review*
* *Tanzania at the Turn of the Century: Background Papers and Statistics*
* *Tanzania at the Turn of the Century: From Reforms to Sustained Growth and Poverty Reduction*

Thailand

Bank Group offices

World Bank Resident Mission
14th Floor, Diethelm Tower A
93/1 Wireless Road
Bangkok 10330, Thailand
Tel: (66-2) 256-7792, ext. 332
Fax: (66-2) 256-7794
Web: http://www.worldbank.or.th

International Finance Corporation
17th Floor, Diethelm Tower A
93/1 Wireless Road
Bangkok 10330, Thailand
Tel: (66-2) 650-9253 through 650-9258
Fax: (66-2) 650-9259

International Information Center 📖
Center for Academic Resources,
5th Floor
Chulalongkorn University
Bangkok 10330, Thailand
Tel (CU): (66-2) 218-2952
Tel (WB): (66-2) 256-7792, ext. 322
Fax (CU): (66-2) 215-3617
Fax (WB): (66-2) 256-7794

MIGA Thailand
(Same address as World Bank)
Tel: (66-9) 851-2046
Fax: (66-5) 322-6527
E-mail: ibadenoch@worldbank.org

Depository and regional libraries

International Information Center
[depository]
Center of Academic Resources
Chulalongkorn University
Phya Thai Street
Bangkok, Thailand
Tel: (66-2) 218-2952
Fax: (66-2) 215-3617

National Institute of Development
Administration [depository]
Library and Information Center
Thanon Serithai
Klong Chan, Bangkapi
Bangkok 10240, Thailand
Tel: (66-2) 377-5070
Fax: (66-2) 375-9026
Web: http://www.nida.ac.th

Thailand Development Research Institute
[regional]

Library and Information Center
565 Soi Ramkhamhaeng 39
Wangthonglang District
Bangkok 10310, Thailand
Tel: (66-2) 718-5460, ext. 429
Fax: (66-2) 718-5461 or 718-5462
Web: http://www.info.tdri.or.th

Khon Kaen University [depository]
Engineering Library
Khon Kaen 40002, Thailand
Tel: (66-43) 362-161
Fax: (66-43) 363-161

Distribution of Bank Group publications

B2S (Books to Stationery)
Jewelry Trade Center Building
12th Floor, South Tower
919/555 Silom Road
Bangrak
Bangkok 10500, Thailand

CentraC Books Distribution Co. Ltd.
306 Silom Road
Bangkok 10500, Thailand
Tel: (66-2) 367-5030 through 367-5041,
ext. 178
Fax: (66-2) 367-5049

Publication discount: 75 percent

Selected titles

- *Back from the Brink: Thailand's Response to the 1997 Economic Crisis*
- *The Dynamics of Education Policymaking: Case Studies of Burkina Faso, Jordan, Peru, and Thailand*
- *Energy Demand in Five Major Asian Developing Countries: Structure and Prospects*
- *Successful Conversion to Unleaded Gasoline in Thailand*
- *Thailand: The Institutional and Political Underpinnings of Growth*
- *Thailand's Macroeconomic Miracle: Stable Adjustment and Sustained Growth*

Timor-Leste

Bank Group offices

World Bank 📖
Avenida dos Direitos Humanos
Dili, Timor-Leste
Tel: (670) 390 324 648, ext. 304
Fax: (670) 390 321 178
Mobile: (61) 407 101 536

Publication discount: 75 percent

Togo

Bank Group offices
World Bank
169 Boulevard du 13 janvier
Immeuble BTCI, 8ème étage
B.P. 3915
Lomé, Togo
Tel: (228) 215569 or 215777
Fax: (228) 217856

Publication discount: 75 percent

Trinidad and Tobago

Bank Group offices
International Finance Corporation
Mutual Center
16 Queen's Park West
Port-of-Spain, Trinidad, W.I.
Tel: (868) 628-5074
Fax: (868) 622-1003

Depository and regional libraries
University of the West Indies [depository]
Main Library
St. Augustine, Trinidad, W.I.
Tel: (868) 662-2002
Fax: (868) 662-9238
Web: http://www.mainlib.uwi.tt

Distribution of Bank Group publications
Systematics Studies Ltd.
St. Augustine Shopping Center
Eastern Main Road
St. Augustine, Trinidad, W.I.
Tel: (868) 645-8466
Fax: (868) 645-8467
[Distributes to the Caribbean]

Publication discount: 35 percent

Tunisia

Bank Group offices
World Bank
1, Blvd. Bab Benat, 1035
Tunis, Tunisia
Tel: (216-1) 436 475
Fax: (216-1) 436 475

Depository and regional libraries
Faculté des Sciences Economiques et de
Gestion [regional]
Université de Sfax Library
Route de l'Aerodrome, Km 4
B.P. 1088
Sfax 3018, Tunisia

Tel: (216-4) 279 034
Fax: (216-4) 279 139

Institut d'Economie Quantitative [depository]
Department d'Assistance a la Recherche
27, rue de Liban
Tunis 1002, Tunisia
Tel: (216-1) 802 044
Fax: (216-1) 787 034

University of Tunis III [depository]
Main Library
29, rue Asdrubal
Tunis 1002, Tunisia
Tel: (216-1) 787 502 or 788 768
Fax: (216-1) 788 768

Selected titles
- *From Universal Food Subsidies to a Self-Targeted Program: A Case Study in Tunisian Reform*
- *Higher Education in Tunisia: Challenges and Opportunities*
- *Tunisie: Étude sur la Strategie des Transports (in French)*

Turkey

Bank Group offices
World Bank
Ugur Mumcu Caddesi 88, Kat 2
06700 Gaziosmanpasa
Ankara, Turkey
Tel: (90-312) 446-3824
Fax: (90-312) 446-2442
Web: http://www.worldbank.org.tr

PIC 📖
(Same address as World Bank)
Tel: (90-312) 468-4527 or 468-4124
Fax: (90-312) 468-4526

International Finance Corporation
Is Kuleleri
Kule II, Kat 3
80620 4. Levent
Istanbul, Turkey
Tel: (90-212) 282-4001
Fax: (90-212) 282-4002

Depository and regional libraries
Middle East Technical University
[regional]
Library
Inonu Bulvari
Eskisehir Yolu
06531 Ankara, Turkey

Tel: (90-312) 210-2782
Fax: (90-312) 210-1119
Web: http://www.lib.metu.edu.tr

Statistical, Economic, and Social Research and
Training Centre for Islamic Countries
[depository]
Library
Attar Sokak No. 4
G.O.P. 06700
Ankara, Turkey
Tel: (90-312) 468-6172
Fax: (90-312) 467-3458
Web: http://www.sesrtcic.org

Bilkent University Library [regional]
06533 Bilkent
Ankara, Turkey
Tel: (90-312) 266-4472
Fax: (90-312) 266-4391
Web: http://library.bilkent.edu.tr

Anadolu University [regional]
Main Library
Yunus Emre Kampusu
26470 Eskisehir, Turkey
Tel: (90-222) 335-2553
Fax: (90-222) 335-2553

Bogaziçi University [depository]
Central Library
80815 Bebek
Istanbul, Turkey
Tel: (90-212) 257-5016
Fax: (90-212) 257-5016

Ege University [depository]
Central Library
Avrupa Documantasyon Merkezi
(Eur. Doc. Centre)
Bornova 35100
Izmir, Turkey
Tel: (90-232) 388-4642 or 388-1741
Fax: (90-232) 388-1100

Distribution of Bank Group publications
Dünya Aktüel A.S.
"Globus" Dünya Basinevi
100, Yil Mahallesi
34440 Bagcilar-Istanbul, Turkey
Tel: (90-212) 629-0808
Fax: (90-212) 629-4689 or 629-4627
E-mail: dunya@dunya-gazete.com.tr

Publication discount: 35 percent

Selected titles
- *Informal Settlements, Environmental Degradation,
  and Disaster Vulnerability: Turkey Case Study*
- *Social Assessment and Agricultural Reform in
  Central Asia and Turkey*
- *Turkey: Informatics and Economic
  Modernization*

Turkmenistan

Bank Group offices
World Bank Liaison Office and International
Finance Corporation
United Nations Building
Atabaev Street, 40
Ashgabat 744000, Turkmenistan
Tel: (993-12) 350-477
Fax: (993-12) 351-693

Publication discount: 75 percent

Selected titles
- *Turkmenistan: An Assessment of Leasehold-Based
  Farm Restructuring*

Uganda

Bank Group offices
World Bank and International Finance
Corporation 📖
Rwenzori House, 1st Floor,
1 Lumumba Avenue, Plot 1
P.O. Box 4463
Kampala, Uganda
Tel: (256 41) 230094, 231061, or 231062
Fax: (256 41) 230092
Web: http://www.worldbank.org/afr/ug

Depository and regional libraries
Makerere University [depository]
Main Library
P.O. Box 16002
Kampala, Uganda
Tel: (256 41) 531041
Web: http://www.makerere.ac.ug/services/
library.htm

Parliament of Uganda [regional]
Library, Research, and Information Services
P.O. Box 16002
Kampala, Uganda
Tel: (256 41) 235461 or 347440
Fax: (256 41) 235461

Distribution of Bank Group publications
Gustro Limited
P.O. Box 9997

Madhvani Building
Plot 16/4, Jinja Road
Kampala, Uganda
Tel: (256 41) 251467
Fax: (256 41) 251468
E-mail: gus@utlonline.co.ug

Publication discount: 75 percent

Selected titles
- *Adult Literacy Programs in Uganda*
- *Case Studies in War-to-Peace Transition: The Demobilization and Reintegration of Ex-Combatants in Ethiopia, Namibia, and Uganda*
- *Health Care in Uganda: Selected Issues*
- *Private Solutions for Infrastructure: Opportunities for Uganda*
- *Uganda: Growing Out of Poverty*
- *Uganda: Policy, Participation, People*
- *Uganda: Post-Conflict Reconstruction*
- *Uganda: Social Sectors*
- *Uganda: The Challenge of Growth and Poverty Reduction*
- *Uganda's AIDS Crisis: Its Implications for Development*
- *Uganda's Recovery: The Role of Farms, Firms, and Government*

Ukraine

Bank Group offices
World Bank
2 Lysenko Street
01034 Kiev, Ukraine
Tel: (380-44) 490-6671, 490-6672, or 490-6673
Fax: (380-44) 490-6670
Web: http://www.worldbank.org.ua

International Finance Corporation
4 Bogomoltsa Street
01024 Kiev, Ukraine
Tel: (380-44) 253-0539
Fax: (380-44) 490-5830

Depository and regional libraries
Ukrainian Academy of Public Administration [depository]
President of Ukraine, Library
20 Eugene Pottier Street
03057 Kiev, Ukraine
Tel: (380-44) 441-7672
Fax: (380-44) 446-9436

Publication discount: 75 percent

Selected titles
- *Land Reform and Farm Restructuring in Ukraine*

- *Land Reform in Ukraine: The First Five Years*
- *Ukraine: Restoring Growth with Equity: A Participatory Country Economic Memorandum*
- *Ukraine: Review of Farm Restructuring Experiences*
- *Ukraine: The Agriculture Sector in Transition*

United Arab Emirates

Depository and regional libraries
Dubai University College [regional]
Library
Al-Masaood Building
Maktoum Street
P.O. Box 14143
Dubai, United Arab Emirates
Tel: (971 4) 207 2617
Fax: (971 4) 224 2151
Web: http://www.duc.ac.ae

Sharjah Chamber of Commerce and Industry [regional]
Library
P.O. Box: 580
Chamber's Building No. 14
Al-Bourj Ave.
Sharjah, United Arab Emirates
Tel: (971 6) 541 444
Fax: (971 6) 541 119

United Kingdom

Bank Group offices
World Bank
New Zealand House, 15th Floor
Haymarket
London SW1Y 4TE, England
Tel: (44-20) 7930-8511
Fax: (44-20) 7930-8515

International Finance Corporation
4 Millbank
London SW1P 3JA, England
Tel: (44-20) 7222-7711
Fax: (44-20) 7976-8323

Depository and regional libraries
British Library [depository]
Overseas English Section
96 Euston Road
London NWI 2DB, England
Tel: (44-71) 412-7743
Fax: (44-71) 412-7563
Web: http://www.bl.uk

Distribution of Bank Group publications
Eurospan
3 Henrietta Street
Covent Garden
London WC2E 8LU, England
Tel: (44-20) 7240-0856
Fax: (44-20) 7379-0609
E-mail: orders@edspubs.co.uk
Web: http://www.eurospan.co.uk

Stationery Office
51 Nine Elms Lane
London SW8 5DR, England
Tel: (44-870) 600-5522
Fax: (44-20) 7873-8242
E-mail: customer.services@theso.co.uk
Web: http://www.theso.co.uk

United States

Bank Group offices
World Bank, United Nations Liaison
1 Dag Hammerskjold Plaza
885 2nd Avenue, 6th Floor
New York, NY 10017, USA
Tel: (1-212) 355-5112
Fax: (1-212) 355-4523

Depository and regional libraries
Library of Congress [depository]
Anglo-American Acquisitions Division
101 Independence Avenue, SE
Washington, DC 20540-4174, USA
Tel: (1-202) 707-9503
Fax: (1-202) 252-3347
Web: http://www.loc.gov

Selected titles
- *Comprehensive River Basin Development: The Tennessee Valley Authority*
- *Intellectual Property Protection, Direct Investment, and Technology Transfer: Germany, Japan, and the United States*
- *Labor Market Flexibility in Thirteen Latin American Countries and the United States*
- *Policies on Imports from Economies in Transition: Two Case Studies*

Uruguay

Depository and regional libraries
Oficina de Planeamiento y Presupuesto
[depository]
Biblioteca
Ed. Libertad (P. Baja)
Luis A. De Herrera 3350

Montevideo 11600, Uruguay
Tel: (598-2) 472-110, ext. 1067
Fax: (598-2) 487-5889

Distribution of Bank Group publications
Librería Técnica Uruguaya
Colonia 1543, Piso 7, Of. 702
Casilla de Correo 1518
Montevideo 11000, Uruguay
Tel: (598-2) 487-2110
Fax: (598-2) 413-448
E-mail: ltu@cs.com.uy
Web: http://www.opp.gub.uy/bibca.htm

Publication discount: 35 percent

Selected titles
- *Competition Policy and MERCOSUR*
- *The Effects of Protectionism on a Small Country: The Case of Uruguay*

Uzbekistan

Bank Group offices
World Bank Resident Mission 📖
43 Academician Suleimanova Street
Tashkent 700017, Uzbekistan
Tel: (998-71) 133-50-02, 133-21-85, or 133-62-05
Fax: (998-71) 133-62-15

International Finance Corporation
(Same address as World Bank)
Tel: (998-71) 133-21-85, 139-49-88, or 120-62-14
Fax: (998-71) 133-05-51 or 120-62-15

Depository and regional libraries
State Library of Republic of Uzbekistan
(named after Alisher Navoi) [regional]
Mustakillik Square, 5
Tashkent 700000, Uzbekistan
Tel: (998-71) 139-43-41
Fax: (998-71) 139-16-58

University of World Economy and Diplomacy
[depository]
Library
Bujuk Ipak Yuli Street, 54
Tashkent 700077, Uzbekistan
Tel: (998-71) 267-58-38
Fax: (998-71) 267-09-00

Publication discount: 75 percent

Vanuatu

Depository and regional libraries
Reserve Bank of Vanuatu [depository]
Library, Research Department
Private Mail Bag 062
Port Vila, Vanuatu
Tel: (678) 233 33
Fax: (678) 242 31

Publication discount: 75 percent

República Bolivariana de Venezuela

Bank Group offices
Banco Mundial
Edificio Torre Edicampo, Piso 9
Avda. Francisco de Miranda con Avda. Del Parque
Campo Alegre
Caracas 1060, R.B. de Venezuela
Tel: (58-2) 267-9943
Fax: (58-2) 267-9828

Depository and regional libraries
Banco Central de Venezuela Biblioteca Ernesto Peltzer [depository]
Torre Financiera
Piso 16, Avda. Urdaneta, Esq. de Santa Capilla
Apartado Postal No. 2017
Caracas 1010, R.B. de Venezuela
Tel: (58-2) 801-8817 or 801-5021
Fax: (58-2) 861-0048 or 801-8706

Instituto de Estudios Superiores de Administración [depository]
Biblioteca Lorenzo Mendoza Fleury
Apartado 1640
Av. IESA, Edificio IESA
San Bernardino
Caracas 1011A, R.B. de Venezuela
Tel: (58-2) 552-8712 or 555-4362
Fax: (58-2) 551-3664
Web: http://www.iesa.edu.ve/biblioteca

Instituto Autonomo de Servicios de Bibliotecas e Información del Estado Merida [depository]
Oficial
Calle 25 Ayachuch
Entre Avenidas 5 y 6 Edificio Invi
Merida, Estado Merida, R.B. de Venezuela
Fax: (58-74) 636-729

Distribution of Bank Group publications
Tecni-Ciencia Libros, S.A.
Centro Cuidad Comercial Tamanaco
Nivel C-2

Caracas, R.B. de Venezuela
Tel: (58-2) 959-5547
Fax: (58-2) 959-5636

Publication discount: 35 percent

Selected titles
*   *Agricultural Trade Policies in the Andean Group: Issues and Options*

Vietnam

Bank Group offices
World Bank
63 Ly Thai To Street
Hanoi, Vietnam
Tel: (84-4) 934-6600, ext. 234
Fax: (84-4) 934-6597
Web: http://www.worldbank.org.vn

Vietnam Development Information Center 📖
63 Ly Thai To Street, Ground Floor
Hanoi, Vietnam
Tel: (84-4) 934-6845
Fax: (84-4) 934-6847
Web: http://www.vdic.org.vn

International Finance Corporation and IFC Mekong Project Development Facility
63 Ly Thai To Street, 7th Floor
Hanoi, Vietnam
Tel: (84-4) 824-7892
Fax: (84-4) 824-7898

IFC Mekong Project Development Facility
Unit 3B, Somerset Chancellor Court
21-23 Nguyen Thi Minh Khai Street
District 1
Ho Chi Minh City, Vietnam
Tel: (84-8) 823-5266
Fax: (84-8) 823-5271

Depository and regional libraries
Institute of World Economy [depository]
Information and Library Section
176 Thai Ha Street
Dong Da
Hanoi, Vietnam
Tel: (84-4) 857-3199, 857-4294, or 857-2295
Fax: (84-4) 857-4316

Institute of Economic Research of Ho Chi Minh City [depository]
Information and Computer Department
175 Hai Ba Trung Street
District 3
Ho Chi Minh City, Vietnam

Tel: (84-8) 829-4641 or 822-5638
Fax: (84-8) 824-3896

Thu Vien Khoa Hoc Tong Hop [depository]
General Sciences Library
69 Ly Tu Trong Street
P.O. Box 341
Ho Chi Minh City, Vietnam
Tel: (84-8) 822-5055
Fax: (84-8) 829-5632

Distribution of Bank Group publications
FAHASA (Book Distribution Co. of Ho Chi
Minh City)
246 Le Thanh Ton Street
District 1
Ho Chi Minh City, Vietnam
Tel: (84-8) 829-7638 or 822-5446
Fax: (84-8) 822-5795
E-mail: fahasa-sg@hcm.vnn.vn
Web: http://www.tlnet.com.vn/fahasa

Vietnam Development Information Center
63 Ly Thai To Street, Ground Floor
Hanoi, Vietnam
Tel: (84-4) 934-6845
E-mail: ctran@worldbank.org

Publication discount: 75 percent

Selected titles
* *Household Welfare and Vietnam's Transition*
* *Poverty, Social Services, and Safety Nets in Vietnam*
* *The Role of the Private Sector in Education in Vietnam: Evidence from the Vietnam Living Standards Survey*
* *Vietnam: Country Framework Report on Private Participation in Infrastructure*
* *Vietnam: Education Financing*

West Bank and Gaza

Bank Group offices
World Bank 📖
P.O. Box 54842
Jerusalem, Israel
Tel: (972 2) 236 6500
Fax: (972 2) 236 6543

International Finance Corporation
(Same address as World Bank)
Tel: (972 2) 236 6517 or 236 6500
Fax: (972 2) 263 6521

Depository and regional libraries
Water and Environmental Studies Center
[regional]

Library
P.O. Box 7
Nablus, West Bank
Tel: (972 9) 238 3124 or 238 1113
Fax: (972 9) 238 7982
Web: http://www.najah.edu/english/Research/watercenter.htm

Palestine Economic Policy Research Institute (MAS)
Library
P.O. Box 2426
Ramallah, West Bank
Tel: (972 2) 298 7053 or 298 7054
Fax: (972 2) 298 7055

Publication discount: 75 percent

Selected titles
* *West Bank and Gaza: Medium-Term Development Strategy for the Health Sector*

Republic of Yemen

Bank Group offices
World Bank
P.O. Box 18152, Hadda Area,
Street No. 40, off Damascus Road,
Sana'a, Republic of Yemen
Tel: (967-1) 413 708
Fax: (967-1) 413 709

Depository and regional libraries
Sana'a University [depository]
Central Library
Ma'in Post
P.O. Box 13732
Sana'a, Republic of Yemen
Tel: (967-1) 250 467
Fax: (967-1) 323 372
E-mail: library@y.net.ye

Selected titles
* *Economic Growth in the Republic of Yemen: Sources, Constraints, and Potentials*

Zambia

Bank Group offices
World Bank
Red Cross House, 2nd Floor
P.O. Box 35410
Long Acres
Lusaka, Zambia
Tel: (260-1) 252-811, 253-219, or 253-223
Fax: (260-1) 254-283

PIC 📖
3rd Floor, Anglo-American Building
74 Independence Avenue
P.O. Box 35410
Lusaka, Zambia
Tel: (260-1) 252-811 or 253-219
Fax: (260-1) 254-283

Depository and regional libraries
Copperbelt University [depository]
Library
P.O. Box 21692
Kitwe, Zambia
Tel: (260-2) 222-066
Fax: (260-2) 223-972

University of Zambia [depository]
Institute of Economic and Social Research
Documentation and Information Unit
P.O. Box 30900
Lusaka, Zambia
Tel: (260-1) 294-131, 295-055, or 294-673
Fax: (260-1) 294-291

Distribution of Bank Group publications
Transafrica Book Sales and Distributors
Company Ltd.
P.O. Box 30023
Lusaka, Zambia
Tel: (260-1) 226-960 or 226-961
E-mail: transafr@coppernet.zm

Publication discount: 75 percent

Selected titles
* *Agricultural Pricing Policy in Eastern Africa: A Macroeconomic Simulation for Kenya, Malawi, Tanzania, and Zambia*
* *Listening to Farmers: Participatory Assessment of Policy Reform in Zambia's Agriculture Sector*
* *Zambia Country Assistance Review: Turning an Economy Around*

Zimbabwe

Bank Group offices
World Bank 📖
Old Lonrho House
88 Nelson Mandela Avenue
P.O. Box 2960
Harare, Zimbabwe
Tel: (263-4) 729-611 or 729-613
Fax: (263-4) 708-659
Web: http://www.worldbank.org.zw

International Finance Corporation
101 Union Avenue, 7th Floor

Harare, Zimbabwe
Tel: (263-4) 794-868, 794-869, or 794-860
Fax: (263-4) 793-805

IFC Africa Project Development Facility Office
Southampton House, 5th Floor
68-70 Union Avenue
P.O. Box UA 400
Harare, Zimbabwe
Tel: (263-4) 730-967, 730-968, or 730-969
Fax: (263-4) 730-959

Depository and regional libraries
University of Zimbabwe [depository]
Library
P.O. Box MP 45
Mount Pleasant
Harare, Zimbabwe
Tel: (263-4) 303-211, ext. 1164
Fax: (263-4) 335-383
Web: http://www.uz.ac.zw/library/index.html

Distribution of Bank Group publications
Rolden Trading and Prestige Books
13 Belgrave House
21 Aberdeen Road
Avondale
Harare, Zimbabwe
Tel: (263-4) 335-105
Fax: (263-4) 335-105
E-mail: books@prestigebooks.co.zw

Publication discount: 75 percent

Selected titles
* *Contraceptive Choice, Fertility, and Public Health in Zimbabwe*
* *Empowering Small Enterprises in Zimbabwe*
* *Why Has Poverty Increased in Zimbabwe?*

Index

classification of member countries, 73–77
classification of proposed projects, 40
Clean Air Initiative for Latin American
    Cities, 103
cofinancing, 50
CommNet, 24, 26
Commonwealth of Independent States, 98
communication technology, 27, 131–32
Compliance Advisor/Ombudsman, 28
compliance monitoring, 41
Comprehensive Development Framework
    (CDF), 36–37, 119
conferences, forums, and summits, 53
conflict prevention and reconstruction, 113–14
  arbitration, 22–23
  publications, 114
  resources, 114
Conflict Resolution System, 27, 28
Conflicts of Interest Office, 28
consultants, 66
Consultant Trust Fund Program, 46
Consultative Group on International
    Agriculture Research (CGIAR), 63
Consultative Group to Assist the Poorest
    (CGAP), 63
contact information, 5, 147–50
Convention on the Settlement of Investment
    Disputes, 22
Cooperative Underwriting Program (CUP), 21
Corporate Secretariat, 26
corporate social responsibility (CSR), 137
corruption and fraud
  combating, 112–13
  publications, 113
  reporting of, 42b
Country Assistance Strategy (CAS), 38–39,
    40, 48, 112
country offices, 25
credits (IDA), 43, 79

D

data, 53
  economic, 115–16
  publications, 117
  resources, 116–17
databases. *See* information
Data on Consultants (DACON), 66
debt relief, 114
  strategies, 37–38, 37b
developing countries, 73–77
  Bank Group objectives and, 4, 5f
  as donor countries, 44
  income levels, 74–76t
Development Committee, 30
  annual meetings, 31

Development Communication Division,
    131
Development Data Group, 115
development economics. *See* economics
Development Education Program, 118
Development Gateway, 63–64
Development Grant Facility (DGF), 51
Development Marketplace, 120
development topics, 109–44. *See also*
    specific topics
disclosure policy, 41. *See also* information
dispute arbitration, 21, 22. *See also* conflict
    prevention and reconstruction
donor countries and IDA, 15–16, 17t, 44, 77

E

Early Child Development (ECD), 118
East Asia and the Pacific, 87–90
  financial crisis, 50
Economic and Social Council, U.N.
    (ECOSOC), 31
economics
  data, 115–16
  development economics, 26, 51
  publications, 117
  research, 51, 115–16
education, 117–19
Education for All (EFA), 118
Education for the Knowledge Economy
    (EKE), 118
effectiveness of aid. *See* aid effectiveness
empowerment and participation, 119–21
energy and mining, 121–22
  Asia Alternative Energy Program, 89
environment, 122–23
environmental assessments (EAs), 40, 56, 61
Environmentally and Socially Sustainable
    Development (ESSD), 24, 40
  Agriculture and Rural Development
    Department, 110–11
  objectives of, 122, 139
  Social Development Group, 139
Environment Department, 122
ethical issues, 27. *See also* corruption
    and fraud
  corporate social responsibility, 137
EU. *See* European Union
European Bank for Reconstruction and
    Development, 62
Europe and Central Asia, 95–99
  transition economies research, 116
European Union (EU), 62, 97
evaluation, operations, 111–12
executive directors (EDs), 9, 169
External Affairs, 26

Multilateral Investment Guarantee Agency
(MIGA) (*continued*)
basic facts, 20b2.6
community impact, 20–21
Compliance Advisor/Ombudsman, 28
contact information, 148
cooperative underwriting program, 21
East Asia and Pacific, 89
Europe and Central Asia, 98
executive vice president of, 10
financial management, 27
funding and lending, 44, 54
general services, 27
government deterrence, role in, 21
human resources, 27
Latin America and the Caribbean, 103
legal services, 21, 54–55
membership requirements, 72, 77
Middle East and North Africa, 106
objectives of, 20
operations evaluation department, 28
policies and procedures, 43
Private Sector, 136–38
products and services, 20, 27, 53–55
regional offices, 25
South Asia, 93
Web site, 20b2.6

N

network vice presidencies, 23–24
sectors of, 23–24
New Partnership for Africa's Development
(NEPAD), 83, 85
Nile Basin Initiative, 85
nongovernmental organizations
(NGOs), 31, 64, 120
North Africa. *See* Middle East and
North Africa
North Africa Enterprise Development, 107
nutrition. *See* health and nutrition
Nutrition Advisory Service, 128

O

Oil, Gas, Mining, and Chemicals
Department, 121
Ombudsman, 28
Operational Manual, 39–42
operational policies (OPs), 39–40
operations, 33–67. *See also* project cycle
evaluation of, 111–12
funding and lending, 43–47
policies and procedures, 28, 39–43
products and services, 47–55
strategies, 34–39

Operations Evaluation Department (OED), 28,
57, 111
Operations Policy and Country Services
(OPCS), 24, 28, 39–42
organizing principles, 23–29

P

Paris Club, 114
Participation and Civic Engagement
Group, 120
Part I countries, 77. *See also* donor countries
Part II countries, 77. *See also* developing
countries
partnerships, 62–64. *See also* United
Nations (U.N.)
bilateral development agencies
(trust funds), 63
institutional, 62–63
NGOs, 64
programmatic, 63–64
PICs. *See* Public Information Centers
policies and procedures, 28, 39–43
operational manual, 39–42
Policy and Human Resources Development
Fund, 44
pollution, 94. *See also* environment
Population and Reproductive Health, 128
Post-Conflict Fund, 113
poverty, 135–36
Consultive Group to Assist the Poorest
(CGAP), 63
IDA focus on poorest countries, 15
IFC, 136
poverty reduction strategies, 37–38
key steps, 37b
publications, 136
resources, 136
Poverty Reduction and Economic Management
(PREM) Network, 24, 136
gender development group, 125
Poverty Reduction Growth Facility, 38
Poverty Reduction Strategies Papers (PRSPs),
38, 79, 119
Poverty Reduction Strategies Sourcebook, 38
president of the World Bank Group, 9–10, 159
as ICSID administrative council chair, 10
managing directors assistance to, 10
office of, 28
private education, 118–19
Private Enterprise Partnership, 98
private sector development, 136–38, 141
Private Sector Development and Infrastructure
(PSI) Network, 24
procedures. *See* policies and procedures
procurement guidelines, 27, 66–67

products and services, 47–55. *See also* funding
    and lending
  ICSID, 55
  IFC, 53–54
  MIGA, 53–55
    legal counsel, 21, 54–55
  World Bank, 51–53
Project Appraisal Document (PAD), 56
project cycle
  IFC, 60–62
  World Bank, 55–60, 55f
projects database, 58, 77
publications, 52–53. *See also specific region*
  African Development Indicators, 52
  agriculture and rural development, 111
  annual reports, 46–47, 150
  conflict prevention and reconstruction,
    114
  contact information, 52b, 149
  East Asia and the Pacific, 90
  education, 119
  empowerment and participation, 121
  energy and mining, 121–22
  environment, 123
  Europe and Central Asia, 99
  Financial Sector Network, 124
  fraud, 113
  gender, 125
  Global Development Finance, 52
  Global Economic Prospects, 52
  globalization, 26
  health and nutrition, 130
  indigenous peoples, 132
  information and communication
    technology, 132
  InfoShop, 58–59
  infrastructure, 133
  labor and social protection, 134
  Latin America and the Caribbean, 103
  law and justice, 135
  Middle East and North Africa, 107
  operations evaluation, 112
  poverty, 136
  Poverty Reduction Strategy Sourcebook, 38
  Private Sector, 138
  Public Sector Group, 126–27
  Resettlement Handbook, 130
  social development, 139
  South Asia, 94
  Sub-Saharan Africa, 86
  sustainable development, 140
  trade, 141
  transportation, 142
  urban development, 143
  water, 144

World Development Indicators, 52, 77
World Development Report, 52
public health. *See* health and nutrition
Public Information Centers (PICs), 25, 26,
    59–60, 183
public notification, 61, 149
Public Sector Group, 126–27

Q

Quality Assurance Group, 28, 57–58, 112

R

regional groupings, 80–81
regional vice presidencies, 25
reproductive health, 128
research. *See also* knowledge sharing
    economic, 51, 115–16
    publications, 117
Resettlement Handbook, 130
Resource Mobilization and Cofinancing
    unit, 44
risk management, 21, 50–51, 53
riverblindness, 85
Robert S. McNamara Fellowships Program, 66
Roll Back Malaria, 128
rural development. *See* agriculture and rural
    development
Russian Federation, 9, 98, 116

S

safeguard policies
    operational manual, 40
scholarships, 65–66
schools. *See* education
sectors, 23–24
    codes for, 179–80
    lending breakdown, 2002, 36f
    public, 126–27
    strategies of, 35–36
    types of, 24
shareholders. *See* member countries
Small and Medium Enterprise
    Department, 137
small states, 80
social development, 139
Social Development Initiative for South East
    Europe, 98–99
Social Protection Advisory Service, 134
South Asia, 91–94
South Asia Urban Air Quality Management, 94
Southeast Europe Enterprise Development, 99
South Pacific Project Facility, 90
staff, 27
    Bank Group, 64–65
    directory orders, 147